Bryan Spinks is an Affiliated Lecturer in Liturgy in the University of Cambridge and Chaplain of Churchill College, Cambridge. He is the author of three previous books, and has written numerous articles on liturgical themes.

The origin of the sanctus as a constituent element in the eucharistic prayer is one of the unsolved mysteries of Christian liturgy, and the author of this study makes a careful investigation into its background and the instances of its occurrence in early Christian literature. In making his enquiry, Dr Spinks rejects certain older theories about the sanctus, and bases his own theory firmly upon primary texts when claiming that the earliest attestations of the sanctus originated in Syria and Palestine.

The sanctus in the eucharistic prayer

The sanctus
in the
eucharistic prayer

BRYAN D. SPINKS

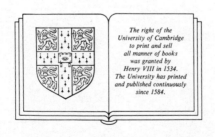

The right of the
University of Cambridge
to print and sell
all manner of books
was granted by
Henry VIII in 1534.
The University has printed
and published continuously
since 1584.

CAMBRIDGE UNIVERSITY PRESS

CAMBRIDGE

NEW YORK   PORT CHESTER   MELBOURNE   SYDNEY

Published by the Press Syndicate of the University of Cambridge
The Pitt Building, Trumpington Street, Cambridge CB2 1RP
40 West 20th Street, New York, NY 10011, USA
10 Stamford Road, Oakleigh, Melbourne 3166, Australia

First published 1991

Printed in Great Britain at the University Press, Cambridge

British Library cataloguing in publication data
Spinks, Bryan D.
The sanctus in the Eucharistic prayer.
1. Eucharistic prayers. Eucharist. Christian church
I. Title
264.36

Library of Congress cataloguing in publication data
Spinks, Bryan D.
The Sanctus in the Eucharistic prayer/Bryan D. Spinks.
p.   cm.
Includes bibliographical references and index.
ISBN 0 521 39307 8
1. Sanctus. 2. Eucharistic prayers. I. Title.
BV194.S25S65 1991
264′.36–dc20

ISBN 0 521 39307 8 hardback

CE

Contents

Preface

As a former pupil of the late Arthur Hubert Couratin, it was perhaps inevitable that sooner or later I should become fascinated by the sanctus in the eucharistic prayer. The sanctus had preoccupied Couratin's friend and mentor, Edward Ratcliff, and Couratin in turn came under the same spell. As he led pupils through the text of the _Apostolic Tradition_, he would raise the questions about its ending which Ratcliff had set out in his now famous article in the _Journal of Ecclesiastical History_ – though rarely mentioning his own support of 'the Master' published in the same journal. I am indebted to Arthur Couratin not only for imparting his technique in assessing liturgical texts, but also for imbuing me with the 'sanctus fascination'. However, my later graduate liturgical studies under Ronald Jasper and the late Geoffrey Cuming, and in Syriac with Sebastian Brock, have been indispensable in equipping me with an independent perspective for investigating its function, and conjecturing on its possible origin. I have found it necessary, therefore, to place this investigation in a context far broader than Couratin and Ratcliff would have thought necessary.

I would like to record my thanks to a number of friends and colleagues who assisted me in this study: to the Revds Dr Anthony Gelston and Professor John Rogerson, Dr G. I. Davies, Dr Stefan Reif and the Revd Dr William Horbury for their assistance with the material in Part I; to Professor Sir Harold Bailey for translating the Armenian texts, and the Revd Professor J. M. Plumley for help with the Coptic; to Professor H. Glahn for information on the Danish rite; to the Revds Professor J. M. Barkley, Dr Bruno Bürki, Dr Howard Hageman and Dr Horace Allen Jun. for help in locating the texts of the many Reformed rites; to the Revd Professor Ronald Feuerhahn for his ever-willing assistance with gathering Lutheran texts; and to Dr Andrea Cervi who kindly translated one of the Strasbourg Reformation

texts. I am also happy to record my thanks to my friends the Revd Dr
Kenneth Stevenson and the late Revd Dr Geoffrey Cuming for their
comments on the earlier drafts of this work which, together with
material already published, was successfully submitted to the University of Durham for the degree of Doctor of Divinity. I would also like to
thank Mr Alex Wright of Cambridge University Press for his interest in
the work and for encouraging its revision for publication.

The views expressed and the judgments made are my own, and I am
responsible for any errors. If the latter are not revealed by other
colleagues now, they will no doubt one day be pointed out to me before
the divine throne by the seraphim, though I hope that, like Arthur
Couratin, they will soften the sharp supervision with that inevitable
glass of sherry!

Lastly I must thank my wife and family who have had to live with 'the
sanctus' for nearly eight years. This work is dedicated to them and to all
those who have joined with me in divine worship in the Chapel at
Churchill College, Cambridge.

Abbreviations

APOT   Charles, R. H. (ed.), *The Apocrypha and Pseudepigrapha of the Old Testament in English*, 2 vols. (Clarendon, Oxford 1913)

AS   *Anaphorae Syriacae* (Pontificium Institutum Orientalium Studiorum, Rome 1939–)

ATR   *Anglican Theological Review*

AV   Authorised Version

BZAW   *Beihefte zur Zeitschrift für die alttestamentliche Wissenschaft*

CBQ   *Catholic Biblical Quarterly*

CD   *Church Dogmatics* (ET. T. and T. Clark, Edinburgh)

CQ   *Church Quarterly*

EL   *Ephemerides Liturgicae*

ETL   *Ephemerides Theologicae Lovanienses*

ET   English translation

ET   *Expository Times*

Gesenius-Kautzch   *Hebrew Grammar* (ET. Clarendon Press, Oxford 1898)

HAT   *Handbuch zum Alten Testament*

HBS   Henry Bradshaw Society

HJ   *Heythrop Journal*

HTR   *Harvard Theological Review*

HUCA   *Hebrew Union College Annual*

IDB   *International Dictionary of the Bible*

JBL   *Journal of Biblical Literature*

JEH   *Journal of Ecclesiastical History*

JJS   *Journal of Jewish Studies*

JLW   *Jahrbuch für Liturgiewissenschaft*

JNES   *Journal of Near Eastern Studies*

JQR	*Jewish Quarterly Review*
JSJ	*Journal for the Study of Judaism*
JSS	*Journal of Semitic Studies*
JTS	*Journal of Theological Studies*
LEW	Brightman, F. E., *Liturgies Eastern and Western* (Clarendon Press, Oxford 1896)
LR	*Liturgical Review* (Liturgical Studies)
LXX	Septuagint
MGWJ	*Monatsschrift für Geschichte und Wissenschaft des Judentums*
MT	*Massoretic Text*
Mu	*Le Muséon*
Nov.T.	*Novum Testamentum*
ns	new series
NTS	*New Testament Studies*
OC	*Oriens Christianus*
OCA	*Orientalia Christiana Analecta*
OCP	*Orientalia Christiana Periodica*
Or.Syr.	*L'Orient Syrien*
OTP	Charlesworth, J. H. (ed.), *The Old Testament Pseudepigrapha*, 2 vols. (Darton, Longman and Todd, London 1983, 1986)
PE	Hänggi, A., Pahl, I. (eds.), *Prex Eucharistia* (Spicilegium Friburgense 12, Editions Universitaires Fribourg Suisse, Fribourg 1968)
PEER	Jasper, R. D. C., Cuming G. J. (eds.), *Prayers of the Eucharist, Early and Reformed* (Pueblo, New York 1987, 3rd edn.)
PG	*Patrologia Graeca*, J. P. Migne
PWHS	*Proceedings of the Wesleyan Historical Society*
QL	*Questions Liturgiques*
REJ	*Revue des Etudes Juives*
RSR	*Recherches de Science Religieuse*
RSV	*Revised Standard Version*
SE	*Sacris Eruditi*
SL	*Studia Liturgica*
SP	*Studia Patrisica*
TDNT	Kittel, G., Friedrich, J. (eds.), *Theological Dictionary of the New Testament* (Eerdmans, Grand Rapids 1964–74)

THAT	Jenni, E., Westermann, C. (eds.), *Theologisches Handwörterbuch zum Alten Testament*, 2 vols. (Zurich/ Munich 1971–6)
TL	*Tijdscrift voor Liturgie*
TRIA	*Transactions of the Royal Irish Academy*
TS	*Theological Studies*
TU	*Texte und Untersuchungen*
VC	*Vigiliae Christianae*
VT	*Vetus Testamentum*
ZAW	*Zeitschrift für die alttestamentliche Wissenschaft*
ZDMG	*Zeitschrift der deutschen morgenländischen Gesellschaft*
ZNTW	*Zeitschrift für die neutestamentliche Wissenschaft*

INTRODUCTION

─────────── ⅏ ───────────

The enigma of the sanctus

FOR Christians of many traditions, the sanctus, *trisagion* or *qeduššah*,[1] is a familiar feature in the eucharistic prayer. It finds a place in almost every classical anaphora, and it has generally been regarded in modern liturgical revision as a necessary constituent of the eucharistic prayer. Its ultimate written source is not a mystery. It is adapted from the song of the seraphim of Isaiah 6:3 which, in different form and on the lips of four living creatures (from Ezekiel), recurs in Revelation 4:8. However, from the viewpoint of the history and theology of Christian liturgy, its occurrence within the eucharistic prayer remains something of a mystery. Why did this biblical song come to be inserted within a prayer in which the church follows the example and command of Jesus at the Last Supper? There is no suggestion in the Gospels that Jesus uttered the sanctus at this meal and enjoined its recitation, nor does there appear to be any evidence to suggest that it was ever a recognised constituent of Jewish meal prayers.

Although in practically all post-fourth-century classical anaphoras, East and West, the sanctus occurs at some point in the first part of the prayer, it is noticeably absent from some significant early texts, namely the *Apostolic Tradition* attributed to Hippolytus, *Testamentum Domini*, from the anaphora of Epiphanius and, according to M. A. Smith, an anaphora alluded to in Narsai's Homily XVII.[2] It is absent from the *Didache* which, in some recent studies, has been regarded as vital for understanding the transition from the Jewish meal benedictions or *berakot* to the Christian eucharistic prayer.[3] It is found in Addai and Mari and Maronite *Sharar*, but although the majority of scholars agree on an early dating for the underlying anaphora, a formidable number have regarded the sanctus here as a later insertion.[4] Justin Martyr, an early witness to the eucharistic liturgy, makes no mention of it; and, although it does occur in Revelation and 1 Clement 34, there is no cogent proof that the context is eucharistic worship.[5] The liturgist is thus left with a number of questions: when, where and why was this biblical song included within the eucharistic prayer?

Inevitably, liturgical scholars have put forward a variety of theories to answer these questions. Two theories have been especially influential in the English-speaking world, and at the very beginning of this study it is necessary to give them some consideration and to state why they cannot be accepted.

THE EGYPTIAN THEORY

Referring to this hypothesis, Geoffrey Cuming rightly observed that whoever first proposed this theory, it certainly owes its authority in England to the writings of Gregory Dix.[6] It has also been espoused by Georg Kretschmar.[7]

In *The Shape of the Liturgy*, while discussing the anaphora in Serapion's euchology, Dix explained that with regard to the preface, the use of the sanctus at Alexandria can be traced in the writings of Origen *c.* 230 CE. Pointing to verbal similarities between the preface of Serapion and that of the Greek eucharistic prayer of St Mark, Dix concluded:

The simplest explanation of these various facts is that the use of the preface and sanctus in the eucharistic prayer began in the Alexandrian church at some time before AD 230, and from there spread first to other Egyptian churches, and ultimately all over christendom.[8]

In support of such a conclusion, Dix cited two references to an article he had written in *Theology* in 1938.[9] On examination of this article, the case rests entirely upon two references in Origen's *De Principiis*, both of which are concerned with an interpretation of the two seraphim of Isaiah which Origen had learnt from his Hebrew teacher. The same interpretation is also given in his Homily on Isaiah.[10] In the first passage, *De Principiis* i. 3,4, Origen links the two seraphim with the two living creatures of Habakkuk (LXX) 3:2. Dix suggested that the exegesis which Origen had learnt from his Hebrew teacher, namely that the two seraphim are the Son and the Holy Spirit, is echoed in Serapion's sanctus where the celestial creatures are described as *timiō-tata*, 'honourable', and he noted that in the anaphora of St Mark they are described as *timiōtata zōa*, 'honourable living creatures', echoing Habakkuk. He inferred from this that Origen was alluding to the sanctus in the Egyptian eucharistic prayer.

Kretschmar approached the evidence from a study of trinitarian origins, finding an Egyptian view which can be traced to Origen and Methodius whereby Christ and the Holy Spirit were conceived of as two supreme heavenly powers standing before God's throne (= seraphim), and a Syrian view whereby God, Christ and the Holy Spirit were ranged side by side as heavenly witnesses. In the middle of the third century, the sanctus was taken up in the Alexandrine eucharistic prayer as a reference to Christ and the Holy Spirit as intermediaries who open up free access to God for the congregation.[11] The immediate context was to counter Sabellianism which regarded the Son and the Spirit simply as modes of the Godhead and not separate persons. However, with the rise of Arianism which taught the inferiority of the Son to the Father, Origen's exegesis was abandoned. Syria received the anaphoral sanctus from Egypt in the fourth century, and here it was addressed to Christ and only later to God the creator. Towards the end of the fourth century the Antiochene school of Diodore adopted the trinitarian interpretation of Alexandria. Kretschmar, in seeking the roots of trinitarian doctrine, traces the view of Origen back to the Ascension of Isaiah and to the writings of Philo. However, for the link between Origen and the Egyptian eucharistic prayer, his authority is Gregory Dix.

However interesting and suggestive these observations might appear, there is in fact little justification for drawing the conclusion which Dix and Kretschmar wished to draw, namely that Origen is our earliest witness to the anaphoral sanctus, and that in the prayer, the seraphim were understood to be Christ and the Holy Spirit. The first passage in De Principiis i. 3,4, does not actually quote the sanctus, and in the second, iv. 3,14, the sanctus which is quoted is that of the biblical text of Isaiah 6:3 and not its adapted anaphoral form. Origen links Isaiah 6:3 with Colossians 1:16, and these are also found together in Serapion and the Coptic fragment in the Coptic Ostrica. However, in the other fragments of the Alexandrine anaphora, and in St Mark itself, it is Ephesians 1:21 which is linked with the sanctus, and not Colossians 1:16. Since in Serapion, Colossians 1:16 comes as a clumsy repetition of Ephesians 1:21, it may have been inserted into the anaphora by Serapion himself or by whoever was responsible for that prayer.[12] Contrary to Dix's conclusion, it would seem that the evidence he presented should be assessed as follows. Origen was concerned with the exegesis of biblical texts, and his exegesis led him to link Isaiah 6:3, Habakkuk 3:2 and Colossians 1:16. He was not expounding a liturgical text. The sanctus in Serapion and in St Mark both show some slight acquaintance with an exegesis linking these passages but it is by no means the same. *Zōa*, for example, does not occur in Serapion and, with due respect to Dix, in St Mark the *zōa* are *not* identified with the seraphim.[13] If Origen was acquainted with an anaphoral tradition which included the sanctus, this is not demonstrated by the passages from *De Principiis*.

In 1938 Dix had cautiously written:

> It begins to look as though *Sarapion* represents, for all its anti-Arian editing, a traditional Egyptian arrangement of the introduction to the Sanctus, which was also in the mind of Origen when he wrote this passage about the Sanctus before AD 225.[14]

What this statement actually means is that it had begun to look like this to Dix, and he admitted that the evidence was 'delicate'.[15] Yet, by the time he came to write *The Shape of the Liturgy*, his 1938 suggestions came to be assured facts of scholarship. Dix had created a false trail which Kretschmar followed – not unlike Winnie-the-Pooh and Piglet in the hunt for the woozle.[16]

THE CLIMAX THEORY

Strangely enough, the first signs of this theory can also be traced to Gregory Dix. In *The Shape of the Liturgy* he suggested that the Egyptian anaphora might have originally consisted of a preface (thanksgiving) terminating with the sanctus.[17] However, the development of this idea into the theory that nearly all early orthodox eucharistic prayers may have terminated with the sanctus is associated with the name of Edward Ratcliff.

Ratcliff's theory was set out in a paper entitled 'The Sanctus and the Pattern of the Early Anaphora'[18] which was concerned with the Verona text of *Apostolic Tradition*. Comparing the Verona text with the evidence of Justin Martyr and Irenaeus on the eucharistic prayer, Ratcliff believed that several things pointed to a later rearrangement of the anaphora. By omitting the epiklesis, Ratcliff joined two paragraphs, both of which were concerned with the idea of divine worship. But,

> there is a want of climax, touching bathos, in the use of the common doxology as the ending of the solemn eucharistic prayer which, alone of all prayers, is introduced by 'Sursum corda', 'habemus ad Dominum'.[19]

On the basis of the Old Latin and Vulgate usage, Ratcliff propounded that the Verona's *adstare coram te et tibi ministrare* ('to stand before you and minister to you') was a translation not of *estanai enōpion sou kai ierateuein soi*, but of *parestanai enōpion sou kai leitourgein soi*. In Theodotion's version of Daniel 7:10 these verbs are found to be juxtaposed in connection with worship from the heavenly host. Ratcliff submitted that the transposed clauses of Daniel 7:10 were combined with Isaiah 6:3, and that the sanctus constituted the conclusion, not merely of the paragraph itself, but of the whole anaphora. Privately he expressed an opinion of what the missing ending might have been.[20] This erudite study of the anaphora of *Apostolic Tradition* ended:

Here this article reaches its limit. If its contention be sound, it raises a number of questions, most of them depending upon the primary question, Why, if the pattern of the ancient anaphora ever conformed with the reconstruction proposed here, was the pattern abandoned? The surviving literature, and not least the historic liturgies, either supply the answers or offer evidence which suggests them. A consideration of the questions and answers, however, must be reserved for a future article.[21]

The argument was taken a little further in 'A Note on the Anaphoras described in the Liturgical Homilies of Narsai'.[22] Here Ratcliff argued that the anaphora outlined by Narsai in Homily XXXII bore witness to an earlier pattern of the anaphora which concluded with the sanctus, while at the same time implying that the sanctus may have had a consecratory function. Although he never wrote the promised article considering the questions and answers, it was his private opinion that all the early anaphoras had ended with the sanctus.[23]

Support for this theory was forthcoming from A. H. Couratin, G. A. Michell and W. Pitt.[24] Couratin asked whether there was any evidence to indicate that the terminating sanctus was sung by the celebrant alone and that the people simply responded with 'Amen'? He appealed to tone XVIII for ferial use in the *Graduale Romanum*; this is the only sanctus chant which continues the melody of the preface. Couratin noted that the first hosanna of the benedictus repeats the notes of *Sanctus Dominus Deus Sabaoth*, and the benedictus repeats the notes of *Pleni sunt cœli*. He suggested that the notes of the second hosanna recalled the *ekphonesis* and the response which concluded the canon missae. Couratin reasoned that, given Ratcliff's argument, the canon missae may originally have ended:

sine fine dicentes Sanctus, Sanctus, Sanctus Dominus Deus Sabaoth. Pleni sunt caeli et terra gloria tua per omnia saecula saeculorum.

R. Amen.[25]

He cited a passage from Tertullian which he interpreted as referring to the sanctus and doxology; from *Apostolic Constitutions* VIII, and from Egypt. For the latter he suggested that the concluding doxology echoed Rev. 4:8, to which it was originally attached in the anaphora.

G. A. Michell, inspired by Ratcliff's hypothesis, turned his attention to the report given by Firmilian of Caesarea in Cappadocia to Cyprian regarding a certain prophetess who apparently celebrated the eucharist, and in particular, to the meaning of *invocatione* and *sacramento solitae praedicationis*. On the basis of trinitarian references in Theodore of Mopsuestia and Ephraem, and the invocation of names in Gnostic prayers, he urged that *invocatione* should be understood as invoking the divine names, and that *sacramento solitae praedicationis* referred to the sanctus. Appealing also to Origen and Ambrose, he wrote:

This cumulative evidence leads to the conclusion that, in Firmilian's view, the second constituent of an orthodox anaphora ought to be the Sanctus, regarded as a proclamation of the holiness and omnipotence of God.[26]

Michell also suggested that in the Byzantine anaphora of Basil, the section as far as the sanctus with its invocation of the Father, Son and Holy Spirit, represented the ancient eucharistic prayer of Caesarea. From this conclusion W. E. Pitt argued that the present Byzantine anaphora of Basil had been extended from its original form by adding material (from St James) after the sanctus; the preface and sanctus represent the earliest stratum.

Ratcliff's study of the anaphora of *Apostolic Tradition* raised some important points about the prayer, particularly regarding the reliability of the Verona text. However, his argument relating to the sanctus rested upon far too many conjectures. We do not know what the underlying Greek was, but the reading of *Apostolic Constitutions* VIII seems preferable to that suggested by Ratcliff. The Old Latin rendering of the LXX and the New Testament is not necessarily a reliable guide for reconstructing the Greek of a liturgical text.[27] But even if Ratcliff's conjectures about the Greek were correct, and even if it echoes the vocabulary found in Theodotion's rendering of Daniel 7:10, there is, logically, no compelling reason for concluding that it led into the sanctus. The fact remains that there is *no* sanctus in Hippolytus, and it is unlikely that a fourth-century reviser would have entirely omitted an existing sanctus at a time when it was becoming a universal feature in anaphoral composition.

I have already questioned the legitimacy of Ratcliff's interpretation of Narsai's Homily XXXII.[28] Ratcliff misused the homiletic material, and his interpretation was based upon four unwarranted assumptions. It is quite possible to interpret the anaphora outlined in the homily in a manner which is consistent with the other two anaphoras described by Narsai.

Similar flaws can be found in the articles by Couratin, Michell and Pitt – though they lose their rationale if Ratcliff's hypothesis falls. Couratin's argument regarding the melody could be reversed; there would be more likelihood of a congregation joining in a sanctus which continued the familiar melody of the preface than in a sanctus with a different melody. Few scholars would agree that Couratin's interpretation of Tertullian is correct, and his interpretation of *Apostolic Constitutions* VIII and the Egyptian doxology are simply speculations. E. Dekkers's interpretation of *invocatio* and *praedicatio* as being synonyms for the eucharistic prayer as a whole is preferable to Michell's;[29] and since recent scholarship has demonstrated that the trinitarian preface of the Byzantine version of St Basil represents a sophisticated reworking of an earlier text, Michell's and Pitt's arguments have been rendered obsolete.[30] Neither the Egyptian theory nor the more elaborate Climax theory provide convincing explanations to the puzzles surrounding the anaphoral sanctus.

This study of the sanctus in the eucharistic prayer is concerned with presenting a developmental argument, and theories of origin are only discussed in the light of a consideration of the texts and contexts. This method seems essential also if the findings are not to be predetermined by *a priori* theories of the origin of the eucharistic prayer itself. Part I is concerned with the background and context of the biblical trisagion and an examination of its quasi-liturgical and liturgical usage in Judaism. Some early Christian references to the sanctus are examined in order to test continuity with Jewish contexts, and for innovation. Part II considers the early anaphoral evidence up to the seventh century, and is particularly concerned with the context and function of the sanctus. The historical and theological background of the liturgical texts is regarded as fundamental to the arguments. In the light of this survey, possible origins of the anaphoral sanctus are discussed. Part III surveys more briefly subsequent development of the sanctus in the eucharistic prayer up to the present, and concludes with a theological reflection on its form and function in future anaphoral composition.

Part I

1

The Old Testament background and setting

THE DIVINE COUNCIL OF YAHWEH

THE ultimate source of the sanctus, that is, the earliest document in which it is recorded, is the book of the prophet Isaiah, whose prophecies are generally dated *c*.742–700 BCE. Here it is usually referred to as the *trisagion*. It occurs on the lips of creatures called seraphim in a vision in which the prophet sees Yahweh on his throne. However, this vision must be seen in the wider context of the Old Testament conception of a Divine Council attending Yahweh.

In an important article entitled 'The Council of Yahweh', H. Wheeler Robinson drew attention to the fact that when Jeremiah asked

Who hath stood in the council of Yahweh
that he should perceive and know his word?   (Jer 22:18)

the word for council, *sôd*, is not a figurative or poetic expression, but reflects a real belief in a divine assembly presided over by Yahweh.[1] There is a large amount of evidence in the Old Testament for the heavenly assembly or council, presided over by Yahweh, and composed of divine attendants, heralds and administrators.[2] The Old Testament itself contains no uniform or systematic account of these celestial beings, but the different books yield what must have been a commonly believed, albeit diverse, angelology.

In Psalm 82:1 we read:

God stationed himself in the divine assembly [*'ª dat'El*]
in the midst of the gods [*'elohîm*] he has judged.

This psalm pictures a courtroom scene in which God, as head of the council, has indicted some beings called *'elohîm* for violating the law.

Although some commentators have suggested that *'elohîm* here means deified kings or patron angels of the nations, it almost certainly reflects the idea that Yahweh called the gods of the nations to a heavenly assize.[3] According to the study of E. T. Mullen, the council motif is common to both Mesopotamian and Canaanite culture, though the influence on Hebrew literature seems to have come from the latter where El assembles with a divine pantheon.[4] Likewise, therefore, Psalm 89:6–9a reads:

Let the heavens praise thy wonders, Yahweh, thy faithfulness in the assembly of the holy ones [*q^ehal q^edôšîm*]. For who in the skies can be compared with Yahweh? Who among the sons of gods [*b^ene 'elohîm*] is like Yahweh? A god ['*El*] feared in the council of the holy ones [*sôd q^edôšîm*] great and terrible above all that are round about him? Yahweh, God of Hosts, who is mighty as you, Yah?

The same idea is expressed in Psalm 29.

Various words are used for the divine assembly: *mô'ed* (compare the Ugaritic *m'd*) (Isaiah 14:13);[5] *'adat'El* (Ps 82:1); *q^ehal* and *sôd q^edôšîm* (Ps 89); *sôd Yahweh* or *'elo^ah* (Jer 23:18; Job 15:8);[6] and, probably,[7] *dôr* (Amos 8:14; Ps 73:15).

In the Canaanite literature the assembly is made up of El and the lesser gods. In Israel, although the celestial beings can be termed gods (Ps 82:1; 8:5), other terms are also used: *b^ene 'elîm* (sons of gods; *bn 'ilm* is the regular term for members of the pantheon in the Ugaritic texts, and recurs in a Canaanite magical plaque from Arslan Tash, dating from the eighth or seventh century BCE);[8] *q^edôšîm* (holy ones); *ṣābā* (host); *'abādîm* (servants); and *m^ešār^etîm* (ministers).[9] To this may perhaps be added *gibbôrîm* (mighty ones, Is 13:3; Joel 3:11). The term *mal'ākîm*, from the root *l'k*, 'to send', also occurs. In some instances it is well known that the *mal'āk Yahweh* is a personification of a theophany, a special self-manifestation of God (see Gen 31:11–13; Ex 3:2–6). However, in certain places in the Old Testament *mal'āk* describes celestial beings who belong to the divine council (see Ps 91:11; 2 Sam 14:17,20). These different names, some of which describe the function of these divine beings, are probably to be regarded as synonyms rather than as different types of celestial being. Together with the stars and celestial bodies (Deut 4:19; Job 38:7), they were believed to make up a numberless celestial entourage.

In the account of the vision of the prophet Micaiah ben Imlah (1 Kings 22:19), the heavenly host stood either side of Yahweh who asked their advice:

Who will entice Ahab, that he may go up and fall at Ramoth-gilead? And one said one thing, and another said another.

At last a *rûaḥ* (spirit) came forward offering advice and volunteering for the task, advice which Yahweh accepted. Clearly a major function of the divine council – who in this context are called spirits – was to advise Yahweh. Thus, in Job 1, the *bᵉne 'ēlîm* assemble, with Satan also in attendance, and put a proposition to Yahweh – which Yahweh accepts. Genesis 1:26, 'Let us make man in our own image, after our likeness', presumably represents God addressing the assembly, and according to Job 38:7, the assembly shouted for joy at the creation. True prophets were those who were privileged to stand in[10] the council of Yahweh and hear the divine decision (Jer 23:21–2; Is 6:1–9; 1 Kings 22:19) – something which Job had not done (Job 15:8). Before Isaiah was admitted, a ritual cleansing was necessary; after being cleansed, Joshua the High Priest was given the right of access 'among those who are standing here' (Zech 3:7).

These celestial beings had other functions also. In the vision of Micaiah ben Imlah, the 'spirit' actually went forth to do the will of Yahweh, and 'servants' and 'ministers' describe something of the relationship and position of these beings *vis à vis* Yahweh. In Joshua 5:14 the captain of the host of Yahweh, with sword in hand, speaks with Joshua. T. H. Gaster summarises their function in the patriarchal and monarchic narratives as to convey the mandates of God to men, to harbinger special events, to protect the faithful and to serve as instruments of divine displeasure against sinners.[11] However, one further important function which the Old Testament attests is that of worship of Yahweh. Thus in Psalm 29:1–2, 9 the *bᵉne 'ēlîm* give glory and worship to Yahweh, and this includes the cry *kābôd*. Psalm 103:19–22 commands the *mal'akim* to bless Yahweh, and Psalm 148:1–2 commands the *sābā* to praise him. This function is also affirmed in the prayer of Ezra (Neh 9:6):

You are Yahweh, you alone.
You have made heaven, the heaven of heavens, with all their host, the earth and all that is on it, the seas and all that is in them; and you preserve all of them; and the host of heaven [*ṣᵉbā haššāmayîm*] worships you.

It is against this wider Old Testament background that the vision of Isaiah must be seen.

THE VISION OF ISAIAH

Chapter 6 of Isaiah marks the beginning of the so-called 'memoir' of the prophet which extends as far as 8:18.[12] This section of the book is introduced with an account of Isaiah's call, 6:1–13, which falls into three parts: A theophany; an act of cleansing; the Commissioning. The actual theophany, including the vision of the seraphim and their antiphonal cry of praise, is recorded in 6:1–3.

In the year that King Uzziah died I saw Yahweh sitting upon a throne, high and lifted up; and his skirts [*šûlîm*][13] filled the temple. Above him stood the seraphim; each had six wings: with two he covered his face, and with two he covered his feet, and with two he flew. And one called to another and said:

Holy, Holy, Holy is Yahweh of Hosts;
The whole earth is full of his glory.

The Peshitta version faithfully translates the Hebrew,[14] but the LXX associates 'high and lifted up' with 'throne', translates *šûlîm* with *doxēs*, and 'above him' (*mimma'al*) with *kuklō autou*.

The theophany is recorded as having taken place in the year King Uzziah (Azariah) died, 742[15] or 736–5 BCE.[16] The details given in 1:1 are not absolutely reliable, and thus it cannot be certain whether or not the vision took place before the death of Uzziah. The vision took place almost certainly in the Jerusalem temple,[17] and it is possible that its context was some specific liturgical celebration.

Edwin Kingsbury has drawn attention to the similarities between the vision of Isaiah and that of Micaiah ben Imlah in 1 Kings 22:19–23.[18] Kingsbury lists five particular elements in the latter:

1 Yahweh was King, seated upon a throne.
2 Some heavenly creatures (all the host of heaven) surrounded Yahweh.
3 Micaiah 'saw' Yahweh.
4 The oracle was merely the relaying of what Micaiah had seen and heard.
5 According to Kingsbury, there is reason to believe that the scene at the 'threshing floor' (v.10) connects this experience with some agricultural feast, at 'the turn of the year'.

Turning to the vision of Isaiah, Kingsbury appealed to the studies of Morgenstern and Mowinckel,[19] arguing that the orientation of the temple in Jerusalem was such that the morning sun at the autumnal equinox shone between the two cosmic pillars Jachin and Boaz, through the doors of the temple into the holy of holies. This made possible the representation of the epiphany of Yahweh in the smoke and incense, the 'skirts' or train of Yahweh. Kingsbury therefore places the occasion of Isaiah's vision, and that of Micaiah's, on the day of the enthronement of Yahweh, the New Year Festival. He finds similar elements to Micaiah's vision in that of Isaiah:

1 Yahweh is King, sitting on a throne.
2 Some heavenly creatures surrounded Yahweh.
3 Isaiah saw Yahweh.
4 Isaiah heard Yahweh's word.
5 The vision was during the enthronement festival.

Other commentators have also connected the theophany of Isaiah with the New Year Festival when Yahweh ascended his throne in order to judge his people.[20]

The New Year Festival and enthronement ceremonies of the Near East have provided a fascinating framework for interpreting the psalms and other Old Testament cultic material.[21] However, the Old Testament itself remains silent on the details and framework of such a festival. As D. J. A. Clines points out, there was no fixed Near Eastern pattern from which the gaps in our knowledge about the Israelite religion can be filled out, and rituals cannot, in any case, simply be reconstructed from the myths with which they were associated.[22] Furthermore, although Israel shared a common cultural background with Canaanite religion, it would seem that Israel reinterpreted and demythologised many of its neighbour's beliefs and practices. The danger of Kingsbury's analysis is that of explaining what we know something about (Isaiah's vision) by reference to something we know nothing about (the New Year Festival). We cannot be certain of such a specific liturgical context for the vision.

As far as the vision of Yahweh is concerned, no attempt is made to specify the form of the enthroned deity. His transcendence is emphasised (on a throne, high and lifted up, and the skirts or hem of his garment are so enormous that the temple, or holy of holies, is filled), and Kaiser rightly observes that the picture Isaiah paints is an indirect one of a powerful figure who transcends all earthly dimensions.[23]

In the vision, the *trisagion* is chanted by the seraphim who stood above Yahweh (LXX: *kuklō autou*, around him), each of which is described as having six wings. The Hebrew expression 'one ... to another' may imply that there were two seraphim only, but verse 6 might be taken to imply that there were several such creatures visible.[24] With two pairs of their wings the creatures reverently concealed their faces and 'feet', which is a euphemism for the genitals.[25] With a third pair of wings the creatures flew. They also, apparently, had hands (v.6).

The reference in Isaiah is the only reference in the Old Testament to seraphim as heavenly beings, but we may presume that the prophet's contemporaries knew something about the form of the creatures of this name. That this is no longer the case today is confirmed by the fact that, although many suggestions have been made regarding their identity and origin, none has won universal acceptance. Gesenius, for example, connected the word *śārāp* with the Arabic *šarufa*, 'to be noble', and interpreted it as meaning a heavenly prince or noble.[26] The majority of commentators, however, identify it with the root *śrp*, 'to burn',[27] and it is possible that, as glowing beings of light, they are connected with the flashing lightning associated with some Old Testament theophanies. Jacob, with the support of Isaiah 14:29 and 30:6 where it is a matter of a flying *śārāp* (serpent), considers a solar or at least an astral origin for these beings.[28] Kaiser, adding Numbers 21:6 and Deuteronomy 8:15 to the above passages, suggests that the seraphim must be thought of as naked winged serpents with human faces and hands as well as with six wings.[29] Karen Joines has cogently argued that they should be regarded as the Israelites' version of the Egyptian symbol of the winged *uraeus*, which was also given human attributes – hands, feet and faces.[30] The association of the throne of the pharaoh with winged serpents is demonstrated archaeologically by the recovered throne of the fourteenth-century BCE pharaoh Tut-Ankh-Amun.[31] Each arm of the throne, which is overlaid with sheet gold and richly adorned with polychrome faience, glass, and stone inlay, is formed by two wings of a four-winged *uraeus* rising vertically from the two back corners of the seat. Joines also cites evidence to show that the winged *uraeus* was known in Palestine.[32] Accepting this identification, J. de Savignac has argued that knowledge of the Egyptian *uraeus* influenced the translators of the LXX, and hence *mimma'al* was rendered *kuklō autou*.[33] Kaiser presumes that they took their name *śārāp* from their painful, burning bite.[34]

Whatever the precise origin of the seraphim, the difficulty lies in explaining why they should have featured in Isaiah's vision. If the vision was inspired by the temple liturgy, or the interior of the temple, we might have expected *cherubim* which decorated the temple and were associated with the Ark in the holy of holies, representing the creatures who surrounded Yahweh.[35] Possibly the glowing coals of the altar of incense (with which a seraph seems to be associated in v.6), or the bronze serpent (2 Kings 18:4) played some part in the formation of the vision. The fact that a function of a seraph in the vision was to use a coal from the altar as a cleansing fire and symbol of atonement might suggest the former.[36] J. de Savignac suggests identification with the latter, called Nehushatan, which was destroyed by Hezekiah.[37] The latter identification would perhaps explain why no further references to seraphim occur in the Old Testament books. It would seem, however, that seraphim could be understood as a distinct type of celestial being. Possibly reflecting the personnel of Royal Courts, the seraphim were envisaged as particular attendants or royal guards who were thought to flank the throne of God.

The first notable action of the seraphim which Isaiah records was the recitation of the *trisagion*. If the context was a liturgical celebration, then the *trisagion* may well have been part of a hymn regularly chanted in the temple liturgy, and it may have been chanted antiphonally as by the seraphim.[38] Engnell, who describes it as 'a burden verse, a cultic formula quoted directly from the ritual of the temple in Jerusalem',[39] cites as an analogy the Egyptian formula applied to pharaoh:

> Pure, Pure is the King of the South and the North;
> Thy Purity is the purity of Horus, Seth, Thot and Sopdu.[40]

This analogy is not a particularly strong one, but even if the vision of Isaiah was not itself directly inspired by a liturgical event in the Jerusalem temple, the *trisagion* could certainly be a cultic liturgical formula. Kaiser observes that the refrain in Psalm 99:3, 5 and 9 seems to be almost in concentrated form in the *trisagion*.[41]

The twofold occurrence of 'pure' in Engnell's analagous formula raises the question of whether or not the *trisagion* of Isaiah is genuine, or whether it represents a later expansion. Engnell himself noted the suggestion of the editor of *Biblia Hebraica* that originally there was only one 'holy' – a view which Engnell regarded as not very creditable, and he argued instead for the genuineness of the threefold 'holy'.[42] More recently, N. Walker, noting that in MT a dividing line, the *paseq*, is found after the first *qādôš*, which draws attention to some peculiarity in the text, and that in 1QIs[a] (ASOR 1950 Plate 5 Line 24) there is a twofold *qādôš*, which the corrector of the text has passed over, suggests that there were originally two readings of this verse, one with one *qādôš*, and another with two, meaning 'exceeding holy'.[43] A later scribe, represented by MT, has attempted to preserve both readings, and placed them together with a *paseq*.

Summing up, one may say that there is a strong presumption that the 'Thrice-Holy' of Isa.vi.3 was in origin, a conflate reading, signifying, 'HOLY, EXCEEDING HOLY'.[44]

The originality of the thrice-holy has been reasserted by B. M. Leiser who, in reply to Walker, pointed out that a *paseq* does not necessarily signify a peculiarity (indeed, Gesenius-Kautzch mentions that one use of *paseq* is as a divider between identical words),[45] and that in view of the corrector's inconsistency, the absence of a correction in 1QIs[a] is not evidence for a reading more ancient than that of MT.[46] A triple repetition is not unknown – Jeremiah 7:4, Ezekiel 21:32 – and in Isaiah 6:3 it is appropriate:

The ancient rabbinical interpretation fits the verse quite well: The first seraph called, 'Holy!' 'Holy!' was the reply. And then in a gigantic chorus, 'Holy is the Lord of Hosts'. Or perhaps the paseq is utilized to introduce a praise and a subsequent *diminuendo* in the reading, giving the impression that the enormous chamber resounded with the cry, 'Holy! (Holy, Holy) is the Lord of Hosts.'[47]

Kaiser is surely correct to reject the suggestion that the threefold repetition is derived from magic and even associated with an apotropaic seraph cult.[48] The threefold repetition serves to emphasise the otherness and transcendence of God.

The formula *Yhwh Ṣᵉbā'ôt* occurs 267 times in the Old Testament,[49] and although it has been suggested that the form *yhwhᵉlōhê ṣᵉbā'ôt* was the original, and that *ṣᵉbā'ôt* stands in genitival or construct relation to *'ᵉlōhê*, it seems more likely that the longer form is a later expansion,[50] though this does not rule out the possibility that an ellipse was intended from the beginning.[51] The question arises, however, as to what *yhwh ṣᵉbā'ôt* actually means? While some scholars have argued that proper names of persons are not used in the construct state in Hebrew, and that *ṣᵉbā'ôt* should be understood in opposition to *yhwh*, J. A. Emerton has argued from inscriptions at Kuntillet 'Ajrud that it is quite possible to understand *yhwh ṣᵉbā'ôt* as 'Yahweh of Hosts'.[52] The problem remains of precisely what 'hosts' means.

Ṣābā seems to be basically a military term, and possibly a tribal detachment. Certainly in 1 Samuel 17:45, 'armies' refers to the host of Israelite armies of which Yahweh is Lord.[53] However, it has also been argued that 'hosts' refers to the stars and astral beings, and/or angels and ministering spirits.[54] According to Patrick Miller's study of the term, it includes both these connotations, and its origin is to be understood against the background of the gods and the heavenly council of the ancient Canaanite pantheon. In the El-Baal-Anat cycle, there was an assembly of gods, a celestial council. El was the theoretical head; there was Baal, Anat, Aṭirat, Aṭṭart, Yamm and Mot, and of less significance, Šăpăs and Koṭar-wa-ḥassis.[55] It included also the sons of El. Yamm's messengers appear as warriors, flaming and with swords, and Miller sees here some connection with the cherubim of Genesis 3:24, and also with the seraphim. In other words, $\d{s}^e b\bar{a}'\hat{o}t$ is another name for the divine council of Yahweh, and the divine council with its heavenly troops join with the armies of Israel. According to Miller, however, $\d{s}^e b\bar{a}'\hat{o}t$ originally referred to the non-human participants.[56]

Against Miller's explanation is the fact that when $\d{s}^e b\bar{a}'\hat{o}t$, absent from the Pentateuch, Joshua and Judges, does appear (in the books of Samuel and Kings) it is in connection with the Ark and the armies of Israel, and refers to Yahweh as the God who made himself known in war. Von Rad urges that it had different meanings for different groups,[57] and thus while its early usage may have been in terms of Israel's armies, it is understandable that $\d{s}^e b\bar{a}'\hat{o}t$ came to be applied to heavenly armies also.[58] According to the analysis of Tryggve Mettinger, there is a clear connection between the Sabaoth title and the temple theology and Zion tradition.[59] The Sabaoth title was the pre-eminent term employed in the Jerusalem tradition for the God who dwelt in the temple, and was indeed the key-word in the classical Jerusalemite theology of the Presence.[60] The title came to stand for the concept of God as king enthroned upon the cherubin throne in the temple. At the time of the Exile, it was no longer an appropriate term, and was replaced by the Šem (Deuteronomy and the Deuteronomistic historical work) and kābôd (Ezekiel and P) theologies.[61]

The LXX renders the phrase sometimes by transliteration (Is 6:3; 37:16), and also by kurios (ho theos ho) pantokratōr (2 Sam 5:10; Amos 5:15, 16) and kurios tōn dunameōn (2 Sam 6:2).[62]

The second part of the seraphim's cry praises Yahweh for his kābôd, his honour and glory, which fills the whole earth. Kābôd carries the meaning of weightiness, honour and prestige, and suggests that which makes God impressive to man, the force of God's self-manifestation.[63] Creation itself reveals his glory (Ps 19), and his mighty theophanies amidst thunder and lightening confront man with his glory (Ps 97:1ff.; Ex 19:16). Indeed, the Priestly writer associates the cloud with glory, whereas in Ezekiel it takes a more concrete form – it leaves like a chariot. But there is another dimension to Yahweh's glory. In Isaiah and Psalms 72:19 and 57:5, 11, it can be something hoped for, and in Deutero-Isaiah the glory of God which will be revealed amounts to Yahweh's salvation for his people. According to Psalm 24, Yahweh of Hosts is the King of Glory. In the trisagion, the various manifestations of his kābôd fill the whole earth. Thus there is a balance between the Holy transcendent God, who is immanent in the world in his glory.

THE VISION OF EZEKIEL

The visions of the divine Throne–Chariot of Ezekiel 1 and 10 are important for a number of reasons. The *trisagion* itself does not of course occur here. Nevertheless, the Book of Ezekiel records two lengthy visions of the divine Throne–Chariot in which the *kābôd* of Yahweh is revealed to the prophet. Like the vision of Isaiah, some of the material in Ezekiel seems to have been inspired by the interior of the Jerusalem temple. Furthermore, the visions mention more celestial beings, which together with other images from Ezekiel reappear in the later development of the liturgical *qeduššah* and the sanctus.

There are well known textual difficulties with the Book of Ezekiel, with regard both to the differences between MT and LXX, and also to the material which can be attributed to the prophet Ezekiel, and that which may be regarded as later editorial work.[64] With regard to the two visions in question, most commentators accept that the theophany in chapter 10 is out of context[65] and is merely an elaboration based on that of chapter 1. However, since these chapters have subsequently affected each other, commentators differ widely on what they regard as original and as editorial in chapter 1.

Chapter 1 purports to describe the vision in which the prophet received his call. The theophany begins with the traditional elements of a great cloud with flashing fire. From the flames appeared four *ḥayyôt* (LXX: *zōa*), having human form. *Ḥayyah* used in the singular usually signifies 'a dangerous animal, untamed, living free, and usually large'.[66] The plural occurrence in Ezekiel 1 is perhaps to be regarded as a general designation for living creatures, deliberately left vague but allowing for a general resemblance to human form. Verses 6–14 give a fuller description of these living creatures, describing attributes of other mammals and birds.

The *ḥayyôt* resemble the seraphim of Isaiah in that they have wings, one pair of which covers the body (v.11), and hands (v.8); and are associated with burning coals of fire. But the similarities end here. The *ḥayyôt* had four wings, not six, and they had four faces – of a man, a lion, an ox and an eagle. The order of the description in verses 6–12, which moves on from the faces and wings to the feet and the hands in verses 6–8, whereas verses 10–12 in fact describe only the details of the faces and wings, is acknowledged by Eichrodt to be strange.[67] However, he rejects Zimmerli's suggestions that the details in verses 7–11a are to be set aside as a subsequent elaboration, suggesting instead that verse 6 conveys a general impression, verse 7 the upright stance of the feet and verse 8 the hands – emphasising the human features – and in verses 10–12 the characteristics of the faces and wings derived from the animal realm are described.[68]

Verses 15–21, which most commentators regard as a later interpolation into the vision, describe four *'ôphannîm* (wheels), which were associated with the living creatures. When the living creatures moved, the *'ôphannîm* moved beside them; when the living creatures arose from the ground, the *'ôphannîm* arose together with them, for the spirit of the living creatures was in the *'ôphannîm* (vv.19–20).

It may be that the inspiration of the vision was a four-wheeled chariot.[69] Zimmerli suggests that each wheel was conceived as a disc, marked with concentric circles, or decreasing in thickness from the centre outwards in such a way that it was hollowed out to form concentric rings. The wheels were full of eyes which were possibly bosses, a form of decoration or strengthening.[70]

Verses 22–8 describe a vault (*rāqîaʿ*) about the heads of the living creatures. Under the vault their wings spread out, touching one another. Above the vault, or platform, is a throne, and seated on the throne is a form in human likeness, presumably Yahweh. The whole is described as like the appearance of the glory of Yahweh.

In its present form, the vision and call of Ezekiel extends to 3:15, where he comes to the exiles at Tel-abib. In MT and LXX 3:12 reads:

Then the spirit took me up, and I heard behind me the voice as of a great earthquake, [saying] Blessed is the glory of Yahweh from his place.

This text reappears in the later Jewish liturgical development of the *qeduššah*, though in modern translations the text is usually emended, reading *berûm* for *bārûk*:

Then the spirit lifted me up, and as the glory of Yahweh arose from its place, I heard behind me the sound of a great earthquake.   (RSV)

Whereas the vision of chapter 1 is of the glory of Yahweh by the river Chebar in Babylon, those described in chapters 8–11, while seen by the prophet in Babylon, are of the temple in Jerusalem, and chapter 10 seems to have been introduced to show that the glory of Yahweh was still at this stage associated with the temple. According to 10:20–1, it was an identical vision to that recorded in chapter 1; in 11:22–5, the glory of Yahweh left the city of Jerusalem.

Although it is clear that chapter 10 is a duplicate of chapter 1, it provides more specific definitions than the latter and is modelled more directly on the iconography of the Jerusalem temple. The living creatures are expressly called cherubim, and in the description of the four faces, that of an ox is replaced with that of a cherub. Furthermore, in verses 2, 6 and 13 of MT the wheels are identified as *galgal*, although the precise significance of this identification remains obscure. Zimmerli suggests that they are wheels under the ark of the covenant, or of the incense brazier set before the ark.[71] However, the identification of the living creatures with the cherubim suggests that the redactor of chapter 10 was attempting to combine the ark sanctuary of the temple with the throne of Yahweh of chapter 1.[72] The speculations about the wheels in chapter 10, which seem to have influenced chapter 1 (vv.15–21), perhaps represent a bold attempt to interpret chapter 1 in terms compatible with a vision modelled directly on the temple interior. But even if this is the case, the vision is not simply a psychedelic description of the temple interior.

The holy of holies of Solomon's temple, with the cherubim of olive wood and gold, their wings covering the poles of the ark of the covenant, is described in 1 Kings 6:19–28 and 8:1–9. However, the form and significance of these latter objects are not uniform throughout the biblical material. Menahem Haran draws attention to two trends of scholarly thought regarding the significance of the ark:

1 It was a chest, a container of objects of great holiness.
2 The ark was the seat of Yahweh, an empty throne.[73]

However, regarding the second view, R. E. Clements notes that the position of the ark in the temple, located lengthwise, is incompatible with its use as a throne, unless we are prepared to accept that Yahweh was thought not to face the congregation in the temple but to be seated sideways on it.[74] According to Haran, there were in fact two quite separate objects which have been brought together by P: there is the ark and, quite separate, the *kappōret*, or throne, supported by the wings of the cherubim. Deuteronomy refers to the ark, but not in association with the *kappōret* and cherubim, and this is also the case for references to the ark in the Former Prophets. In Ezekiel, however, it is the throne which is described, and there is no reference to the ark. Both Haran and Zimmerli see the Throne–Chariot of Ezekiel as reflecting a time after the loss of the actual ark.[75] It is only P who links them together, and in the description of Solomon's temple it is clear that the ark and its poles are separate from the *kappōret* and cherubim. The ark may have been, therefore, a chest and the footstool of Yahweh. The wings of the cherubim carried the platform on which Yahweh was seated. However, M. Metzger has argued that the cherubim were not part of the throne but were protectors of the shrine and the ark, while the ark itself should not be regarded as the 'empty throne' of Yahweh, but as a portable support for his invisible throne, like the 'boxes' in actual Egyptian examples.[76]

The identity of the creatures designated cherubim is only slightly less mysterious than that of Isaiah's seraphim. According to Dhorme, they were Babylonian intercessory deities;[77] Kapelrud traces them to Sumerian door-divinities;[78] W. F. Albright suggested that they were winged sphinxes of Syria and Palestine, as represented at Byblus, Hamath and Megiddo, c.1200–800 BCE, a view shared by Metzger;[79] and De Vaux suggested winged sphinxes from Egypt.[80] More probable may be the case presented by R. H. Pfeiffer who, citing three Assyrian texts where *kuribi* are mentioned, concluded that cherubim derive from the Assyrian root *karabu* (to bless), and were akin to guardian angels.[81] It is probably better to speak of Assyrian parallels rather than identity and origin. In the Old Testament the cherubim have various functions or, rather, appear in a variety of contexts. In Genesis 3 (J) and in Ezekiel 28:13–14, we encounter a cherub in 'Eden, the garden of God', implying that in some sense they were in the service of Yahweh. These creatures adorned the walls of the temple, and Yahweh can be said to ride (drive)[82] or be enthroned upon them (Ps 18:10–11 and 80:1–2). But whatever their Mesopotamian or other origin, Haran correctly observes that 'out of all this pre-Israelite heritage the image of the cherubim succeeded in becoming the centre of the sacral–cultic symbolism of the First Temple in Jerusalem'.[83]

Although the cherubim and *kapporet* of the holy of holies seem to have influenced chapter 10 of Ezekiel, and may have played some conscious part in the form of the vision contained in chapter 1, there are distinctive elements in the latter which are significantly different from the earthly counterpart. The cherubim described by P and in 1 Kings each had two wings, whereas Ezekiel's *ḥayyôt* had four. Ezekiel's creatures also had four faces, and the cherubim, *kapporet* and ark of 1 Kings give no suggestion of 'wheels', although 1 Chronicles 28:18 does refer to the 'golden chariot of the cherubim that spread their wings and covered the ark of the covenant of Yahweh'. There is something to be said for Bertholet's suggestion that the description of the Throne–Chariot had in mind the mobile stands of the temple (1 Kings 7:27–39) as a model.[84]

Mettinger has argued that in both chapter 1 and 10, God's throne is a central motif, showing a continuity with the concept of the enthroned king of the Zion–Sabaoth theology.[85] However, the throne is no longer occupied by *yhwh ṣᵉbā'ôt*, but God's *kābôd*.[86] The most likely explanation for this is the supposition that God's abandonment of his city to an enemy had made the designation unusable; *kābôd*, however, turned out to be a reasonable designation for the God who both leaves and returns to the city.[87]

The first occurrence of the sanctus, therefore, is as an acclamation of praise on the lips of the winged serpent-like creatures called seraphim which succinctly proclaimed the transcendent holiness of Yahweh of Hosts, who is immanent in the world through his glory. The chant may have been a regular part of the temple liturgy, pre-dating the eighth-century BCE context in the Book of Isaiah in which it is recorded.

Both Isaiah and Ezekiel claim to have a small glimpse of the heavenly reality, and they describe their visions using terminology from other Old Testament theophanies, and they use images from the temple. The concepts underlying these visions were apparently still common currency at the time of the compilation of the Book of Daniel. The vision of the judgment scene in Daniel 7 with the 'Ancient of Days' (*'attîq yômîn*) seems to draw upon Ugaritic mythology where El, 'Father of Years', sits enthroned, surrounded by the gods of the Ugaritic pantheon.[88] However, the vision also echoes the vision of Ezekiel and the concept of the divine council which Isaiah and Ezekiel presuppose. The throne of the Ancient of Days had flames of fire and wheels (*galgillîm*) which were burning fire. Furthermore, El is surrounded by innumerable beings:

A thousand thousands ['*elep 'alᵉpîm*; LXX; *chiliai chiliades*] served him,
and ten thousand times ten thousand [*wᵉribbô ribwān*; LXX *muriai muriades*]
stood [*yᵉqûmûn*; LXX *pareistēkeisan*] before him.[89]

The (heavenly) court then sat in judgment. This vision of Daniel, together with those of Isaiah and Ezekiel, provided the material for the descriptions in later Judaism of the appearance of God in heaven, and the worship offered to him by celestial beings.

2

⚜

The worship of heaven and the qeduššah *in Judaism*

THE heavenly visions of the Old Testament provided the material and inspiration for the descriptions and assertions in later Judaism of the appearance of God in heaven, and the worship offered to him by celestial beings. Although by no means exclusively limited to the *trisagion*, or *qeduššah* as it is termed in Judaism, this particular acclamation of praise was considered in some circles to be an important element in the angelic repertoire. The extension of the biblical ideas can be traced in the Qumran literature, the Old Testament Pseudepigrapha, the *yorde merkāvāh* or *Hekhalot* literature, and in the evolving prayers of the Synagogue.

THE QUMRAN COMMUNITY

The discovery of scrolls in a number of caves near the ruins of Qumran on the Dead Sea – the Dead Sea Scrolls – has given scholars a much broader picture of the variety of religious beliefs in Judaism during the period 100 BCE – 100 CE. Amongst the writings which originated within the community itself (many scholars identify them as Essenes), one basic belief was the idea of a cosmic struggle between light and darkness, represented by the Sons of Light and the Sons of Darkness. The sectarians of the Qumran Community believed that they were engaged in a struggle with their enemies which reflected a cosmic struggle between the Spirits of Light and the Spirits of Darkness – an angelic struggle. M. Mansoor describes it as follows:

With God in heaven, under the leadership of the prince of light [1QM 13:10] are all the hosts of angels, who gladly and willingly serve God, who sing His praises, who compose His retinue, and fight His battles. To the prince of light God has apportioned the righteous. He had His angels enlighten the hearts of the elect, lead them to righteousness, truth and purity. Angels lead them to repentance and strengthen them in the doing of what is good. The righteous are taken up into their ranks at some time. Everything that is good and pure has its origin in the realm of the prince of light. However, over and against Him stands the angel of darkness. Angels are classed in two main groups – good and evil – whose respective functions are strongly linked with the fundamental dualistic teachings of the Sect. The Almighty is surrounded by His angels, and the Sect looks forward to praising Him ultimately in their company. The angels participate in the eschatological event. The members of the Community have fellowship with the good angels. This fellowship involves participation in the heavenly songs of praise for the Almighty.[1]

The fellowship which Mansoor refers to must be seen in the context not simply of the eschatological war, but of the origin of the Sect in its opposition to the Jerusalem cult. The Sect believed that the Jerusalem temple and its priesthood were defiled, and saw itself as the true Israel, and its priests as the true priesthood. It had its own calendar, priesthood and liturgies, and table fellowship was an important feature. There were detailed regulations ensuring the purity of those taking part, and meals were eaten in strict conformity with the hierarchical order of the community. An Aramaic fragment from Qumran is said to describe a sacred meal in the heavenly temple, a meal in which the sons of Zadok were to take part.[2] The writings of the community stress that God and his angels dwelt in their midst and, therefore, that the community stood in the midst of God and his angels. Thus 1QS 11:7ff:

God has given them to His chosen ones as an everlasting possession, and has caused them to inherit the lot of the Holy Ones. He has joined their assembly to the Sons of Heaven to be a Council of the Community, a foundation of the Building of Holiness, an eternal Plantation throughout all ages to come.[3]

This idea is also found in 1QH 3:19–22, and 1QH 11. In 1QSb the priestly leader is said to be 'like an angel of the Presence in the holy dwelling, to serve the glory of the God of hosts [for ever. And thou] shalt be a faithful servant in the temple of the kingdom, sharing the lot of the angels of the Presence, and in the council of the community [with the holy ones] for ever, and for all eternity, for all they commandments are [sure]'[4] – though these particular blessings may be for the end-time.

The union of the sectarians with the angelic host implies that the community joins in the praises given to God by these holy ones:

For the multitude of the Holy Ones [is with thee] in heaven, and the host of the Angels is in thy holy abode, praising thy Name.   (1QM 12)

Indeed, praising the Name as an important angelic function is also implied in 4Q Dib Ham:

Give thanks ...
[Bless] His holy Name unceasingly
... all the angels of the holy firmament
... [above] the heavens.

Of specific importance are the two fragments published by Strugnell in 1960 under the title 'The Angelic Liturgy'.[5] In the first fragment, the seven 'sovereign Princes' are the seven chief angels who bless the holy ones, both celestial and earthly, and it is possible that this was thought to coincide with the Sabbath offering. The second fragment is a description of the activity of the heavenly entourage of the Divine Throne–Chariot of Ezekiel 1, which on palaeographical grounds Strugnell dated between 75 and 50 BCE:

the [ministers] of the Glorious Face in the abode of [the gods] of knowledge fall down before Him, [and the Cheru] bim utter blessings. And as they rise up, there is a divine small voice ... and loud praise; [there is] a divine [small] voice as they fold their wings.

The Cherubim bless the image of the Throne–Chariot above the firmament, and they praise the [majesty] of the fiery firmament beneath the seat of His glory. And between the turning wheels, Angels of Holiness come and go, as it were a fiery vision of most holy spirits; and about them [flow] seeming rivulets of fire, like gleaming bronze, a radiance of many gorgeous colours, of marvellous pigments magnificently mingled.

The spirits of the Living God move perpetually with the glory of the wonderful Chariot. The small voice of blessing accompanies the tumult as they depart, and on the path of their return they worship the Holy One. Ascending, they rise marvellously; settling, they [stay] still. The sound of joyful praise is silenced and there is a small voice of blessing in all the camp of God. And a voice of praise [resounds] from the midst of all their divisions in [worship of] ... and each one in his place, all their numbered ones sing hymns of praise.

There is no *qedušša̅h* here, but the speculation on Ezekiel seems to echo the Targum of Jonathan (1 Kings 19:20 – they who bless silently) and Isaiah. The angelic beings utter blessings, praise and sing hymns of praise, all presupposing a wider background of the divine council.

The question of whether the *qedušša̅h* was used in liturgies of Qumran (it would not be out of place in the Angelic liturgy quoted above) has been raised by Moshe Weinfeld.[6] Weinfeld has argued that the opening sentences of the so-called 'Hymn to the Creator', 11Q Psa Col.24 lines 9–15, echoes the Synagogue *berakah Qedušša̅t ha-shem* to which Isaiah 6:3 is attached.[7] His observations are extremely suggestive, but too much weight is placed upon linguistic echoes. The fact remains that *qeduššah* itself is not yet attested in the Qumran liturgical literature.

THE OLD TESTAMENT PSEUDEPIGRAPHA

The Old Testament Pseudepigrapha are those pseudonymous Jewish works, or probable Jewish works, which date from the centuries immediately before and after the beginning of the Christian era, and carry the name of an Old Testament personage.

However, those engaged in the study of this diverse literature are far from agreeing on what books should be included within this designation, and there seems to be little certainty on the question of dates, provenance, original language and whether a work may be classified as 'Jewish', 'Jewish–Christian' or 'Christian'.[8] This study follows the list compiled by J. H. Charlesworth which is based on the following criteria:

First, the work must be at least partially, and preferably totally, Jewish or Jewish–Christian. Second, it should date from the period 200 BC to AD 200. Third, it should claim to be inspired. Fourth, it should be related in form or content to the Old Testament. Fifth, it ideally is attributed to an Old Testament figure, who often claims to be the speaker or author.[9]

With the exception of the *Ladder of Jacob*, references have been limited to those works listed in Charlesworth's 'primary' list, though the *Ascension of Isaiah*, which in its present form is a Christian work,[10] has been deliberately omitted from consideration here.

Commenting upon his criteria for defining Pseudepigrapha, J. H. Charlesworth writes:

It is important to note that the documents collected according to these criteria are predominantly apocalyptic, or related to this genre, and some are expansions of Old Testament narratives.[11]

Apocalyptic literature is generally described as dealing with eschatology and the cataclysmic intervention of God in history, and the unveiling of the secrets of future history. However, Christopher Rowland has pointed out that an equally important emphasis in apocalyptic literature is the revelation of things *as they actually are* in the heavenly world.[12] In certain parts of apocalyptic literature it is not so much the description of the last stages of the historical process which is to the fore, but a mystical insight into the world above and the perception of its secrets.

Within many of these apocalyptic books of the Pseudepigrapha we find descriptions of heavenly ascensions and relatively detailed accounts in which the host of heaven, and finally God, are seen by the apocalyptist. According to Mary Dean-Otting, the origin of such ascensions are the Old Testament figures of Enoch, Moses, and Elijah, who 'ascended' rather than died.[13] Sometimes the ascension is simply to heaven and the heaven of heavens (Ethiopic Enoch), but in many there are several heavens – five (3 Baruch), seven (Testament of Levi, Slavonic Enoch) or ten (Slavonic Enoch). These visions, which in many ways represent the beginnings of *merkāvāh* mysticism, seem to have their basis in the biblical visions of 1 Kings 22; 19ff, Isaiah 6:3ff, Ezekiel, 1,3:22–4 and 10, and Daniel, 7:9–10 and are, therefore, not unconnected with the ideas of the 'Angelic Liturgy' of Qumran. Ithamar Gruenwald points out that, taken together, these biblical verses display the following characteristics:

1 God is sitting on a throne.
2 He has the appearance of a man, and particularly that of an old white-haired man (Ezekiel, Daniel).
3 God is sitting in a palace (1 Kings, Isaiah, Daniel).
4 Fire occupies an important position in the vision (Ezekiel, Daniel, and under the altar in Isaiah).
5 God is accompanied by angels who minister to him (1 Kings, Isaiah, Ezekiel, Daniel).
6 The angels render hymns (Isaiah and Ezekiel).[14]

It is the latter feature which is of interest, since in addition to testifying to the growing belief in a wide variety of groups or ranks of celestial beings (thrones, authorities, powers and so forth), and that certain ranks had the function of praising God, several of the Pseudepigrapha record the words of the angelic heavenly liturgies and chants.

In chapter 48:1–4 of the Testament of Job, for example (dated variously from the first century BCE to the first century CE), one of Job's daughters chants verses in the angelic language; in chapter 49 another daughter adopts the language of the archons and praises God for the creation of the heights. Another daughter speaks in the language of the cherubim.[15] In the *Apocalypse of Abraham* (a haggadic midrash on Genesis 15:9–17, and perhaps dating from 80–100 CE), chapter 17 tells how Abraham is taught an eternal song which calls on the 'mighty one, holy, Sabaoth'.[16] In chapter 18 there is a vision in the seventh firmament of the throne of God. Fire is under the throne, and round it are the 'all-seeing ones, reciting the song'. Whether the song here refers to the chant in chapter 17 or to the *qeduššah* is unclear. Under the throne are four fiery living creatures who are singing. Each has four faces – of a lion, a man, an ox and an eagle. Each has six wings; two wings cover their faces, two their feet and two are spread out for flying straight forward. Behind the living creatures Abraham sees a chariot with fiery wheels, and each wheel is full of eyes.

In some of these works direct reference is made to Isaiah 6:3. *The Testament of Adam* is dated by S. E. Robinson to the middle or late third century CE. It is regarded as being Jewish, but has been heavily christianised in its middle section which deals with prophecy.[17] In the first section, the Horarium, Adam informs the reader:

> The fourth hour is the 'holy, holy, holy' praise of the seraphim. And so I used to hear, before I sinned, the sound of their wings in Paradise when the seraphim would beat them to the sound of their triple praise. But after I transgressed against the law, I no longer heard that sound.

Here we have the simple affirmation that in Paradise one can hear the *trisagion*, but if a person is not 'a heavenly man' then he can no longer hear the seraphic chant.

The *trisagion* is also mentioned in the third section, the Hierarchy, but this particular section has been christianised.

The Testament of Abraham recounts the archangel Michael's attempt to gain the soul of Abraham, and is extant in numerous languages. Charlesworth believes that it is a Jewish composition of the first century CE, although the actual date and original language are debatable.[18] There are two recensions in Greek.[19] In recension A of chapter 3, as Abraham and Michael approach a city, they find a large tree:

> As they [Abraham and the Archistrategos] went from the field toward his house, by that path there stood a cypress tree and at God's command the tree cried out in a human voice and said, 'Holy, holy, holy is the Lord God who summons him to those who love him!' And Abraham concealed the mystery, for he thought that the Archistragos had not heard the tree's voice.[20]

There is nothing to suggest that this reading in recension A (recension B is rather different) is the deliberate work of a Christian redactor, and it seems to present us with a variant of the *qeduššah*. It should be noted that in this apocalypse, the chant, which is a mystery, is heard on *earth* from the *tree*.

In the *Testament of Isaac* (which, according to Box, is to be dated 400 CE and might be Christian or Jewish, but according to Stinespring is second century CE, and either Coptic Christian or Egyptian

Jewish)[21] Isaac, who is at the point of death, converses with angels, and ascends to heaven under the guidance of the angel of Abraham. In 6:1–6 we are told:

After this the angel took me to heaven and I saw Abraham. So I prostrated myself before him and he received me graciously, he and all the godly ones. Then they all came together and did me honor because of my father. Then they took me by the hand and led me to the curtain before the throne of the Father. So I prostrated myself before him, and worshipped him with my father and all the saints, while we uttered praises and cried aloud, saying 'Most holy, most holy, most holy is the Lord Sabaoth! Heaven and earth are filled with your sanctified (holy)[22] glory.'

Exactly the same chant occurs later in 6:24. The form of the *qeduššah* – heaven and earth, and 'holy' glory – may suggest the influence of Christian liturgy, but not necessarily so.[23] The same is true of the *qeduššah* endings found in the Books of Adam and Eve (widely accepted as dating from the first century CE, and composed in a Semitic language) where in the Apocalypsis Moisis 43:4–5 there are a number of alternative endings:

> Even thus spake the angel, and ascended into heaven, glorifying (God) and saying: 'Alleluia'.
> (Holy, holy, holy, is the Lord, in the glory of God the Father, for to him it is meet to give glory, honour and worship, with the eternal life-giving spirit now and always and for ever. Amen.)
> (Holy, holy, holy is the Lord of Hosts. To whom be glory and power for ever and for ever. Amen.)
> (Then the archangel Jael glorified God, saying, Holy, holy, holy Lord, heaven and earth are full of thy glory.)[24]

The editor of the edition in R. H. Charles, L. S. A. Wells, commented

Doxologies are later additions. The first paragraph occurs in C, the second in Arm, the third in Slav.[25]

In his more recent edition, M. D. Johnson simply notes that a number of manuscripts all have the *trisagion* as an ending.[26] It is not clear at all whether these are Christian additions, or a variety of Jewish and christianised forms of *qeduššah*.

More obviously Jewish is the prayer which Jeremiah prays after he has offered a sacrifice, in 4 Baruch 9:2–6; S. E. Robinson gives this work an upper limit of 136 CE, and believes it to have a Palestinian provenance;

Holy, holy, holy, incense of the living trees, true light that enlightens me until I am taken up to you, for your mercy I plead, for the sweet voice of the two seraphim I plead, for another fragrant odour of incense. And may Michael, the archangel of righteousness who opens the gates for the righteous, be (the object of) my attention until he leads the righteous in. I implore you, Almighty Lord of all creation, unbegotten and incomprehensible, in whom all judgment was hidden before these things existed.

This prayer, which is concerned with intercession rather than simply with praise, and which accompanied a sacrifice, begins with the thrice-holy of the *trisagion*, but nothing else. Nevertheless, the hint is made that the *trisagion* will be sung if the voice of the two seraphim is granted to Jeremiah.

Another text of significance is the *Ladder of Jacob*. Charlesworth places this text in a secondary list of Old Testament Pseudepigrapha, and suggests that far from being a medieval composition by Slavs, it dates from second-century CE Palestine.[27] More recently, H. G. Lunt suggests that it is a Jewish story composed in Jewish–Greek, for a Palestinian audience.[28] Chapter 2, as published by M. R. James, contains an ascent to heaven with a prayer which includes the following:

Before the face of thy majesty the six-winged Seraphim fear, and hide their feet and their face with their wings, and with the others they fly, and sing ... (*two lines missing: no help from Rec.2 which omits this invocation*) Highest, with twelve faces, many-named, fiery, lightening-formed, holy one! Holy, holy, holy, Jao, Jaova, Jaoel, Savakdos, Chadob, Sabaoth, Omlelech, Elaber, Ame (?) S'me barech, eternal king, strong, mighty, very great, long-suffering, Blessed One, that fillest heaven and earth and the sea and the abyss and all aeons with thy glory.[29]

It is unfortunate that two lines of the invocation, or song of the Seraphim, are missing: the context suggests that the *trisagion* followed – particularly with a repetition of the thrice-holy, the mention of Sabaoth and glory. Although it displays something of a magic formula with a series of names for God, it does seem to be a prayer with a much expanded *qeduššah*.

The two most notable works which contain the *qeduššah* are, however, 1 and 2 Enoch.

In 1 Enoch (Ethiopic Enoch and the Parables of Enoch) a distinction has been made between 1 Enoch 1–36, 72–end, and the Parables of Enoch 37–71 simply for reference purposes. Although 1 Enoch is generally regarded as a Jewish work, J. T. Milik, on the strength of the absence of fragments from Qumran, has argued that the Parables are to be regarded as Christian additions.[30] However, Milik's arguments relating to the Parables have been rejected by Fitzmyer, Knibb and Mearns,[31] and according to Charlesworth the overwhelming consensus is that Ethiopic Enoch 37–71 is Jewish.[32] In a special study of the Parables David W. Suter writes:

Examination of the heavenly ascent and the oath traditions in the Parables of Enoch leads to the conclusion that the work is Jewish rather than Christian in origin and that it belongs to an early stage of the Merkavah tradition.[33]

The link with the *merkāvāh* tradition is also emphasised by C. Rowland and I. Gruenwald.[34] As to the date of the Parables, Suter writes:

On the basis of the typological examination of the ouranology and angelology of the Parables, its likely use by Matthew, and the examination of its relation to the events of the first centuries BC and AD, it appears that the work was composed sometime between the last quarter of the first century BC and the fall of Jerusalem in AD 70.[35]

In 1 Enoch 36:4, the seer says that the Lord of Glory works wonders and shows the greatness of his work to angels, spirits and men so that they might praise and bless him, and in 1 Enoch 104:6 the righteous are promised that they will become companions of the host of heaven – an idea similar to that of Qumran. The same idea is found in the Parables, 1 Enoch 39:6–7. In 29:11ff, the seer says of the Lord of spirits:

Blessed is he, and may he be blessed, from the beginning and forever more. There is no such thing as non-existence (lit. 'ceasing') before him. (Even) before the world was created, he knows what is forever and what will be from generation to generation. Those who do not slumber but stand before your glory, will bless you. They shall bless, praise, and extol (you) saying, 'Holy, Holy, Holy, Lord of the Spirits; the spirits fill the earth.'
    And at that place (under his wings) my eyes saw others who stood before him sleepless (and) blessed (him) saying,
    Blessed are you and blessed is the name of the Lord of the Spirits forever and ever.
And my face was changed on account of the fact that I could not withstand the sight.

Thus the seer hears the *qedušša̱h* chanted by 'those who sleep not', though it is not the biblical text which is recited. The Parables continue:

And after that I saw a hundred thousand times a hundred thousand, ten million times ten million, I saw an innumerable and uncountable (multitude) who stand before the glory of the Lord of the Spirits.   (40:1)

The seer saw four presences – archangels – who bless, praise, pray and supplicate. In 47:1–2, at the coming of the Son of Man in judgment, the prayers of the righteous, together with their blood, shall ascend where the holy ones, with one voice, supplicate, pray, praise, give thanks, bless and will pray to God for them. We thus have the concept of a mingling of earthly and heavenly worship and supplication. In 1 Enoch 61, an angel reveals to Enoch that the Elect One will be placed on the throne:

And he will summon all the forces of the heavens, and all the holy ones above, and the forces of the Lord – the cherubim, seraphim, ophanim, all the angels of governance, the Elect One, and the other forces on earth [and] over the water. On that day, they shall lift up in one voice, blessing, glorifying and extolling in the spirit of faith, in the spirit of wisdom and patience, in the spirit of mercy, in the spirit of justice and peace, and in the spirit of generosity. They shall all say in one voice, 'Blessed [is he] and may the name of the Lord of the Spirits be blessed forever and evermore.'
All those who do not sleep in heaven above shall bless him; all the holy ones who are in heaven shall bless him; all the elect ones who dwell in the garden of life [shall bless him]; every spirit of light that is capable of blessing, glorifying, extolling and sanctifying your blessed name [shall bless him]; and all flesh shall glorify and bless your name with an exceedingly limitless power forever and ever.

Here we have an eschatological picture of the End, when the righteous and the celestial beings – including cherubim, seraphim and ophanim (the latter having become a separate class of angelic beings – cf. 1 Enoch 71:7) – together praise God in heaven. The *qeduššah* in the Parables, we may note, is a song of heaven, and not earth.

Although Daniélou regarded Slavonic Enoch as a Jewish–Christian work the consensus opinion seems to be that, although it may have Christian interpolations and although the relationship between the two recensions presents problems, the work may be regarded as a Jewish work.[36]

In its present form, Slavonic Enoch records the ascent of Enoch, carried on the wings of two men (angelic beings) through ten heavens, though the original seems to have referred only to seven heavens; certainly only seven are given a full description. In each of the heavens Enoch encounters varied groups of celestial beings who praise God in pleasant and unceasing voices. Thus, in the sixth heaven are seven bands of angels who organise singing and glorious praise. In their midst are six (seven in recension B) Phoenixes, Cherubim and six-winged ones having but one voice and singing in unison. And their song is not to be reported; and the Lord is delighted by his footstool.   (19:6)

Recension B reads:

having but one voice and singing in themselves. Their song is not to be reported; the Lord is delighted by his footstool.

In the seventh heaven, Enoch encounters more celestial beings, arranged in hierarchies. Recension B 20:3–21:1 reads:

And all the heavenly armies assembled, according to rank, advancing and doing obeisance to the Lord. And then they withdrew and went to their places in joy and merriement, in immeasurable light, but gloriously serving him by night, nor departing by day, standing in front of the face of the Lord, carrying out his will – with all the army of cherubim around his throne, never departing, and the six-winged ones covering his throne, singing in front of the face of the Lord.

Recension A has a much more complicated celestial hierarchy, with specific angelic classes arranged in steps according to their rank which would bow down to the Lord and would again go to their places in joy and felicity, 'singing songs in the boundless light with small and tender voices, gloriously serving him'. However, Recension A goes on to quote the *qeduššah*:

Cherubim and seraphim standing all around his throne, six-winged and many-eyed; they cover his entire throne, singing with gentle voice in front of the face of the Lord.
  Holy, Holy, Holy, Lord Lord Sabaoth,
  Heaven and earth are full of his glory.

If Recension A is an expansion of Recension B, it would seem that the redactor felt it necessary to elaborate on the heavenly songs by giving the *qeduššah*, which is attributed to cherubim and seraphim. Since it is generally agreed that any Christian additions are to be found in A rather than B, it might be the case that this *qeduššah*, which is close to the eucharistic sanctus, was inserted under the influence of Christian liturgical usage. There can be no certainty in this matter.

    Enoch, it should be noted, is anointed and becomes like one of the glorious ones and is invited to stand before the Lord's face to eternity (22:6). We may presume that he thus joins in the songs of the heavenly host.

    On account of the many uncertainties which surround the diverse literature described by the term 'Old Testament Pseudepigrapha', and which originated from diverse groups with diverse interests, it is impossible to draw any firm conclusions. Some of the apocalypses in this material record the ascent of an Old Testament seer to heaven, where the seer learns some of the secrets of heaven, including the names of some of the ranks of celestial beings and their liturgical chants. While the chants vary, the *qedussah* is often included, and while some instances may be the work of Christian redactors (Apocalypse of Moses; Testament of Isaac; 2 Enoch), others occur in works which scholars regard as emanating from Jewish groups. The form of the *qedussah* varies, illustrating that the biblical text was not sacrosanct in these circles. In one instance the *qedussah* is heard on earth (Testament of Abraham), and it can be used as a prayer by man to God (4 Baruch); otherwise it is a heavenly chant. It would seem that in some Jewish circles the *qedussah* and other chants were regarded as secrets of the heavenly world which angels and righteous men sing now, and which they would sing together in heaven in the age to come.

MERKAVAH MYSTICISM

In discussing the Old Testament Pseudepigrapha, reference has already been made to the *merkāvāh* tradition. Deriving its name from the Hebrew term *Ma'aśeh Merkāvāh* (the work of the Chariot), which in rabbinical writings describes one of the two branches of the esoteric teachings of ancient Judaism (the other being *Ma'aśeh Bereshit*, the work of Creation), it has been the subject of important studies by G. Scholem, I. Gruenwald and P. Schafer.[37] The literature of the mature period of this movement, the *Hekhalot* (Divine Palaces) literature, is preserved in a number of books:

> Re'uyot Yehezkel
> Hekhalot Zutreti
> Hekhalot Rabbati
> Merkāvāh Rabbah
> Ma'aśeh Merkāvāh
> Sefer Hekhalot (3 Enoch or Hebrew Enoch)
> Masekhet Hekhalot

According to Gruenwald, the three main subjects dealt with are: heavenly ascension; the revelation of cosmology, and other secrets; and the special method of studying and memorising the Torah.[38] Central to the tradition, however, is the study of God's glory and celestial throne, with considerable speculation on the visions of Ezekiel 1 and 3. Lawrence Hoffman argues that this movement emerged out of the

Hellenistic milieu of the second century CE, if not earlier.[39] However, it would be quite wrong to identify the *merkāvāh* movement solely with the Hekahlot literature. As Hoffman points out:

> In fact we have no record whatever of *merkavah* organizations, calls, meetings, leaders, social structure – nothing that a student of human organizations would point to as illustrating the development of a group. We have instead legends about rabbis, some well known, like Yochanan ben Zakkai and Akiba; a literature detailing visions of people who attained the mystical vision; and prayers galore illustrative of *merkavah* values and *merkavah* style. So we should speak not of the *merkavah* 'group' but of a *merkavah* 'tendency' to which many a rabbi may well have leaned at one time or another.[40]

It seems fairly clear that the Angelic Liturgy of Qumran, where there is speculation on the *merkāvāh* (throne–chariot), and the heavenly ascents noted in the Old Testament Pseudepigrapha are expressions of this movement or 'tendency'[41] and bear witness to its wide diffusion and to a date earlier than that suggested by Hoffman. The visions of the Book of Daniel seem to be connected in part with this speculation, and the Targum of Ezekiel, where there is already some considerable elaboration of the biblical text, may itself be the work of this movement.[42] Although concern with the Book of Ezekiel may suggest a Babylonian origin, the stories of Rabban Yohanan ben Zakkai (*c*. 1–80 CE) and his disciple Rabbi El'azar ben 'Arakah indicate that it was equally a Palestinian movement.[43]

The importance of this tradition for the sanctus lies in its revelations concerning divine songs of heaven and liturgical hymns of the angels which, we may presume, were sung in certain circles of this diffuse movement.[44] According to Scholem, many of these hymns originated in Palestine, certainly not later than the third century CE, and probably earlier.[45] Quite a number of these hymns include *qedušsah*.

In *Re'uyot Yehezkel*, the *qedušsah* is sung by angels in the second heaven and these angels are renewed every day and recite their hymns from sunrise to sunset. In the *Sefer ha-Razim*, before the angels sing the *qedušsah*, they immerse themselves in streams of purity and wrap themselves up in garments of white fire. In *Hekhalot Rabbati*, the major *Hekhalot* tractate, Rabbi Ishmael is told:

> Between firmament and firmament is hung water; between water and water, fire; between fire and fire, water; between water and water, fire and hail and water. Fire burneth more fiercely and there is a wall of fire on either side of the throne and seraphim standing before Him and saying, 'Holy, holy, holy is Yahweh of Hosts' and beasts uttering praise, 'Blessed be the glory of Yahweh

from His [dwelling] place. And the firmament saith, 'The Lord reigneth He is apparelled with majesty', And the seas and the rivers utter praise and say, 'To Him who divided the Red Sea into parts' etc.[46]

In chapter 11 Rabbi Ishmael gives a detailed description of the worship and ministry of the angelic host. Regarding the holy beasts, in language which echoes the Qumran fragment, Ishmael reveals:

But among the holy beasts there is none that precedeth or delayeth because their height is one and their breadth is one and their clothing is one and their strength is one and the crowns of their heads are one and their splendour is one. And the creatures are arranged at the four feet of the throne, one over against the other: one wheel over against another, one ophan over against another, one beast over against another, one cherub over against another and one melody over against another. And they open their mouths in song, in thanksgiving, in fear, in fright, in terror, in trembling, in shaking, in shivering, in cleanliness and in holiness and in a still small voice, as it is said, 'and after the tumult [sic] a still small voice'.

And they lift up the *Merkāvāh* with a sound of songs, with praise and with laud. They do the holy hallow, the pure applaud, the messengers exalt, the wheels rejoice, the cherubim praise, the beasts bless, the seraphim give utterance, the troops magnify, the angels make music and they are divided into three groups of a thousand thousands and myriad of myriads. One group saith, 'Holy, holy, holy', and kneeleth and falleth prostrate; and the second group saith, 'Holy, holy, holy', and kneeleth and falleth prostrate; and the third group saith, 'Holy, holy, holy is Yahweh of Hosts, the whole earth is full of His glory', and it kneeleth and falleth prostrate. And the beasts from under the throne of glory answer after them and say, 'Blessed be the glory of the Lord from His [dwelling] place.'

Similarly, in *Ma'aśeh Merkāvāh*, a short text published by Scholem, we are informed that the chariots of fire in the first palace say 'Holy, holy, holy, Yahweh of Hosts, all the earth is full of Thy glory', and the flames in the second and third palaces answer 'Blessed be the glory of Yahweh from His place.'[47]

In *Sefer Hekhalot*, known as 3 Enoch or Hebrew Enoch, we encounter the mystical tradition as it had developed in the sixth and seventh centuries CE. From the literary point of view the book is affiliated to the Enoch tradition. The first part describes Enoch's translation to heaven and his transformation into Metatron, or a *Synthronos* – one seated alongside God. Chapter 13 describes Metatron's crown, and then in chapter 14 we encounter a highly complex angelology. *Qeduśśah* occurs at a number of points in this work and is chanted by special hosts of angels, the *ḥayyôt*, the great Prince, the heavenly bodies and the Seer. According to *Hekhalot Rabbati*, it is amongst the 'principal songs' heard by Ishmael and learnt by him. And in *Maʿaśeh Merkāvāh* we find a *berakah* which includes *qeduššah*:[48]

> Blessed art thou Yahweh my God and my maker great and terrible,
> Life of the worlds, powerful over all the Chariot.
> Who is like thee, powerful in the height?
> Prosper me in all my limbs
> And I shall meditate at the gates of wisdom and examine the ways
> of perception
> And watch at the chambers of the Law and meditate on the hidden
> things of blessedness;
> And may they be treasures to me, for wisdom is before Thee,
> And protect me from all angry [spirits] who attend, so that
> they may become friends to me before Thy presence,
> And I shall know Thy holiness is for ever,
> And I shall bless Thy holy name for ever
> And I shall sanctify Thy holy and great name
> And the great Seal shall be on all the limbs of my body
> as it is written, and I shall cry 'Holy, holy, holy is Yahweh
> of Hosts, the whole earth is full of His glory.
> Blessed art thou, Yahweh, Life of the Worlds.[49]

The *merkāvāh* tradition, as it blossomed in this particular literature, bore witness to the importance of the *qeduššah* amongst this 'tendency' in Judaism. The chant came to be included in hymns, whether appropriate to the context or not, and the occurrence of *qeduššah* within a *berakah* suggests that it may well have occurred as a regular feature in the personal *berakot* of some adherents to this widely diffuse movement.

THE SYNAGOGUE PRAYERS

The Synagogue liturgy provides for a Morning (*Shaharit*), Afternoon (*Minha*) and Evening (*'Arvit*) Service daily, plus an additional (*Musaf*) service on Sabbaths and festivals.[50] The *qeduššah* occurs in three places within the Synagogue liturgy: in the *Yoṣer*, the first *berakah* before the *shema* in the Morning Service (*qeduššah dᵉ yoṣer*); in the third *berakah* (*Qeduššat ha-shem*) of the *Amidah* (*qeduššah dᵉamidah*); and at the end of the service, originating in the *Bet Midras* after the readings and exposition (*qeduššah dᵉ sidra*). A great deal of discussion has taken place concerning which of these was the first to make its appearance in the public liturgy, and at what date.[51]

It was not until the Gaonic period (c. 600–1100 CE) that a more or less fixed wording of the Synagogue prayers came to be determined and were written down; until the close of the Talmud, the principle that found acceptance was 'They who write down prayers are as they who burn the Torah.'[52] The first prayer book known to us is that of Amran Gaon (d. 871) who composed an order (Seder) for use in Spain; roughly a century later, Saadiah Gaon (d. 942) issued a prayer book.[53] Although the texts of these collections are by no means identical, they are both identified as belonging to the 'Babylonian' ritual. There was also another distinct ritual, the 'Palestinian' ritual. However, this latter sank into oblivion with the eclipse of Palestinian Jewry at the time of the Crusades, and the Babylonian rite ultimately predominated.[54] In Egypt, the Palestinian rite seems to have been preserved in many of the liturgical fragments of the Cairo Genizah. Although certain more recently developed rites – the Italian, Ashkenazic and Romanian – show the influence of the 'Palestinian' ritual, the predominant influence on all modern rites is undoubtedly 'Babylonian'.[55]

The scholarly investigation of the origins and development of the Synagogue prayers has tended to concentrate on the historical and philological issues, and the reconstruction of their 'original' form.[56] Generally the 'Palestinian' rite has tended to be regarded as older, and hence more 'original', than the 'Babylonian' texts. Furthermore, shorter texts of the same prayer tended to be regarded as the earlier versions. In recent years, however, another approach, the form-critical method, has been pioneered by Arthur Spanier and Joseph Heinemann.[57] This method is concerned with the development and employment of diverse liturgical forms and patterns in the actual setting of the Synagogue. Heinemann maintains that the liturgy was long circulated in oral form, and thus there was no single Urtext, but different oral versions. It is now recognised that in the Tannaitic and Amoraic periods there was a variety of alternative texts which were used in worship. It has also become clear from the form-critical method that not only is it questionable to regard the Palestinian texts as more original, but a text which comes down in the Babylonian sources may also be of Palestinian origin.

It has long been recognised that the qedušśot of the Synagogue berakot, with their accompanying angelology, were due to the influence of the merkāvāh tradition,[58] but there has been little agreement either on the extent or the date of this influence. Heinemann noted:

Only once in the Tannaitic sources (and this only toward the end of the period) do we find any mention of the *Qeduššah*, viz., the description of the sanctification of God by the ministering angels on high, which has its roots in the theophanies of the prophets Isaiah and Ezekiel. Its core is the recitation of two verses from the biblical accounts of those theophanies – *Isaiah* 6:3 ('Holy, holy, holy is the Lord of hosts; the whole earth is full of His glory'), and *Ezekiel* 3:12 ('Blessed be the glory of the Lord from His place'). Scholars are in disagreement as to whether this solitary Tannaitic passage (Tosafta Berakot, I,9) refers to the *Qeduššah* in the *amidah*, or in the *Yoser* (the first benediction before the recitation of the *Sema*). But there is reason to believe that *both* forms of the *qeduššah* came into being during, or even before, the Mishnaic period, the only question being to what extent either had been accepted as an integral part of the statutory worship in all places during this period.[59]

The form-critical approach, together with more recent studies on the Cairo Genizah fragments, has meant that the late date previously given to the Synagogue *qeduššot* is in need of considerable revision.

*Qeduššah d*ᵉ *Yoṣer*

In Seder Amran Gaon (SAG), the daily *Yoṣer* blesses God for the light and darkness, the luminaries, and mentions the exultation of God by the heavenly host:

They all take upon themselves the yoke of the kingdom of heaven, one from the other, and give leave one to another to hallow their Creator: in tranquil joy of spirit, with pure speech and with holy melody they all respond in unison in fear, and say with awe: Holy, holy, holy is JHWH of Hosts: The whole earth is full of his glory. And the Ophanim and the holy Chayoth with a noise of great rushing, upraising themselves towards them praise and say: Blessed be the glory of JHWH from his place. To the blessed God they offer pleasant melodies.[60]

The text of the Sabbath *Yoṣer* is considerably longer.[61]

The date of the *Yoṣer* itself has been disputed. Some scholars believed that it formed part of the temple liturgy as outlined in *Tractate Tamid*, but others believe this is a reference to the *Ahabah* prayer. Heinemann argued that all three *berakot* of the *shema* are old, not because of some presumed origin in the temple liturgy, but because they originated as a single unit in the popular prayer of the Synagogue, and from the popular worship entered the morning service of the temple priests. Since the temple service was before sunrise, *Yoṣer* was never adopted there.[62]

Louis Finkelstein, whose liturgical views have been popularised in the English-speaking world by C. W. Dugmore,[63] believed that the original form of the *Yoṣer* originated in the temple and was shorter than the form used in the Synagogue.[64] Indeed, Zunz fixed the 'original' form of this *berakah* at forty-five words.[65] The Palestinian Genizah fragments published by Jacob Mann provided shorter texts of the *Yoṣer* which did not contain *qeduššah*, leading Mann to posit a late date for inclusion of *qeduššah*.[66] However, the explanation for this latter seems to be that it was for *private* recitation. In Seder Saadia Gaon (SSG), an ordinance, also found in one manuscript of SAG, notes that the individual recital of the *Yoṣer* must be without *qeduššah*, since it is only possible to recite *qeduššah* when ten men are present.[67] Furthermore, the recent research of Ezra Fleischer now indicates that Mann's conclusion is inaccurate. Fleischer has examined some of the Piyyutim, especially those found in the Cairo Genizah.[68] The early Piyyutim were composed to create a parallel with the text of the prayer. Fleischer concludes that the Piyyutim associated *Yoṣer* and *qeduššah*, and this would not have been possible unless the latter had been included in the *Yoṣer*. The Piyyutim indicate that *qeduššah* was used on Sabbaths and holidays, but not semi-holidays and weekdays. Only in some Palestinian communities was *qeduššah not* recited, and this was atypical.

In the texts of SAG, the Sabbath *Yoṣer* has three main insertions: 'All shall thank thee'; 'God the Lord'; and 'To the God who rested.'[69] The second of these seems to be the work of the later *merkāvāh* tradition,[70] and it was probably this type of expansion leading up to *qeduššah* which was resisted in Palestinian circles rather than *qeduššah* itself.

In *Yoṣer* it is 'ministering spirits' who recite the *qeduššah*, while it is the *'ôphanîm* and *ḥayyôt* who respond with Ezekiel 3:12. The words 'upraising themselves towards *them*' is in some texts rendered as 'towards the *seraphim*', thus identifying the ministering spirits.

A fragment of a *Yoṣer* from the Cairo Genizah published by Schechter uses phraseology from Daniel 7:10:

Creator of ministering spirits, tens of thousands stand before him, myriads upon myriads surround his throne, all are beloved, all are pure.[71]

Qeduššah d^e 'amidah

This occurs with the third *berakah* of the *'amidah*, Qeduššat ha-shem. The nucleus of this *qeduššah* is Isaiah 6:3, Ezekiel 3:12 and Psalm 146:10, and to these scriptural verses various additions have been made. It is first mentioned in connection with Rabbi Judah ben Ilai in the middle of the second century CE. According to Finkelstein, this *berakah* was composed *c*. 10–60 CE, but without *qedušśah*.[72] He believed that in Babylon the *'amidah* remained more fluid than in Palestine, and it was in Babylon that the *merkāvāh* mystics added *qedušśah* and changed the wording of the *berakah*. On the other hand, Kohler believed that it was introduced shortly after *qedušśah d[e] Yoṣer*, and under the influence of the Essenes. It was subsequently altered in some rites to allow private recitation without the angelic song, but the *qedušśah*, so he argued, is the core of the *berakah*.[73]

Finkelstein's views concerning the development of *qedušśah d[e] 'amidah* and *Qedušśat ha-shem* centred on the opening words of the latter. In SAG it reads:

From generation to generation give homage to God, for he alone is high and holy, and *they* praise our God.

In SSG it reads:

You are holy and your Name is holy, and holy beings each day offer you their praise.

Clearly both these versions refer back to the *qedušśah*. However, in the Palestinian rite the *berakah* consists of seven words, which Finkelstein regarded as the *Urtext*:

You are holy, and your Name inspires awe, and there is no other God than you.

Here there is no reference to heavenly beings, and the *berakah* shows less connection with the *qedušśah*, and can stand alone without it.

SAG forbids the recital of *qedušśah* unless ten people are present; Palestinian usage demanded at least seven.[74] Thus, the Palestinian version may well represent a version for private recitation; furthermore, as has been noted above, different versions do not necessarily mean later developments, but may have existed side by side. Fleischer's study referred to above suggests that in fact *qedušśah d[e] 'amidah* was recited in Palestinian communities in the morning prayers and holidays, and also in the *Musaf* for Rosh Hashanah, and all the services for the Day of Atonement.[75]

The form of the *qedušśah d[e] 'amidah* varies amongst different rites, and undoubtedly it was in the Babylonian communities that the expansion of the mystical elements took place. The angelology is very restrained: holy beings. The occurrence of holy seraphim in some versions would appear to make explicit the 'they' who 'sanctify [Thy

Name]' in the highest heaven. In contrast to the *qeduššah d^e Yoṣer*, where the song belongs to the holy beings, in this *qeduššah* it is made explicit that Israel joins in and makes the chant its own together with the angelic beings.

Qeduššah d^e sidra

The context of this *qeduššah* has been thoroughly analysed by Liebreich.[76] It consists of:

1 *Qeduššah* (Isaiah 6:3). Ezekiel 3:12, 15:18, with the Targum Onkelos of Isaiah 6:3.
2 The initial biblical verses: Isaiah 59:20–1 and Psalm 22:4 suggesting the theme of repentance and redemption.
3 Scripture verses which link the *qeduššah* with the *berakah*.
4 The *berakah* (*ubā l^esiyyôn*).
5 A concluding passage from scripture – Psalm 30:13, and in some texts also Psalm 19:15.

This *qeduššah* was recited after the conclusion of the reading of the prophets and was of *Bet Midras* origin rather than the Synagogue (though study was closely connected to worship). Of significance is the fact that in this *qeduššah* no angelic beings are mentioned, though clearly the seraphim are presupposed by the biblical quotation. Also of interest is the apparent doublet: the biblical text of Isaiah 6:3 is followed by the Aramaic Targum version, which explains the holiness of Yahweh as *in heaven* as well as on earth.

Although Jewish scholars differ as to which is the earliest of these three Synagogue *qeduššot*, the weight of scholarship has been in favour of *qeduššah d^e Yoṣer*.[77] Fleischer has shown that *qeduššah* was used in Palestine in the *Yoṣer* and *'amidah* at an early date, and *Tosafta Berakot* I, 9 demonstrates that a *qeduššah* was already customary towards the end of the Tannaitic period at the very latest. In the light of the Pseudepigrapha and *Hekhalot* literature, it is quite probable that *some groups* of Jews used *qeduššah* in their Synagogue prayer in the first century CE.

In this diverse literature emanating from very different Jewish groups between the first century BCE and the sixth century CE (Qumran – 3 Enoch) the following tendencies can be detected in relation to Isaiah 6:3:

1 Certain privileged men are taken to heaven and witness the angelic chants, including *qeduššah*.

2 Certain groups who have this knowledge can use *qeduššah* in hymns and prayers; eventually, through the culminative influence of these groups, *qeduššah* became part of the Statutory Synagogue prayers, and Israel itself (*qeduššah dᵉ 'amidah*) can take part in the song of the seraphim.

3 In the apocalypses the angelology is complex, but in the *Hekhalot* hymns and Synagogue *berakot* the angelology which accompanies *qeduššah* is somewhat more restrained.

4 In the *Hekhalot* literature and Synagogue *berakot* the biblical text of Isaiah 6:3 (and Ezekiel 3:12) is reproduced without change. An exception is *qeduššah dᵉ sidra* where the Targum version appears with the biblical texts. In the Pseudepigrapha, however, even excluding the possible Christian interpolations, there are examples of considerable adaptation of the biblical text.

3

Continuity and influence in early Christian documents

IN continuity with Judaism, Christianity inherited the concepts of angelic beings, God enthroned in heaven and, at least in some circles, the idea that the redeemed would be like angels (Lk 20:36; cf.Mk 12:25). It inherited the *trisagion* through its use of the Book of Isaiah as canonical scripture, and through the various groups which conserved, copied and edited many of the Old Testament Pseudepigrapha. A number of early Christian documents also bear witness to the continuing influence on Christianity of the Jewish liturgical and quasi-liturgical use of the *qeduššah*.

Within the New Testament it has been claimed by David Flusser that the song sung by the heavenly host in Luke 2:14 is a diminished Greek paraphrase of the Aramaic Targum on Isaiah 6:3 as found in *Qeduššah d^e sidra*.[1] Flusser places a great deal of weight upon vague linguistic echoes, and his view is highly speculative. The context in Luke warrants a new song to mark the occasion, not the *qeduššah* which was the eternal song of the heavenly host. However, even if Flusser's claim is doubtful, there are nevertheless two other New Testament references which indisputably relate to the *qeduššah*.

Although the text itself is not quoted, Isaiah 6:3 is directly referred to in John 12:41. In explaining why the Jews refused to believe in Jesus despite the many signs he had performed, the evangelist refers to Isaiah 53:1 and 6:10. He then adds:

Isaiah said this because he saw his glory and spoke of him.

Here the evangelist interprets 'I saw the Lord' as referring to Jesus. B. Lindars notes that in the Targum this statement is rendered as 'I saw the Lord's glory', and R. E. Brown compares this with John 1:14 where the glory of the Lord is revealed in the incarnation.[2] The Fourth Gospel thus gives the *trisagion* a christological application.

The other reference is Revelation 4:8. Whereas the first three chapters of this book are concerned with letters to the seven churches, in chapter 4 a door in heaven opens and the seer is told:

Come up hither, and I will show you the things which must come to pass hereafter. (4:1)

The seer is spiritually translated to heaven, and remains there until the close of chapter 9.[3] As in the Enoch literature, he hears many celestial songs, acclamations and prayers. The very first chant he hears is a variant of Isaiah 6:3, sung by four living creatures (*tessera zōa*). The fact that the seer is in the presence of twenty-four elders and the living creatures has suggested to many scholars that we have here an early Christian liturgical tradition, which may have its roots in Jewish worship.[4] P. Prigent concludes his analysis of chapter 4:

The heavenly liturgy of Revelation 4 is not a pure invention of the seer. It takes over, adapting them to the literary genre of a book, the great moments of an actual liturgy the sources of which are Jewish and which in turn prepares the way for a many-structured liturgical elaboration which can be inserted in a larger whole.[5]

The occurrence of a sanctus in Revelation 4:8 is explained by a number of studies as being a Christian adaptation of Jewish liturgical usage, particularly of *qeduššah d^e Yoṣer*; to quote Lucette Mowry, in chapters 4 and 5 'we have material which bridges the gap between Jewish Synagogue worship and later Christian worship'.[6] A. Cabaniss goes even further, and suggests that Revelation reflects a Christian liturgy with a structure of scripture, homily, prayer and eucharist, though his method is to argue backwards from later liturgical practice. The implication here is that we have in Revelation 4:8 an embryonic anaphoral sanctus.[7]

Although the majority of commentators have noted that the seer's description draws upon the imagery of Isaiah, Ezekiel and Daniel, it has been left to Gruenwald and Rowland to develop the insights of R. H. Charles and see Revelation 4 as a reflection, not so much of an earthly liturgy (Jewish–Christian or Christian), as of Jewish mystical tendencies of the type found in the Old Testament Pseudepigrapha.[8] Gruenwald remarks:

The Merkavah vision in Revelation IV is an interesting example of how Jewish Merkavah material was recast in the new Christian environment.[9]

Rowland, who dates Revelation 4 to the sixties CE, asserts that it 'shows no evidence whatsoever of Christian influence, and, treated in isolation, it is quite clear that it is entirely Jewish in its inspiration'.[10] Although in Revelation we may well have early Christian hymns, the visions of chapter 4 and 5 seem to have their roots in *merkāvāh* rather than in the Synagogue liturgy.

The seer sees the throne of Yahweh surrounded by twenty-four thrones with twenty-four elders and the four living creatures, each with six wings. The vision of the throne is inspired by Ezekiel 1, though there are obvious omissions; there is no mention of the wheels of the chariot, and the living creatures are not bearers of the throne. The twenty-four elders are variously identified as glorified men, a college of angels (originally star gods), representatives of the twenty-four priestly orders, and angelic representations of the faithful.[11] The living creatures are akin to the *ḥayyôt* of Ezekiel, but each one is identified with one of the four faces of the creatures of Ezekiel 1:10ff.[12] However, imagery from Isaiah 6 is also used for the four living creatures; they have the six wings of the seraphim, and sing (*legontes*, which in such a context implies singing or chanting) the song of the seraphim or, rather, an adaptation of it.

R. H. Charles suggests that the seer followed the LXX rendering of *ṣᵉbā'ôt* with *Pantokratōr* and inserted *Kurios ho theos* from Ezekiel;[13] in fact Amos 5:15–16 renders *Yhwh ṣᵉbā'ôt* by *Kurios ho theos ho Pantokratōr*. In place of Isaiah's text 'The whole earth is full of his glory', the text here describes the *Pantokratōr* in the terms of Revelation 1:4, 8 as Lord of past, present and future.[14] Noting the grammatical irregularity, Martin McNamara states:

It is clear that in the divine Name we are in the presence of a designation whose individual terms are left throughout undeclined. We appear to be here in the presence of a traditional designation for God.[15]

McNamara examines and rules out Hellenistic and Septuagintal influence, but notes parallel ideas in the late work *The Alphabet of Rabbi Akiba* in explanation of the divine Name of Exodus 3:14.[16] However, more fruitful are the Targumim, where there are precedents for taking the divine Name to imply God's creative activity in the first and a future creation.[17] Targum Pseudo-Jonathan paraphrases Deuteronomy 32:39 thus:

I am He who is and who was and I am He who will be

giving an Aramaic tripartite form of the divine Name, of which, McNamara suggests, Revelation 4:8b seems to be a servile rendering into Greek.[18] The Fragment Targum and Neofiti Deuteronomy 32:3 says:

It is not possible for any of the angels on high to recall the glorious Name until they say Holy, Holy, Holy, three times.

It may be that Revelation is dependent upon these paraphrases, or they may all be dependent upon the same early tradition which, McNamara suggests, may have been liturgical.[19] Thus, although there are probably liturgical echoes in the vision of chapters 4 and 5, the sanctus of Revelation 4:8 seems to be a variant *qeduššah* comparable to those encountered in the Pseudepigrapha. Whether or not one accepts Rowland's view of the Jewishness of chapter 4, it would seem that the context of Revelation 4:8 is more akin to the *qeduššot* of the Pseudepigrapha and *merkāvāh* texts than to the setting it was given in the Synagogue liturgy.

Merkāvāh mysticism may also be the inspiration or influence upon 1 Clement 34:6 and Aphrahat's Demonstration XIV.

In 1951 the Dutch scholar W. C. van Unnik published an article entitled '1 Clement 34 and the Sanctus' in which he challenged the hitherto accepted view that 1 Clement 34:6–7 bore witness to a (eucharistic) liturgical sanctus at Rome *c*.96 CE.[20] Van Unnik lists the previous literature, and there is no point in repeating it here. 1 Clement does discuss the eucharist in chapters 40–2, and recent studies have regarded chapters 59–61 as reflecting the content of early eucharistic prayers.[21] However, van Unnik's penetrating analysis of chapter 34 has made it extremely difficult to regard the sanctus in verse 6 as a direct liturgical allusion. He criticised the view, represented for example by Lightfoot, that in chapter 34 the ministrations on earth are the copy and counterpart of the angelic ministrations in heaven.[22] Van Unnik argued that the context of chapter 34 is eschatological and concerned with judgment. In a painstaking analysis of verses 4–8 he sees a gap between verses 6 and 7:

Vs 6 gives the reason for the contents of the will of God in vs 5; vs 7 describes a meeting of the church which serves the will of God amongst the afflictions and dangers of this world, longing for the end. Therefore it is impossible to see a direct parallelism between the two. *Consequently this passage does not speak of the heavenly 'Sanctus' which is imitated on earth.*[23]

Van Unnik concludes that Clement is simply quoting from scripture, and this view has been endorsed by Donald A. Hagner's study of Clement's use of scripture.[24] Hagner observes:

The first part of this quotation agrees exactly with Dn 7:10, according to Theodotion, except for the transposition of clauses, Clement beginning with *muriai* rather than *chiliai*. Clement has *eleitourgoun* in the *chiliai* clause with Theodotion against the 'Old Greek' or 'LXX'. The words *muriades muriadōn kai chiliades chiliadōn* found in Rev.5:1 (alluding to Dn 7:10) reveal the sequence *muriai–chiliai* found in Clement. This indicates no direct connection, but suggests either that this order was in current use, or that the order could be altered freely. The second half of Clement's quotation agrees exactly with Is.6:3 as found in the LXX except for the substitution of *he ktisis* for *hē gē* (A, B and א). B differs from A and in the further slight variant *ekekragen* for *ekekragon*. Clement has either combined the texts himself, or borrowed the combination from some other source.[25]

However, we might ask what prompted Clement to combine these two pieces of scripture? According to R. M. Grant, Clement used a florilegium.[26] However, van Unnik relied on Dugmore and Finkelstein, working with the view that *qeduššah* in Jewish prayers was late. In the light of Fleischer's findings, and the Schechter fragment of a *Yoṣer* which combines Daniel 7:10 with Isaiah 6:3, liturgical usage could have influenced Clement. But influence could have come from *merkāvāh*. In a paper entitled 'Hellenistic–Jewish Rhetoric in Aphrahat' read at the 1980 Symposium Syriacum, Robert Murray drew attention to the similarity between the themes of 1 Clement and Aphrahat's Demonstration XIV.[27]

Aphrahat, the 'Persian Sage', was probably born *c*.260–75 CE, and died in the persecution of King Sapor the Great *c*.345 CE. In Demonstration XIV Aphrahat includes what Robert Murray calls a wisdom passage about creation. Aphrahat includes a consideration of the wise man, whose wisdom allows him a vision of heaven (whether it is himself or someone else is not clear).

> He is shown that which he knew not;
>   he gazes into that place and is tested;
>   his reason is amazed at all that he sees.
> The Watchers hasten to serve Him
>   and the seraphim cry 'Holy' to his glory,
> flying with their swift wings,
> white and resplendent their garments,
> veiling their faces from his splendour,
>   rushing swifter than the wind.

Murray suggests that although the Demonstration is much longer and much later than 1 Clement, both may reflect a common Hellenistic topos, which has a hint of mysticism parallel to the *Hekhalot* mysticism. Certainly this is speculative, but the possibility cannot be ruled out that Clement was influenced by the widespread diffusion of Jewish mysticism. Likewise it is possible that Aphrahat's spirituality produced this particular passage quite independently of Jewish mysticism; yet it is well known that East Syrian Christianity, of which Aphrahat was a product, developed under the influence of the strong Jewish communities of Adiabene.[28]

Less speculative is the continuing influence seen in the *Passio sanctarum Perpetuae et Felicitatis*.[29] This *passio* is generally dated *c.*200 CE, and is not only an account of the trial and sufferings of the African martyrs, but is also an apocalypse in its own right, reminiscent of the Book of Revelation and the Shepherd of Hermas. It is mainly concerned with the imprisonment, trial and martyrdom of a young matron, Vibia Perpetua, and includes her visions and those of her fellow prisoner, Saturus. The visions reflect a variety of apocalyptic images, reminiscent of the *Hekhalot* literature, 1 Enoch, the Shepherd of Hermas and the Ascension of Isaiah.[30] In the vision of Saturus, there is an account of the ascent of the martyrs to heaven, in three stages. At the third stage is the heavenly city, and at the entrance to God's divinity there stood four angels. The martyrs entered heaven:

And we entered, and we heard singing [*dicentem*] with one voice *hagios, hagios, hagios*, without ceasing.

'With one voice' finds parallels in 2 Enoch and *qedussah d^e Yoser*, and 'without ceasing' is found in Qumran's Angelic Liturgy and 2 Enoch. Although the *passio* is in Latin, the sanctus is in Greek, which chapter 13 perhaps implies is the language of paradise. The literary genre of the *passio*, and its context, suggest a *qedussah* of the Old Testament Pseudepigrapha type or an allusion to Revelation 4:8, and it bears witness to the continued belief passed on from certain circles that those who ascend to heaven would hear the ceaseless chanting of the *qedussah*. The person addressed, however, appears to be Christ.[31]

A similar influence is found in *The Ascension of Isaiah*. This is a composite work, made up of three separate sections: the martyrdom of Isaiah (1–5), the Testament of Hezekiah (3:13–4:18), and the Vision of Isaiah (6–11). It would seem that the first is a Jewish work dating from the second century BCE, while the other two are Christian compositions dated from about the end of the second century CE.[32] A Palestinian provenance is probable.[33]

The vision of the third section begins when King Hezekiah and all the people of the court together with Isaiah heard 'a door which had opened and the voice of the Holy Spirit'. Gruenwald notes that from the date given, the writer was concerned to describe a different vision to that of Isaiah 6.[34] Isaiah fell into a trance and an angel came to show him a vision. The prophet ascended above the firmament, through six heavens, and finally into the seventh heaven. In the first five heavens there was a throne, with angels on the right and angels on the left. Those on the right had greater glory than those on the left, and they all praised with one voice. Those on the left also gave praise after them, but with an inferior voice, and a different praise (7:14–15).

In the sixth heaven there was no throne, nor angels on the left (8:1ff.). Power was given to the prophet and he joined with the angels:

> And there they all named the primal Father, and His Beloved, the Christ and the Holy Spirit, all with one voice.   (8:17–18)

This seems to be a reference to the seraphim, or at least to the *trisagion*, interpreted as praise of Father, Son and Holy Spirit. Later, in the seventh heaven, Isaiah saw all the righteous in heaven, like angels. He also saw 'The Lord' (= Christ) and the angel of the Holy Spirit.

Even though the *trisagion* is not quoted, the work is clearly inspired by the vision of Isaiah 6, and it indicates that, as in Revelation 4 and 5, there were certain Christian circles which inherited and developed the ideas of the early *merkāvāh* tendency in Judaism.

It has been suggested that Tertullian is a witness to the early use of a liturgical sanctus, with reference to his work *De Oratione*.[35] In *De Oratione* 3, speaking of the Name of God, 'Father', Tertullian wrote:

> Yet when is the name of God not holy and hallowed [even] of itself, seeing he hallows others from within himself, and those angels that stand around cease not to say to him, Holy, holy, holy [*Cui illa angelorum assistentia non cessat dicere: sanctus, sanctus, sanctus*]? Consequently therefore we also, angels-designate if such our merits are found to be, already here are learning [to use] that heavenly address to God and that service of the glory that is to be.[36]

The context is a discussion of the Lord's Prayer, and particularly the hallowing of God's name. Tertullian seems to be arguing that, by virtue of the Lord's Prayer, Christians have the privilege of hallowing God's Name, just as the angels who surround God hallow him with their own appointed chant, the thrice-holy. However, there is certainly a hint that (cf. Qumran) Christians will become like angels and will then participate in the heavenly hallowing with *qedussah*.

In these documents we find the idea that Christians will be like angels and will therefore be able to hear, or themselves sing, the *trisagion* and, at least in Revelation, the *passio* and the Ascension of Isaiah (and possibly Aphrahat and 1 Clement) *merkāvāh* influence is discernable.

Although 1 Clement can no longer be cited with confidence as evidence of Synagogal influence, *Apostolic Constitutions* VII.35 bears witness to this influence on some Christian groups.

The *Apostolic Constitutions* (AC) is regarded as the work of an Arian or semi-Arian compiler – possibly a bishop – in the region of Antioch c.360 CE.[37] However, it is a composite work. Books 1–6 are an expansion of the *Didascalia*; 7:1–32 are a reworking of the *Didache*; and much of Book 8 is a rewriting of the *Apostolic Tradition*. There is also material in Books 7 and 8 which so far has eluded liturgical scholars in the tracing of the original sources.[38]

K. Kohler seems to have been the first to draw attention to the similarity between six prayers (AC 7:33–8) and seven *berakot* of the Sabbath *'amidah* of the Synagogue, and he suggested that the former represented Essene prayers which had been taken over by Christians.[39] W. Bousset, unaware of Kohler's work, also argued that these prayers had a Jewish origin; they were Hellenistic Jewish prayers which had been interpolated by Christians.[40] E. R. Goodenough developed Bousset's insights, linking the prayers to the type of Judaism represented by Philo.[41] Although dissenting from the idea of a specific 'Philo Judaism', Louis Bouyer has argued that these prayers were originally Hellenistic Jewish Synagogal prayers which originated in Alexandrian Judaism.[42] The more recent detailed analysis of these prayers by David Fiensy reaches the following conclusions:[43] The prayers are indeed Jewish Hellenistic Synagogal prayers, which the compiler of AC has expanded; the source was probably *oral*, though perhaps it was written down before the compiler of AC appropriated it; the characteristics of the prayers lead to the conclusion that they date from 150–300 CE, and that the provenance was Syria.[44]

Fiensy does not seem to consider the possibility that these prayers could be Jewish–Christian Synagogal prayers. It seems strange that the compiler should have borrowed one Jewish source amongst other Christian documents, parts of which clearly indicate the Jewish cradle of Christianity. Although following Fiensy's analysis here, we allow the possibility that these prayers originated from Jewish–Christian circles.

The third prayer of AC 7:33–8 seems to echo the *Qeduššat ha-shem* in theme, and contains the sanctus. According to Fiensy, paragraphs 1, 2, 5, 7 (first part) and most of 9 and 10 are mainly the work of the compiler. On the other hand, where the holiness of God is its theme, and where sanctus occurs, these belong to the original source: 'Apart from some interpolations in this section, very little of the vocabulary is typical of the compiler.'[45]

The context of the sanctus is that of the created order declaring the greatness of God. Various angelic beings are mentioned – an army of angels and intellectual spirits, and the seraphim who, with six-winged cherumbin, cry out together the sanctus. Other groups call out Ezekiel 3:12 – archangels, thrones, dominions, sovereignties, authorities and powers. Israel sings Ps.68:17 about the chariot of God.

Whereas Bousset and Goodenough argued that 'thrones, dominions, sovereignties and authorities' might reflect a common Jewish angelology which is also found in Colossians 1:16, Fiensy is prepared to accept that the compiler has himself inserted the reference from Colossians 1:16. On the other hand, Fiensy accepts that the form of the sanctus which, as will be seen, became standard in several anaphoras, is thoroughly Jewish:[46]

And holy seraphim, together with the six-winged cherubim, singing to you the triumphal song, with never-silent voices cry out,
  Holy, holy, holy, Lord Sabaoth,
  the heaven and the earth are full of your glory!
And the other throngs of hosts, archangels, thrones, dominions sovereignties, authorities, powers, crying out, say,
  Blessed be the glory of the Lord from its place!

Eric Werner has pointed out the Jewish precedents for uniting 'heaven' and 'earth' in Isaiah 6:3. The Targum of Isaiah in *qeduššah d^e sidra* mentions heaven and earth; furthermore, Werner quotes a midrashic passage where Isaiah 6:3 is linked with Jeremiah 23:24.[47] However, if this was originally a Jewish prayer, there is the possibility that the compiler replaced the biblical text with this emendation, which he also has in his anaphora in Book 8. At the very least, however, we have in this prayer evidence that, as in the Synagogue and in the *Hekhalot* literature, some groups of Christians, at an earlier date than AC, had prayers within which the sanctus could be inserted. Here the use of Ezekiel 3:12 suggests that the Synagogue pattern was indeed the parent model.

In conclusion, therefore, it appears that the various Jewish uses and associations of the *trisagion* discussed in the previous chapter persisted in Christianity. It is from this context that we can turn to look directly at the sanctus in the eucharistic prayer.

Part II

4

৯৫

The sanctus in the East Syrian and Syro-Byzantine eucharistic prayers

ADDAI AND MARI

IT is generally accepted that the anaphora which underlies the East Syrian anaphora of Addai and Mari, and its 'twin', the Maronite anaphora called *Sharar*,[1] is a very early composition, reflecting the Jewish–Christian communities of Syria, with parts dating back to the third century and possibly earlier.[2] However, although the sanctus is found in both versions of this anaphora, it has almost unanimously been regarded as a later interpolation. This view seems to have originated with E. C. Ratcliff in his reconstruction of the 'original form' published in 1929. Ratcliff wrote:

The clauses that introduce this have no connexion with what precedes them. They have no relevance except to the Sanctus; and the whole passage coming in between an address of praise to the Creator and Redeemer and a thanksgiving for salvation and grace is out of place. As in the Roman Rite so in the East-Syrian the Sanctus is an intrusion.[3]

Ratcliff's later opinion, echoed by W. E. Pitt, was that in fact Addai and Mari had always contained the sanctus, but as the termination of the anaphora.[4] Nevertheless, the view that the sanctus in its *present* position represented an intrusion was subsequently endorsed by Gregory Dix, Bernard Botte and Louis Bouyer.[5] In 1966 W. F. Macomber published the Mar Esa'ya text of Addai and Mari, the manuscript of which he dated tenth to eleventh century, and which is regarded as our earliest witness to the text.[6] Although the sanctus is contained in this text, Macomber at that time endorsed Ratcliff's view.[7] Such a view has been repeated more recently by J. M. Sánchez Caro, H. A. J. Wegman and Jean Magne.[8]

Ratcliff's arguments for regarding the sanctus as an interpolation rested on two premises:

1 The clauses introducing the sanctus appear to have no connection with what precedes them.
2 Coming between an address of praise to the creator and a thanksgiving for salvation and grace the sanctus is 'out of place'.

On the basis of these two opinions, Ratcliff classed the East Syrian sanctus with the Roman sanctus, as an intrusion.

It is difficult to understand by what criteria Ratcliff arrived at the liturgical law that if it is to be authentic, a sanctus *must* always connect with what precedes it, or why a sanctus is 'out of place' between praise of the Creator and thanksgiving for salvation. It is these assumptions which are questionable.

To begin with, what does an interpolated sanctus look like? We are fortunate in having one example of a sanctus which textually and contextually is an intrusion and out of place. The anaphora of the *Apostolic Tradition* is without a sanctus, as is its expanded form in *Testamentum Domini*. However, both these anaphoras are used in the Ethiopic Church and have had a sanctus added. The interpolations here, therefore, offer at least some idea of what an interpolated sanctus might look like.

Apostolic Tradition (*Dialogue and short thanksgiving*)	*Ethiopic Apostles* (*Dialogue and short thanksgiving*) (*Intercessions*)
You sent him from heaven into the Virgin's womb; and, conceived in the womb, he was made flesh and was manifested as your Son, being born of the Holy Spirit and the virgin. Fulfilling your will and gaining for you a holy people, he stretched out his hands when he should suffer, that he might release from suffering those who have believed in you.	And for these and for them all, rest their souls and be propitious unto them, thou who sentest thy Son from heaven into the bosom of the virgin. He was carried in the womb, was made flesh and his birth was revealed of the Holy Spirit. Unto thee, before whom stand thousand thousands and myriad myriads and the holy angels and archangels and thine honourable creatures that have six wings, the seraphim and cherubim with two of their wings they cover their face, with two of their wings they cover their feet, and with two wings they fly from end to ends of the world. Continually as they hallow thee and praise, with

> all them that hallow thee and praise
> thee, receive our hallowing also which
> we utter unto thee:
> Holy, holy, holy . . .
>> Holy, holy, holy . . .
> Truly the heavens and earth are full of
> the holiness of thy Glory in our Lord
> and our God and our Saviour Jesus
> Christ thine holy Son. He came and
> was born of the virgin, that he might
> fulfil thy will and make a people for
> you. He stretched out his hands to the
> passion, suffering to save the sufferers
> who trust in thee.[9]

There are good grounds for concluding that the sanctus here is an interpolation: textual grounds, since the earlier forms of the anaphora have no sanctus; contextual grounds, since the sanctus in the Ethiopic version, which is based on the Egyptian form of the sanctus, certainly has no connection with what precedes it. It begins abruptly within a passage which rehearses the incarnation in the past tense, introducing a statement concerning praise offered by the celestial host in the present tense. There is no connection either in terms of a transitional clause, though this in itself is not necessarily indicative of interpolation (see below). However, in addition, it does not fit in with the general sense of the passage. In this example, the textual and contextual grounds *together* point to interpolation.

When the sanctus in the anaphora of Addai and Mari is examined in the light of this example, it is difficult to find grounds to justify Ratcliff's assertions.

Firstly, there is no textual evidence to support his argument. The sanctus is found in all the manuscripts, and is common to both Addai and Mari and *Sharar*. It is generally accepted by scholars that the material common to both these anaphoras represents the earliest strata. The sanctus, therefore, has as much claim to antiquity as any other part of the common material. If any of the common material can be given a third-century date, then the same can be claimed for the section which contains the sanctus.

Secondly, Ratcliff's claim does not hold contextually. The anaphora praises the name of God who created the world(s) and its inhabitants; *Sharar* gives Glory to the Name who created the worlds and its inhabitants – both using phraseology which is thoroughly biblical.[10]

God is creator of heaven and earth, the heavenly world and the lower earthly world (perhaps a variant reading of *Sharar*, 'their inhabitants' is to be preferred). In heaven the Name is worshipped without ceasing, and the sanctus, far from being 'out of place', is a quite logical inclusion, since it is the praise which the inhabitants of the heavenly world continually offer to God. This is wholly in accord with the ideas found in early Christian literature – Revelation, 1 Clement and the ouranology of the Ascension of Isaiah. In Addai and Mari the sanctus remains the song of heaven, the celestial glory, to which is added the thanksgiving of mortals, and it coheres with the overall concept of offering in the anaphora.[11] The hallowing of God's Name in heaven and earth, the concern of this first part of Addai and Mari, is reminiscent of the *berakot* with *qeduššah* which we quoted earlier from *Ma'aśeh Merkā-vāh*. Jacob Vellian has pointed out the strange similarity between the Synagogue *Yoṣer* with its *qeduššah* and the *berakah* which follows it, *Ahabah*, and Addai and Mari.[12] Talley also points to *Yoṣer* with its *qeduššah* as a possible inspiration, though he suggests that the whole of the opening section as far as sanctus may have been added to an earlier strata of thanksgiving (for redemption) and intercession, the addition being due to Jewish influence.[13]

In *Sharar* the thought is slightly different in that 'Glory' is offered to the Name, and the sanctus is made part of the praise of the congregation; here, like the seers in the Pseudepigraphal literature who ascend to heaven and join the heavenly praise, the Christian congregation are permitted on earth to join in the heavenly chant, as well as making their own thanksgiving for redemption.

Although it is not impossible that the address to the Name of God, revealed as Father, Son and Holy Spirit, is original to the anaphora (though not the explicit reference to the Trinity),[14] most commentators accept that the anaphora was originally addressed throughout to Christ, who has been given the Name (*kurios* = Yahweh = Creator = God) and is a hymn to Christ as God.[15] In this anaphora it would seem that the sanctus is addressed to Christ, or the God who is both creator and became incarnate.[16] Such an address we have already observed as early as St John's Gospel.

The introduction to the sanctus is a combination of Daniel 7:10 with Isaiah 6:2 – a combination already encountered in a *Yoṣer* fragment and in 1 Clement 34. The angelology is not particularly complex:

Addai and Mari	*Sharar*
Heavenly beings	
angels	heavenly angels
spiritual beings	
ministers of fire and spirit	ministers of fire and spirit
cherubim	cherubim
holy seraphim	seraphim

Addai and Mari has a slightly more elaborate angelology than *Sharar*, though it is impossible to be dogmatic about which is 'more original'. Four groups are found in AC 7:35 – host of angels, intellectual spirits, holy seraphim and six-winged cherubim. The *qeduššah de Yoṣer* mentions holy beings and ministering spirits. The idea of fear in *Sharar* is found in *qeduššah de Yoṣer*; glorifying is found in the Apocalypse of Moses; 'crying out and saying' in the Testaments of Abraham and Isaac; 'bless' and 'glorify' are found in 1 Enoch 61. All of this is not incompatible with a third-century date, and in a more recent article, W. F. Macomber also accepts that the sanctus is original to the common underlying anaphora.[17] Thus, against Ratcliff and many other scholars, our suggestion is that in Addai and Mari we have evidence of the sanctus as part of the anaphora in East Syria in the third century.

JERUSALEM

The anaphora traditionally associated with Jerusalem is that of St James which has come down to us in a variety of versions, though the principal ones are the Greek and Syriac. Since it was used by chalcedonians and monophysites we may assume that there was a common tradition by the fifth century. However, the Mystagogical Catecheses attributed to Cyril deal in part with the anaphora, and thus bear witness to the Jerusalem anaphora, or some parts of it, in the fourth century. According to Massey Shepherd, a sermon of Eusebius of Caesarea delivered sometime between the years 314 and 319 CE at the opening of the new cathedral at Tyre, also bears witness to the Jerusalem anaphora.[18]

Shepherd calls attention to the paragraph preceding the final bidding of Eusebius' sermon which has marked affinities with the 'Preface' and Anamnesis–oblation of the anaphora of St James and, indeed, with some passages of Cyril. The textual affinity of Eusebius' words with the 'Preface' of James may be exhibited as follows (emphasising the verbal agreements):

Such is the great temple which the Word, the great *Creator* of the universe, hath builded throughout the whole world beneath the *sun*, having fashioned upon *earth* that intelligible image of those things that lie beyond the vaults of *heaven*; so that by the *whole creation* and by the rational, living beings upon earth, His Father is honoured and reverenced. But the region above the heavens and the models there of the things on earth, and the *Jerusalem* above, as it is called, and *the heavenly* Mount Sion, and the supramundane city of the living God, in which the myriad *choirs* of *angels* and *assembly of the first-born written in heaven*, honour their Maker and sovereign Ruler of the universe with *praises* [*theologiais*] unutterable and inconceivable to us – such as no mortal can worthily *hymn*.

Although the sanctus as such is not quoted, it is clearly alluded to, and when compared with the evidence of Cyril and the anaphora of St James there is indeed a reasonable probability that Eusebius is here an independent witness to the anaphora used in the area under the jurisdiction of Caesarea, and therefore of Jerusalem, though this cannot be taken as certain. What it would bear witness to is a eucharistic prayer which began with praise of God by the whole creation, particularly in heaven by choirs of angels and the saints who praise God with 'praises', presumably the sanctus.

The Mystagogical Catecheses (MC) attributed to Cyril of Jerusalem (*c*.348) deal in part with the anaphora. Cyril's authorship of these particular homilies has been questioned, and it has been suggested that they are really the work of his successor, John (387–417).[19] Recently E. Yarnold has suggested that Cyril was the author, but that they represent the older Cyril rather than the younger Cyril of the other catecheses.[20] However, whether by Cyril, older Cyril or John, the MC have been accepted as an important witness to the ancient anaphora of Jerusalem. This view was challenged by G. J. Cuming in an article in 1974 in which he argued that Cyril bears witness to an anaphora of the Egyptian type.[21] In a communication read at the Oxford Patristic Conference in 1983, the present writer argued against Cuming's interpretation of the evidence and, while accepting that there are curious differences between MC and the anaphora of St James, urged that Cyril was nevertheless a witness to the Jerusalem rite which is a quite distinct Syrian rite.[22]

The anaphora is the subject of MC 5. It is important to bear in mind that the material is catechetical and does not yield the accuracy demanded by modern liturgical scholarship. Where Cyril agrees with the anaphora of St James we may check his accuracy, but where he disagrees it is difficult to know whether he knew a different text or was simply relying on memory or the licence of a preacher and orator. The order of the anaphora he described included an opening dialogue, praise of God by mentioning creation, sanctus, epiklesis and intercession for the living and the dead. There is no mention of thanksgiving for redemption, and institution narrative or anamnesis–oblation. It is possible that Cyril passed over these. However, E. Cutrone has argued that had these elements been present, Cyril's concern for *eikon-mimesis* – the identification of the believer with Christ – would have induced him to make a great deal of such material. His silence suggests its absence.[23] Indeed, John Fenwick has argued very strongly that at the time of Cyril such features were not part of the Jerusalem anaphora, and their appearance in the anaphora of St James is the result of a reworking of the Jerusalemite material with the anaphora attributed to St Basil in one if its earlier recensions.[24] What is significant for this study is that MC *does know* of the existence of the sanctus.

The sanctus which MC alludes to occurs early in the anaphora, seemingly as part of an *oratio theologica*:

After this we make mention of heaven, and earth and sea; of the sun and moon; of the stars and all the creation, rational and irrational, visible and invisible; of Angels, Archangels, Powers [*dunameōn*], Dominions [*kuriotētōn*], Principalities [*archōn*], Authorities [*exousiōn*], Thrones [*thronōn*]; of the Cherubim with many faces; in effect repeating that call of David's, 'Magnify the Lord with me.' We make mention also of the Seraphim, whom Isaiah by the Holy Spirit beheld encircling the throne of God, and with two of their wings they cover the face, with two the feet, and with two flying, and saying Holy, holy, holy Lord of Sabaoth [*kurios Sabaoth*]. For this reason we rehearse this hymn of praise, handed down to us from the seraphim that we might join in hymns with the hosts of the world above.

Allowing for the homiletic nature of the passage, it is valuable in a number of ways for establishing the probable context and rationale of the anaphoral sanctus at Jerusalem in the fourth century.

1 MC does not mention 'thanksgiving', but simply lists the various items mentioned in the prayer. It seems that rather than thanking God for creation, it was a prayer about the *creation itself*; the mention of creation seems to be regarded as praising God, and mention of the celestial creation logically leads to the sanctus. The thought is slightly different from that encountered in Addai and Mari. Here the existence of the creation, visible and invisible, is itself a form of praise, and leads to the verbal praise of the seraphim (cf. Neh 9:6).

2 While MC makes it clear that the congregation recites the sanctus (that we might join in), grammatically it remains the chant of the

seraphim. Whether the congregation joined in with the single recitation, or whether a congregational recitation followed, is a matter for
conjecture.

3 The quotation from Psalm 34:3 is woven into the anaphoral material
as part of the catechetical style. There are no grounds for endorsing
Kretschmar's suggestion that it actually formed part of the introduction
to the Jerusalem sanctus.[25]

4 In comparison with Addai and Mari and the Jewish Synagogue
qeduššot, the angelic hierarchy is complex, and seems more deliberately
thought out. Four classes from Colossians 1:16 – suggested by creation,
rational and irrational – have been introduced; Powers (dunameōn) has
been introduced from Ephesians 1:21, and the angelic classes have been
increased to nine. However, there is no attempt to reproduce the
scriptural order. Whether Cyril was quoting from memory, or was
quoting them in a deliberate, ascending order, is unclear.

5 G. Dix and G. J. Cuming pointed to the archaic features of the
sanctus passage – covering the face (of God) rather than 'faces' of the
seraphim, and kurios Sabaoth – as Egyptian features.[26] It more
probably simply reflects use of the LXX.

6 We are fortunate that Cyril actually explains how he understood the
function of the anaphoral sanctus:

i It is rehearsed 'that we may join in hymns with the hosts of the world
above'.
ii Cyril immediately adds: 'Then having sanctified ourselves with these
spiritual hymns, we beseech God, the Lord of all, to send forth his Holy
Spirit.'

This seems to suggest that the recitation of the sanctus was a means of
'sanctifying' the congregation. Perhaps it is putting too much weight on
this homiletic material, but it may imply that the singing of the sanctus
was necessary for the actual supplicatory part of the anaphora; the
congregation made a 'spiritual ascent' and, having sanctified themselves, standing before God like the seraphim, they then asked for a true
communion and the descent of the Spirit, and favours for the living and
dead. The reference to spiritual hymns (plural) may mean that some
other chant (benedictus?) was already part of the Jerusalem sanctus,
but Cyril does not quote any other chant than the sanctus at this point.

The anaphora of St James exists in a number of versions, but the
primary versions are the Greek and Syriac.[27] The terminus ad quem for
its creation is the monophysite split, and the Syriac translation was
probably made relatively soon after 451 CE.[28] A version of the

mid-sixth century may be recovered from commentators on the Syrian rite.[29]

In comparison with MC 5, the anaphora of St James presents us with a rather expanded structure of the anaphora:

    Dialogue
    Eucharistia and sanctus
    Thanksgiving for redemption
    Institution narrative
    Anamnesis–oblation
    Epiklesis
    Intercessions
    Doxology

Thus, in comparison with MC 5, a block of material now appears between the sanctus and epiklesis. Furthermore, it has long been recognised that there is some dependence between St James and the anaphora of St Basil, though the direction of the dependence is disputed.[30] John Fenwick's recent thesis demonstrates that St James appears to be a conflation of the Cyrilline Jerusalem eucharistic prayer with an earlier version of St Basil, giving the Jerusalem anaphora a similar structure to the Cappadocian anaphora of Basil.[31] Since, however, the Jerusalem anaphora already contained a eucharistia for creation with sanctus, this particular part has not been subjected to so many additions from the Cappadocian anaphora.[32]

In the Greek version,[33] after an initial build up of praise verbs (remarkably similar to the *Gloria in excelsis*)[34] directed to the creator of all creation, the prayer continues speaking of creation itself 'hymning God', leading to the celestial host and the seraphim. In this respect, to divide the sanctus as a separate unit beginning with 'angels' is artificial, since there is a logical progression from the heaven of heavens and all their powers to the sun and moon, the spirits of righteous men, angels and archangels. Bouyer aptly comments:

This first part, which mentions the Father only, is unified by a summary of the whole of creation, which is invited to join unanimously in the hymn of the Seraphim. All creation is, as it were, summed up in the heavenly Jerusalem, the festal assembly, the Church of the first-born whose names are written in heaven . . . the spirits of the righteous and the prophets, to whom are joined the souls of the martyrs and the prophets.[35]

It is almost as though this *oratio theologica* has deliberately been constructed around the recitation of the sanctus. Perhaps this reflects the eschatology of the Jerusalemite Church, regarding itself as part of the new Jerusalem, and already part of heaven?

Fenwick notes that in comparison with Cyril, some inversion has taken place, though this is perhaps to place too much weight on MC reproducing a correct textual sequence.[36] It is significant that the sermon of Eusebius gives some support to elements in James which are not actually mentioned by Cyril.

This whole *oratio theologica* has been constructed from biblical quotations – 2 Thessalonians 1:3, Colossians 1:16, Revelation 7:17, Psalm 148:3–4, Nehemiah 9:6, Hebrews 12:22–3, Ephesians 1:21, Ezekiel 10:12, Revelation 4:8 as well as Isaiah 6:2–3. The celestial classes mentioned are exactly the same as those mentioned by Cyril, though those from Colossians 1:16 are arranged in their biblical order. The cherubim with many faces have become the cherubim with many eyes, and Powers are 'fearful'. In comparison with Cyril (and the LXX) certain changes have been made in the immediate context of the sanctus: the face (of God) has become 'their faces', and the hymning of the seraphim is now described in more elaborate style – with unwearying mouths and never-silent doxologies (variant reading: theologies), singing, shouting out, glorifying, crying out and saying. The sanctus itself is described as 'the victory hymn of your magnificent glory'.

The post-sanctus, as is characteristic of the Syro-Byzantine family, continues with a linguistic pick-up from the thrice-holy of the sanctus. This whole section of the anaphora, according to the study of Fenwick, derives from St Basil.

In comparison with the Greek text, it is clear that the Syriac is a translation, and in this particular section, for example, the Syriac translator has had to invent adjectival forms, for example, sixfold wings. A number of points can be noted:

1 The list of the creations which *glorify* the creator is slightly shorter than the Greek, and Hebrews 12:22–3 is followed immediately by the angelic hierarchy.

2 The angelic hierarchy of Colossians 1:16 has a different order: principalities, authorities, thrones and dominions. Principalities, *risanwata*, represents a direct translation, the Peshitta using *arcaws*. Whereas the Greek has 'fearful powers', the Syriac has 'powers that are above the world'. The Syriac adds 'heavenly armies' from Revelation 19:14, making ten classes of angelic beings.

3 In the Greek the seraphim cry one to another, in the Syriac they fly one to another.

4 The vocal activity of the seraphim appears to be slightly different: glorifying (*msbhnn*) crying out (*mz'qin*) calling (*q'in*) and saying, though although the words may thus be translated in English, it may be that the Syriac translator believed he was fairly representing the Greek.

Thus, if the sermon of Eusebius is a trustworthy witness to the Jerusalem anaphora, it would appear that from at least the beginning of the fourth century, that anaphora opened with a statement of the creation hymning God and leading into the sanctus. The context of the sanctus is different from that of Addai and Mari, though both are connected with the creation. At Jerusalem, it would seem, the sanctus was addressed to God the creator, though Cyril in the Catecheses shows knowledge that it was connected with the Son (Cat.14.27), and the tenth-century commentator on the Syriac anaphora of St James, Moses Bar Kepha, knew of three interpretations of the sanctus, including that it was addressed to Christ who Isaiah had seen sitting on the throne.[37]

CAPPADOCIA

Asterios Sophistes was born in Cappadocia and lived in Antioch and Syria. His Easter Homilies which are dated *c.*335–41 CE have been edited by M. Richard.[38] According to the study of these homilies by Hans-Jörg Auf der Maur, Asterios is one of our earliest witnesses to the liturgical use of the sanctus.[39]

In Homily XVI 13–15, Asterios proceeds from commenting upon Ps.8:3a to the entry into Jerusalem, and the cry 'Hosanna to the Son of David. Blessed be he who comes in the name of the Lord' (Mt 21:9). Asterios applies Ps.8:3a to those newly baptised at the Easter Vigil. the newly enlightened who once defiled their mouth with immodest songs now praise God in the Holy Spirit and sing the hymn of praise 'never heard before'. Auf der Maur considers the possible meanings of 'hymn of praise' and rules out psalms, the creed or the Lord's Prayer. On the basis of passages in Gregory of Nyssa's *De Baptismo* and John Chrysostom's Homily 18 on 2 Corinthians 3, he concludes that the hymn seems to be the sanctus in which the people of the 'baptised' may join with the priest and the seraphim.[40]

In Homily XV.16, which is also a homily for early morning on Easter Day, there is a further reference to the sanctus. Here Asterios dwells on the glorification and exaltation of Jesus. The ascension and enthronement of Jesus he regards as the fulfilment of the prophetic word in Psalm 8:2b:

Therefore, since the seraphim and the six-winged ones, all the rational spirits who celebrate the liturgy together with them, behold the body of Christ, radiating over them, they praise and glorify Christ for the sake of the astounding miracle, not because of the human nature in itself but for the sake of him who bears it – and they sing – holy, holy, holy, Lord Sabaoth. Others cry out: 'Blessed be the glory of the Lord from this place – that is, from this adored body.'[41]

A further parallel is found in Homily XXIX on Psalm 18, though this is not an Easter psalm:

Yet who are these, angels, archangels, the cherubim and the seraphim? The cherubim proclaim the glory of God; for the prophet Ezekiel hears them say 'Blessed be the glory of the Lord from this place.'

The heavens proclaim the glory of God (Ps 18:2a). The seraphim proclaim the glory; for Isaiah hears them cry out 'Holy, holy, holy, Lord Sabaoth. Heaven and earth are full of his glory.'

The heavens proclaim the glory of God (Ps 18:2a). For the evangelist Luke heard them and said: 'And there was with the angel a great multitude of the heavenly host, who praised God and said: Glory to God in the highest, and on earth peace, among men of goodwill' (Lk 2:13–14).[42]

From this survey, Auf der Maur concluded that the sanctus, which is cited by Asterios in conjunction with Ezekiel 3:12 as in the Synagogue *qeduššot*, first entered the *Easter* anaphora from the morning prayers used at the Easter Vigil (cf. AC 7), and then became a regular feature of the anaphora.[43] He suggests that the tradition in Cappadocia represented by Asterios probably goes back to the third century. As apparently with Addai and Mari, the sanctus mentioned by Asterios was addressed to Christ.

Quite possibly the anaphora of St Basil had a Cappadocian origin.

The name of St Basil the Great has been attached, at least from the fifth century, and quite possibly before that date, to the text of a eucharistic liturgy. Although it exists in several versions – Byzantine Greek, Armenian, Syriac, Alexandrine Greek, Coptic (Sahidic and Boharic) and Ethiopic – it is reasonably clear that we have two basic texts:

1 The short text which is represented by the Coptic and Alexandrine Greek.
2 The longer text represented by the Byzantine Greek.

For many years the relationship between the two texts was surrounded by confusion on account of an assertion attributed to Proclus,

Bishop of Constantinople (434–46) that Basil had shortened a longer liturgy. However, it is now clear that this assertion and its attribution are untrustworthy, and the shorter version represents an earlier version than the longer text. In a study in 1931, H. Engberding demonstrated by a comparative study of the various texts of Basil that the Egyptian text is actually 'pre-Basiline'.[44] St Basil, so Engberding suggested, was responsible for re-writing the anaphora to produce the longer text. This view found further support in the publication in 1960 of a Coptic fragment.[45] In an appendix, B. Capelle argued that the Byzantine version had been reworked by St Basil himself, at least from the opeining dialogue as far as the sanctus. A similar assessment was also made by Bobrinskoy.[46] This assessment has now been expanded considerably by John Fenwick, who has subjected the whole of the anaphora (Engberding, for example, did not include the intercessions) to a very thorough analysis, tracing the expansions in the various versions. Fenwick suggests that an *Urtext* (Ur-Basil, underlying all other versions) of a Cappadocian anaphora was expanded at various times by Basil himself, and this accounts for the reason why all the versions are called after the saint. Whereas the redactor of St James worked by conflation, St Basil worked by expansion, using scripture and theological enrichment.[47]

In the shorter or Alexandrine text, the opening address, or evocation, calls upon God the Father, describing his eternal existence and everlasting sovereignty. A. Houssiau comments:

It thus calls on the eternal God, the creator, and the Father of Jesus Christ; there is no sign here of Trinitarian consideration.[48]

The prayer describes God as the one who made all things, visible and invisible, and who sits on the throne of glory. This reference to the throne room leads to the adoration given by the celestial beings who stand before and around the throne.

The opening description of God, 'Master, Lord, God of truth . . . and regard what is low' has no parallel in the longer Byzantine text, but some parts are attested to in a Sahidic fragment, showing that it certainly belongs to the Egyptian recension of Basil. Fenwick, noting the biblical base – Jeremiah 1:6, Psalms 30:6, 54:20 and 112:6 – suggested that Basil himself added this, and later discarded it in later revisions of the anaphora.[49] However, this may be an Egyptian addition, and Basil was certainly not the only anaphoral writer – expander who was able to quote from scripture! In the subsequent section of the anaphora, material is used from Nehemiah 9:6 as well as the angelic orders of Colossians 1:16 and Ephesians 1:21. We may note a number of points:

1 Standing *beside* God (*hoi parastēkousin*) are the seven celestial orders – angels, archangels, principalities, authorities, thrones, dominions and powers – in the same order as in Syriac James. 'Standing beside' may be an Egyptian stylistic feature.[50]
2 Standing *around* God are the cherubim with many eyes and the seraphim with six wings.
3 In the Coptic version the sanctus is described as 'the hymn of glory'.
4 The Coptic gives the activity of the seraphim as 'ever singing' and 'saying', while the Greek has 'hymning', 'shouting out' and 'saying'.

In the longer or Byzantine text, there is general agreement that the opening thanksgiving to the sanctus has been expanded by Basil himself. Some of the material found in the Egyptian recension is absent, but the whole opening section has been enriched theologically, and a great deal more scriptural quotation and allusion has been added – from Psalm 50:17, Romans 12:1, Hebrews 10:26, Psalms 105:2 and 25:7, Matthew 11:25, Colossians 1:16, Wisdom 7:26, 1 John 5:20, John 1:9, 14:17 and Romans 8:15. It has been given a trinitarian structure. God is praised, and 'this our reasonable service' is offered.[51] The reference to the throne of glory no longer leads immediately to the sanctus, but the prayer proceeds to mention the Son, who is the Logos, and the Holy Spirit. The third person of the Trinity now provides the transition to the sanctus:

By whose enabling the whole reasonable and intelligent creation does you service and renders you unending praise and glory; for all things are your servants. For angels . . .

The result is that now the sanctus is addressed to the Trinity rather than to the Father and creator as in the shorter text, and the amplification has resulted in rather an abrupt transition to the sanctus. Having simply the longer text before our eyes, it would easily be possible to conclude that the sanctus is an intrusion, and therefore a later addition. The shorter text gives the sanctus a more logical context. Fenwick is hesitant on this point, though there is no reason to regard the sanctus in the shorter text as an intrusion.[52]

Capelle notes that in comparison with the Egyptian text, an 'inversion' of the angelic orders has taken place (now in the same order as in Greek James) and finds the same order in Basil's works, concluding that the saint himself made the rearrangement.[53]

One may therefore conjecture that the *Urtext* known to Basil in the first decades of the fourth century contained the sanctus in praise of the creator, and this is still evident in Egyptian Basil. After further reworking of the text, the longer version gives us a trinitarian setting for a sanctus which is introduced very abruptly, looking more like an interpolation. If this is correct, the versions of Basil bear witness to the very opposite of one of Ratcliff's premises; abruptness *may be* the result of reworking by a redactor, upsetting an earlier contextually logical sanctus.

The Egyptian anaphora attributed to St Gregory Nazianzen (329–30 to 390) is found in both Greek and Coptic recensions. There are also Armenian and Syriac anaphoras attributed to Gregory, but apart from the attribution, they have little in common with each other or with the Egyptian anaphora.

It was the view of Baumstark that the Egyptian anaphora was the ancient anaphora of Nazianzen which Gregory had himself expanded and which was later taken to Egypt, possibly by Syrian monks.[54] However, a characteristic of the anaphora is that it is addressed throughout to the Son.[55] Jungmann, in his classic study *The Place of Christ in Liturgical Prayer*, 1925, argued that it was a monophysite product dating from the sixth century.[56] Hammerschmidt, in his edition of the Coptic (Boharic) text, 1957, suggested that it dated from between the last years of the fourth century and the early part of the fifth century,[57] though he accepted that it had been 'Egyptianised'. Recently the Greek text has been examined by José Manuel Sánchez Caro and Albert Gerhards. Sánchez Caro considered the 'I-thou' style of the post-sanctus, comparing it with the homilies and poems of St Gregory, and concluded that this section could well have been written by the saint, reflecting his anti-Arian stance.[58] Gerhards took this further to suggest that the anti-Arian Cappadocian anaphora had been expanded, quite probably by Proclus of Constantinople, in an anti-Nestorian stance, and had then been subsequently Egyptianised.[59] He points out that the *oratio theologica* consists of two sections which have been joined together:[60]

1 The opening praise, consisting of,
  i   Dialogue
  ii   Verbal praise to God
  iii Theological statements
2 The praise of the angels.

The apophatic adjectives, the so-called negative theology, have parallels in Gregory's writings, but they may also represent the common stock of a particular theological epoch.[61] As the text now stands, however, this whole section of praise leading to the sanctus seems to have been expanded, and Egyptian elements have been wedded with Syrian elements, as is indicated by the deacon's interruptions. Gerhards points out that the Syrian understanding of the sanctus seems to have been amalgamated with an Egyptian understanding.[62] The introductory praise leads to an angelological list, but each class of angelic being has a particular liturgical activity. After this, within a statement that the Father and the Spirit are made known through the Son, petition is made that the voice of the Church may be joined with the voice of the seraphim. This may not necessarily be an Egyptianising, since such petitions are found in some late Syriac anaphoras.[63] However, it does reflect the Egyptian pattern, as found in Serapion, of praise, petition, sanctus. Gerhards suggests that the liturgical understanding on which the anaphora is based has the imprint of the platonic mimesis idea, namely that the earthly liturgy is merely a copy of the heavenly liturgy;[64] however, such an idea finds echoes in the Bible itself. We may note that when mention is made of the seraphim, the material in this anaphora is reminiscent of that found in St James.

It is extremely difficult to estimate what, if anything, in this section of the anaphora goes back to fourth-century Cappadocia. However, against the very popular thesis of Jungmann, both Sánchez Caro and Gerhards have shown that Gregory, in his writings against the Arians, made the equation of Christ=God, and Gerhards cites the *Didache*, the Apocryphal Acts of Thomas and John, Addai and Mari, *Testamentum Domini* and Armenian Gregory to show that contrary to Jungmann's view, early eucharistic prayers in *some* places were addressed to Christ.[65] It may be that this Egyptian anaphora bears witness to an earlier Cappadocian custom, seemingly attested to by Asterios Sophistes, of the anaphoral sanctus being addressed to Christ.

ANTIOCH

Little is known of the Antiochene anaphora before the fourth century. Massey Shepherd has suggested that the anaphora of Hippolytus might have derived from Antioch,[66] and Robert Grant has suggested that passages on the works of God in creation and providence developed by Theophilus of Antioch in *Ad Autolycum* i.6–7 (probably written before 180 CE) might echo a eucharistic preface.[67] However, it is only in the fourth century that firm, datable material comes to light with the writings of St John Chrysostom and Theodore of Mopsuestia, and the anaphoras of *Apostolic Constitutions* VIII, of John Chrysostom and possibly of the Apostles.

In an appendix to *Liturgies Eastern and Western*, F. E. Brightman collected together from Chrysostom's writings what appear to be definite references to the liturgy of Antioch 370–98.[68] An even more searching analysis has been made by Frans Van de Paverd.[69] Thus for evidence of initial praise of God, Van de Paverd cites passages from *In Mt*. Hom. 25–6, 3, *In ep.II ad Cor*. Hom. 2, 5, *In ep.I ad Cor*. Hom. 24, 1, and for the sanctus, *In ep.ad Ephes*. Hom. 14, 4, *In illud: vidi Dominum* 6, 2–3, 4, *De baptismo Christi* 4, 1, *In Mt*. Hom. 19, 3, *De ss.Martyribus* 2 and *In illud: vidi Dominum* 1, 1 and 3.[70] Such a selection is extremely convincing, though it presupposes a certain structure and content in the anaphora of Antioch.

Although probably reworked for use at Mopsuestia, Theodore's Homilies 15 and 16 on the eucharist were probably preached at Antioch before 392, and are therefore a useful witness to the usage of Antioch. It would seem from Homily 16 that the sanctus came near the beginning of the anaphora, after praising the greatness of the Father, the Son and the Holy Spirit. Theodore is useful, not so much for the form of the sanctus as for its rationale. The congregation sing in a loud voice 'as if we were also singing that which the invisible natures sing: Holy, holy, holy, is the Lord of Sabaoth, the whole heaven and earth are full of his praises'.[71] Theodore saw it as a revelation of the Trinity in three persons, revealed by the thrice-holy. He continues:

It is necessary, therefore, that the priest also should, after having mentioned in this service the Father, the Son, and the Holy Spirit, say: 'Praise and adoration are offered by all the creatures to Divine nature.' He makes mention also of the seraphim, as they are found in the Divine Book singing the praise which all of us who are present sing loudly in the Divine song which all of us recite, along with the invisible hosts, in order to serve God. We ought to think of them and to offer a thanksgiving that is equal to theirs. Indeed, the Economy of our Lord granted us to become immortal and incorruptible, and to serve God with the invisible hosts 'when we are caught up in the clouds to meet our Lord in the air, and so shall we ever be with the Lord', according to the saying of the Apostle. Nor are the words of our Lord false, who says that the children of God 'are like the angels of God, because they are the children of the resurrection'.[72]

Theodore, it would seem, saw the eucharist as the offering equal to the praise offered by the heavenly host (cf. Addai and Mari).

W. F. Macomber has drawn attention to a prayer quoted by the Syrian theologian, Cyrus of Edessa, which is similar to a prayer quoted in Narsai and attributed to Theodore.[73] Neither version has the sanctus, but the prayer in Cyrus includes an institution narrative. Macomber suggests that the prayer probably occurred in Theodore's commentary on the Gospel of St Matthew which is no longer extant.[74] He concludes that Theodore thus bears witness to a eucharistic prayer which lacked the sanctus.

The prayer is without doubt full of the Logos-anthropos christology of Theodore, and since *Testamentum Domini* and the anaphora of Epiphanius bear witness to the continuing existence of eucharistic prayers without the sanctus, there is no reason why Theodore should not also have been acquainted with such prayers. However, too much should not be read into this prayer. The form in Narsai, which Macomber suggests is the more original, does not include the institution narrative: neither versions contain an epiklesis or intercessions. Yet these elements were common in eucharistic prayers by the time Theodore was writing. The prayer may reflect Theodore's attempt to recreate the type of prayer he believed Jesus used at the Last Supper. Whatever the origin, it is indisputable that in the Catechetical Homilies Theodore knew an anaphora of the classical Syro-Byzantine shape, and it included the sanctus.[75] Both Chrysostom and Theodore bear witness to an Antiochene anaphora which began with praise to God the Holy Trinity, in which the heavenly host and the sanctus are mentioned.

The relationship between the anaphoras of St John Chrysostom and the Apostles, and their relationship if any with Chrysostom himself are far from settled questions.

In his study *Der Ursprung der Chrysostomusliturgie*, Georg Wagner subjected the text of the anaphora of John Chrysostom to a careful comparison with Chrysostom's writings, and concluded that 'Goldenmouth' could be the author of the Greek anaphora which bears his name.[76] Few scholars, however, have been entirely convinced that the saint authored this anaphora. Geoffrey Cuming has pointed out that the presence of an identical phrase in a liturgy and in the writings of a Father may indeed be explained as evidence of common authorship; but it may be that the Father quoted from a liturgy, or both may have drawn on a common source.[77] Thus the apophatic adjectives which appear in the anaphora of St John Chrysostom could reflect the Anomoean controversy to which Chrysostom devoted several sermons, but they could also reflect the common stock of theological phrases in vogue at that time.[78] However, more recently, Robert Taft has argued that the sequence of these adjectives found in the anaphora can only be paralleled in the writings of Chrysostom.[79] It is possible that Chrysostom expanded the liturgy of Antioch which he brought with him to Constantinople in 398.

In an article in 1937, H. Engberding drew attention to the similarities between the Greek anaphora of St John Chrysostom and a Syriac anaphora entitled the Apostles or Twelve Apostles.[80] He suggested that perhaps the Syriac might preserve an earlier version of the anaphora. This suggestion was pursued by A. Raes and G. Khouri-Sarkis, both of whom concluded that the Syriac preserved an earlier version of an anaphora which had been expanded in the Greek recension.[81] The relationship between these two anaphoras is undeniable, but it may be an oversimplification to regard the Syriac version as being nearer to the older use of Antioch. One of the problems with the vast number of Syriac anaphoras of the Syro-Byzantine family is that many of them are abbreviations or conflations of texts, and their authors made additions and alterations of their own which may appear 'primitive', but which are certainly not original! The Syriac of the Twelve Apostles, in the opinion of S. P. Brock, points to the translation being made in the sixth or seventh centuries,[82] and this is also the view of G. Wagner.[83] Twelve Apostles might, therefore, simply be a conflation; however, it might also reflect an earlier Greek text which was also the ancestor of the present Greek anaphora of St John Chrysostom, the common ancestor being the, or an, anaphora of Antioch.

In the Greek text, the sanctus is woven into the opening praise of the anaphora, and is presented as a sacrifice of praise offered in heaven;[84] after a thanksgiving for the creation and redemption of the worshippers, thanks is given for 'this service' ('tes leitourgias tautes') and God is asked to receive the eucharistic action as well as the praise of the heavenly host (cf. Theodore of Mopsuestia and Addai and Mari). The thought behind this is close to that expressed by Chrysostom himself in Homily 25 on Matthew:

Wherefore, as you know, the Priest also enjoins to give thanks for the world, for the former things, for the things that are now, for what hath been done to us before, for what shall befall us hereafter, when that Sacrifice is set forth.

For this is the thing both to free us from earth, and to remove us into heaven, and to make us Angels instead of men.

Wagner cites parallels to the negative epithets in *De incomprehensibili contra Anamoeos* 3, 1, and a similar vocabulary is to be found in *Ad eos qui scandalizati* 2.[85]

The angelology is more akin to Addai and Mari than to Jerusalem or Cappadocia – something which might be expected in view of the fact that both originate from a similar geographical area.[86] Chrysostom simply mentions thousands of angels, myriads of archangels, cherubim and seraphim. In the earliest manuscript they simply sing the triumphal hymn. The transition to the post-sanctus is reminiscent also of Addai and Mari, 'With these powers [hosts] ... we also cry and say.' The thrice-holy pick-up is given a trinitarian application.

The sanctus pericope in the Syriac Twelve Apostles is even shorter, and seems less contextually connected with the opening praise than the Greek anaphora. This led G. J. Cuming to postulate that the Apostles was originally an anaphora which lacked a sanctus, and one was later inserted.[87] This, however, seems to overlook the thought-pattern of the opening of the anaphora, which is different from Greek Chrysostom. The thought seems to be:

It is our duty to praise and glorify you,
for [gyr]   1   You brought us out of not-being into being (creation and red-
               emption of mankind) ... because of this we give thanks to you.
for [gyr]   2   Around you stand the cherubim ... glorifying with never-silent
               mouths and voices.

This may be paraphrased: 'we praise you because you have created and redeemed us, and because you are worshipped in heaven by the heavenly host'. Admittedly this is different from Chrysostom, but it is not out of context.[88] Nevertheless, if this is a conflation of a Greek text, the different context of the sanctus might be purely accidental, as a result of conflation and omission. In the angelology the cherubim have four faces (Ezekiel and Revelation), and the heavenly armies (cf. Syriac James) have been added. The vocal activity is identical to that of Syriac James.

If these two anaphoras bear witness to Antioch, they are not early enough to indicate whether the sanctus was ever addressed to the Son. In the two texts we have, the praise of God has been given a trinitarian setting (cf. Addai and Mari), though the sanctus itself is addressed to the creating and redeeming God.

The composite character of the AC has already been noted.[89] It is generally dated c.360, in the region of Antioch. Chapter 8 contains a eucharistic liturgy with a lengthy anaphora which is in part a vast expansion of that found in *Apostolic Tradition*, borrows material from the Jewish Synagogal prayers of AC 7 and, it is assumed, from current Antiochene anaphoral usage. Bouley comments:

There is no reason to assume, however, that the order and structure of the ana-phora were the result of his own initiative. These were known to him because they were characteristic of the public liturgy with which he was familiar, and indeed, at least on occasion his own prayer was perhaps actually used in the liturgy.[90]

If this view is correct, it has a significant implication for the sanctus. While the compiler used the anaphora of the *Apostolic Tradition*, he inserted a great deal of extra material, including a sanctus. This suggests that in *c*.360 the compiler did not regard the *Apostolic Tradition* anaphora as entirely adequate, and was aware that an Antiochene anaphora at that time would normally include the sanctus. The compiler was a collector of sources, who found it difficult to discriminate; he tended to amalgamate and duplicate. In respect of the sanctus, therefore, we might expect a composite form which is a result of amalgamating material. However, the compiler was also an Arian, or had semi-Arian sympathies, and was therefore concerned with God the creator and Father as distinct from the Son. If the anaphora of Antioch was ever addressed to the Son, including its sanctus, it is unlikely to be reflected in this compilation. Thus, although it pre-dates the evidence of St John Chrysostom and Theodore of Mopsuestia, it may not be regarded simply as a local variant of the anaphora of Antioch *c*.360.

The anaphora opens with the familiar 'Grace' of the Syro-Byzantine family, and proceeds to praise God the creator. Creation is rehearsed in descending chronological order; first the Son is brought into existence, and through him are made the heavenly powers, cherubim and seraphim, the beings of Colossians 1:16 in reverse order, with archangels and angels. This might suggest the appearance of the sanctus, but the descending order seems to be part of the compiler's elaborate rehearsal of creation – perhaps suggested to him by the angelology of the sanctus – but it is unlikely that the compiler has omitted an 'original' sanctus at this point. Metzger observes:

The inspiration behind the description is both biblical and hellenistic; the description of the universe is based on biblical cosmology, but some parts of it draw on Stoic physics and physiology.[91]

The rehearsal of creation continues, and then transfers to the Old Covenant salvation history from Adam as far as Joshua and the Canaanites. Then, as W. H. Bates points out, 'the Sanctus seems to have been placed abruptly between the sections of the prayer which describe the work of God in Christ in the Old Testament, and the work of God in Christ in the New'.[92] In fact, the compiler passes from the old Joshua to the new Joshua, but without doubt the sanctus occurs as an intrusion into the flow of the text.

It is interesting to speculate on whether the sentence *Huper apantōn soi hē doxa, despota pantokratōr* (Glory be to you for all things, Almighty Lord) is a concluding doxology to the rehearsal of Old Testament salvation history, or the opening of the sanctus pericope, reintroducing the notion of praise. Short doxologies are found in *Didache* 9 and 10, *Testamentum Domini* and Syriac Apostles. On the other hand, it is slightly reminiscent of the opening of *Sharar*, and it is tempting to ask whether or not this is the opening of a eucharistic prayer (that of Antioch?) which the compiler had inserted or joined to other material. If the passages which subordinated the Paraclete and the Son are removed, together with the first set of angelic classes (since angels and archangels are duplicated), we have something not altogether unlike Addai and Mari, or more particularly, *Sharar*. It would certainly be in keeping with the compiler's method to amalgamate angelologies and subordinate the Son. It might just be possible, therefore, that this section preserves something of the opening of the anaphora of Antioch of the early fourth century. However, whether or not this suggestion has any substance, in this anaphora the transition from salvation history to the sanctus is contextually abrupt.

The context of the sanctus is rather different from that so far encountered. It is not linked with the worship of the creation as in James, but is more akin to the heavenly sacrifice of praise in Greek Chrysostom. However, the compiler has given it a christological function in line with his own theology. Worship is offered to God by all bodiless and holy orders, including the Paraclete and, above all, Jesus 'your angel and the chief general of your power'. Only then comes the heavenly host, similar to Greek James, but with 'eternal armies' (cf. Syriac James, 'heavenly armies'), and after mention of cherubim and seraphim, reference to angels and archangels in terms of Daniel 7:10. It might, therefore, suggest that the compiler combined a Jerusalemite or Cappadocian angelology with a simpler Antiochene one. After the sanctus and Romans 1:25, the prayer proceeds in the usual Syro-Byzantine manner with a trinitarian (though qualified) application of the thrice-holy.

The evidence from Antioch – which is generally later than for Jerusalem and Cappadocia – confirms that praise and thanksgiving led to the sanctus. The evidence suggests that praise was offered to Father, Son and Spirit, and the sanctus was regarded as a sacrifice of praise offered in heaven, to which the church added its eucharistic action. The peculiar nature of the anaphora of AC 8 does not allow us to use this as direct evidence of the anaphora of Antioch, though it confirms that at that time, $c.360$, the sanctus was an accepted part of the anaphora in this area also. It is possible that the pericope which introduces the sanctus in this anaphora might preserve something of the *oratio theologica* and sanctus of the Antiochene anaphora before $c.360$.

THE LATER EAST SYRIAN TRADITION

Although theologians such as Ephraim and Aphrahat shed some light on the eucharistic liturgy in East Syria, they do not provide any evidence on the anaphoral sanctus. As we have seen, Aphrahat alludes to the sanctus in a passage which Murray suggests echoes the Jewish mystical tradition;[93] Ephraim mentions the sanctus, though not in a eucharistic context, but interestingly, he understands it as being addressed to Christ.[94] Cyrillonas, writing $c.396$, knows of the sanctus in a eucharistic context, and also seems to understand that it was addressed to Christ.[95] For other information we must rely on Narsai's liturgical homilies, and the two other East Syrian anaphoras, Theodore the Interpreter and Nestorius.

The origin of the anaphoras attributed to Theodore and Nestorius is uncertain, though it is highly unlikely that they were composed by either Theodore or Nestorius. Writing $c.$ 531, Leontius of Byzantium accused Theodore of having no respect for the anaphora of the Apostles (Twelve Apostles?) or for that of St Basil, but compiled his own.[96] Some of the manuscript headings of these two anaphoras describe them as translations made from the Greek by Mar Abbas and Mar Thomas, suggesting an early sixth-century date for the Syriac. Certainly both seem dependent upon a Greek text. However, this information from the manuscripts is late, and its accuracy is called into question by the fact that Narsai's Homily XVII seems to presuppose the existence of an anaphora or anaphoras of the type represented by Theodore and Nestorius.[97] Narsai was professor at Edessa from 437–57, and then at Nisibis until his death in $c.502$. In the liturgical homilies, Narsai in fact seems to be commenting on an anaphoral tradition in general rather than on one particular anaphora, and seems to switch with ease between parts of Nestorius and parts of Theodore. However, unless the homilies have been interpolated, they suggest that versions of Theodore and Nestorius were in existence in the fifth century.

In Homily XVII Narsai explains that the priest, after the anaphoral dialogue, recounts the glory of the incomprehensible Divinity, the cause of intelligible and sensible beings, the Creator who is revealed as a Trinity in three hypostases, Father, Son and Holy Spirit. The watchers and the cherubim together with the seraphim sanctify God, and the people answer 'Holy, holy, holy.'[98] Narsai continues with an explanation of the thrice-holy; there is one Lord, but known as Father, Son and Holy Spirit. The sanctus is thus given a trinitarian application.

Homily XXI is a baptismal homily and describes the baptismal eucharist. Much less information is given here about the opening of the eucharistic prayer, though the anaphora certainly contained the sanctus. In this homily Narsai turns to Isaiah 6:4ff. to explain the function of the sanctus. The coal which touched Isaiah's lips was in fact the mystery of the body and blood of Christ. The priest fulfils the role of the seraph, bringing the body and blood of Christ to the sinner.

In the homily on the Church and the Priesthood there is only a brief reference to the anaphora, and a mention of a thrice-holy. This is either a reference to the sanctus, or possibly a reference to the thrice-holy at the commixture.[99]

Allowing for the homiletic nature of the material, it would seem that at the time of Narsai, the East Syrian anaphoral tradition gave praise to God the creator, revealed as Father, Son and Holy Spirit, and led into the sanctus which could also be understood as a proof-text of the Trinity.

There is general agreement amongst scholars that the anaphora of Nestorius is a skilful conflation of both Byzantine Basil and Greek Chrysostom (or earlier versions of these) and Addai and Mari.[100] The opening *gehanta* praises God in terms very similar to Greek Chrysostom, though the theologising tendency of the latter is heightened. The compiler has adapted the reference in Greek Chrysostom to 'this ministry' to form an independent lead into the sanctus. It is noticeable that only angels and archangels are mentioned, showing that a simple angelology is not necessarily a sign of antiquity. However, it seems to confirm that in the area of Antioch, and in East Syria (Addai and Mari) Daniel 7:10 formed part of the sanctus *Formelgut*. The post-sanctus picks up in characteristic Syro-Byzantine manner. It explicitly states that God made his worshippers on earth worthy to become like those who glorify him in heaven – thus making explicit the thought implied in Addai and Mari. The sanctus is thus part of the praise offered on earth to God for his magnificence and glorious nature and deeds.

With regard to the anaphora of Theodore, it has been argued by Georg Wagner that this is an East Syrian adaptation of the anaphora of Antioch which Theodore of Mopsuestia commented upon in his homilies.[101] However, that anaphora was of the Syro-Byzantine shape, not the East Syrian; furthermore, the anaphora of Theodore seems to be dependent upon Addai and Mari and Nestorius. It may be, therefore, that this anaphora is a compilation based upon Theodore's catechetical homilies with material from Addai and Mari, and even Nestorius.[102] It certainly reflects Theodore of Mopsuestia's rationale for the sanctus. The anaphora explicitly says that the sanctus is offered as praise by the angelic beings, using the characteristic East Syrian verb for the offering of verbal praise, *slq*.[103]

For before thee, O God the Father of Truth, and before thy only-begotten Son our Lord Jesus Christ, and before the Holy Spirit, stand a thousand thousand and myriad myriads of holy angels; these for the joy of their lives, in the constancy of their wills, hallow thy great and holy name in constant praise. And thou hast, my Lord, in thy grace, made even the feeble race of mortal men worthy to lift up glory and honour, with all the companies of those on high, to thy Almighty Sovereignty, even with those who at all times before the majesty of Thy holiness lift up their voice to glorify thy glorious Trinity which in three persons co-equal and undivided is confessed, crying and praising without ceasing, calling one to another and saying.[104]

The sanctus in this anaphora is very much part of the sacrifice of praise which is offered to God in conjunction with the oblation.[105]

Thus, in East Syria, we find theological elaboration which centres praise on the Trinity; the sanctus explicitly becomes part of the Church's oblation of praise, and bread and wine, and the angelology introducing it is severely reduced.

CONCLUDING SUMMARY

In the Syro-Byzantine and East Syrian traditions it has been argued that our earliest example of a Eucharistic Prayer containing the sanctus is probably Addai and Mari and its Maronite twin, *Sharar*. The older argument that it is a later addition to the anaphora is hard to justify. The sanctus has a logical setting and function, and, as with the other 'common material' in Addai and Mari and *Sharar*, could be given a third-century dating. Eusebius may give us an early fourth-century attestation for Jerusalem, and Asterios the first part of the fourth century for Cappadocia. For Antioch, AC gives us a mid-fourth-century date. In these areas the sanctus occurs in the first part of the Eucharistic Prayer as part of the *oratio theologica*. Beyond this there are a number of differences.

In Addai and Mari/*Sharar* it occurs as the praise of the heavenly hosts to the Name (Christ, or Name revealed as Father, Son and Holy Spirit) who is creator and redeemer. From the evidence of Asterios, the anaphora in Cappadocia may also have addressed the sanctus to Christ, and this is possibly confirmed by the anaphora of Gregory which is addressed to the Son. The Jerusalem tradition addressed the Father as creator, and this too is the case in Egyptian Basil and in AC 8; in Byzantine Basil, Greek Chrysostom and Syriac Apostles a trinitarian application becomes more obvious, and this is made explicit in the later West Syrian tradition.

The Jerusalem tradition stands apart in that it is a hymn of creation to the creator, rather than of the church to God making mention of the angelic praise. In Basil, the sanctus is introduced in the praise of God by mention of the throne room (the logical link being broken in Byzantine Basil); in Addai and Mari/*Sharar* it is the praise of heaven to which is added the thanksgiving of mortals; in Greek Chrysostom the eucharist is offered along with the sanctus. Although it is a chant of the congregation, contextually it remains the song of heaven in Addai and Mari, Eusebius and James, AC 8, Greek Chrysostom, Syriac Apostles, Egyptian and Byzantine Basil, and Nestorius. *Sharar*, Cyril, Theodore of Mopsuestia, John Chrysostom, Narsai, the anaphora of Theodore, and Gregory, all make explicit that it becomes also the chant of the church. As far as angelology is concerned, Jerusalem and Cappadocia (together with the compiler of AC 8) have a complex angelology, using mainly Colossians 1:16, adding from Ephesians 1:21, with angels, archangels, cherubim and seraphim. East Syria and Antioch have a similar angelology, both ignoring Colossians 1:16, but using Daniel 7:10.

In so far as there is any comparison with the use of the *qeduššah* in Judaism, the *Hekhalot* hymns and *qeduššah d^e Yoṣer* are the nearest, in that they praise the Name of God the creator who is worshipped in heaven. The similarity is, however, minimal.

5

_SM_

The sanctus in the Egyptian and Western eucharistic prayers

THE EGYPTIAN TRADITION

THE anaphoras of Egyptian Basil and St Gregory of Nazianzen bear witness to the Syro-Byzantine (or Cappadocian) influence in Egypt. However, the Greek anaphora of St Mark, its Coptic recension (St Cyril), together with various Greek and Coptic fragments and the anaphora in the collection attributed to Serapion of Thmuis, bear witness to a quite distinct indigenous Egyptian anaphoral pattern. In this pattern, characteristics include intercessions before the sanctus, an epiklesis before the institution narrative, and the use of 1 Corinthians 11:26 in the anamnesis (_katangellete_). Some of these distinct features may themselves be later changes to an earlier, quite distinct anaphoral pattern. The fragments include the Strasbourg Papyrus Gr. 254 (fourth to fifth century), the Deir Bala'izah papyrus (sixth to seventh century), a Coptic wooden tablet of the eighth century, the Manchester Papyrus (sixth century), the Louvain Coptic papyrus (no longer extant) and the Barcelona anaphora.[1] The fragments suggest that this distinct pattern was found in Upper and Lower Egypt, and therefore to refer to the pattern as Alexandrine in an exclusive sense is inaccurate.

In his magisterial study, 'L'Anaphore Alexandrine de Saint Marc', R.-G. Coquin carefully examines the Greek and Coptic recensions, tracing their growth by comparing them with earlier fragments.[2] However, the gradual evolution presupposed by Coquin has in recent years been called into question by a number of scholars working quite independently.

Coquin assumed, as did the original editors, that the Strasbourg Papyrus Gr.254 was a _fragment_ of an earlier version of St Mark. However, in 1974 E. Kilmartin described the fragment as a 'eucharistia', strongly hinting that the papyrus was a complete prayer.[3] Subsequently W. H. Bates, H. A. J. Wegman and G. J. Cuming have argued persuasively that 'Strasbourg' is a *complete eucharistic prayer*, representing the earliest Egyptian pattern which subsequently underwent considerable metamorphoses in its evolution to the pattern of St Mark.[4] Important in these studies is the analogy with the structure of the Jewish *berakot* and the significance of the short doxology of the papyrus. Although this interpretation is not the only possible one,[5] their view is gaining considerable acceptance.[6] If, therefore, Strasbourg is a complete early Egyptian anaphora, it gives us an example of an anaphora with the following structure:

1 Thanksgiving, or blessing for creation.
2 Oblation – Malachi 1:11
3 Intercessions

These items are brought to a conclusion by the short doxology, 'through whom be glory to you to the ages of ages' (*di ou soi doxa eis tous aiōnas tōn aiōnōn*). This pattern, which Cuming dated to the third century, would be significantly different from that of *Apostolic Tradition*, Addai and Mari, and the Jerusalem pattern attested to by Cyril. It also has significant implications regarding the sanctus. Contrary to the view of Dix and Kretschmar, it would indicate that, far from originating in Egypt, the sanctus here represents a later development, some time in the fourth century. A consideration of the sanctus as it appears in St Mark and the various fragments, and Serapion, may shed some light on this development.

There are four manuscripts of the medieval Greek St Mark: a roll at the University of Messina (twelfth century); Vat. Gr. 1970 (twelfth century); 2281 (thirteenth century); and the Pegas manuscript of the sixteenth century.[7] The text used here is that of Vat. Gr. 1970. There are many medieval manuscripts of the Coptic recension which is named after St Cyril. The Hunt MS 403 and the printed edition of Tuki have been used here.

As with Greek and Syriac James, so with this anaphora the two versions have influenced each other, and thus it is not always easy to identify the 'original' reading. On the whole, the Coptic version is probably to be preferred. The Greek text shows considerable assimilation to the texts of Greek St James and Byzantine Basil.

Greek Mark	Coptic Cyril
For you are the One who is above all Principalities and Authorities and Powers and Dominions and every name that is named not only in this Age but in that which is to come.	For you are God, who is above all Principalities and all Authorities and all Powers and all Dominions and every name that is named not only in this Age but in that which is to come.
Beside you stand thousands and thousands and myriads of myriads of armies of holy angels and archangels.	For you are He beside whom stands the commanders of thousands of thousands and the commanders of myriads of myriads of the angels and holy archangels who serve you.
Beside you stand your two most honourable living creatures, the many-eyed cherubim and the six-winged seraphim who with two wings cover their faces, and with two their feet and with two they fly, and *cry out one to another with unwearying mouths* and *never silent theologies the triumphant* and thrice-holy *hymn singing, shouting out, glorifying crying out and saying to the glory of your great majesty*: [sanctus]	For you are He beside whom stand two most honourable living creatures, those to whom belong six wings and many eyes, the seraphim and the cherubim. With two wings they cover their faces because of your Godhead which cannot be seen and is inconceivable. With two they cover their feet, flying with the other two.
For at all times all things sanctify you. But with all those who sanctify you, receive, Lord God, also our sanctification as with them we hymn and say:	For at all times all things sanctify you. But with all those who sanctify you, receive also our sanctification as we sing to you saying:
The People: [sanctus]	*The People*: [sanctus] 'their faces because of your Godhead' is omitted from Tuki, [whose text is defective at this point]

Unlike the Syro-Byzantine and East Syrian anaphoras, the sanctus here is *not* part of the opening *oratio theologica*. St Mark/St Cyril gives the following pattern:

1 Thanksgiving for creation and redemption
2 Oblation
3 Intercession
4 Sanctus
5 Epiklesis
6 Institution narrative
7 Anamnesis
8 Epiklesis
9 Doxology

Since each of these items is generally dove-tailed into the next, such an outline obscures the fact that although *textually* the sanctus remains a hymn of praise, *contextually* it occurs within intercessions and serves as a transition to further intercession, namely the first epiklesis. In fact, in comparison with the Strasbourg papyrus, the theme of redemption has been added to 1, and 4–8 are simply an extension of 3, the intercessions. We shall return to this observation later.

The Greek version of the sanctus pericope has a long duplication, and the words in italics are identical with Greek James, which is probably the source of the duplication. In addition there are slight differences between the two versions. The Coptic has 'commanders' of angels and archangels who 'serve you'. The Greek version describes the cherubim as having many eyes, and the seraphim as six-winged, whereas the Coptic has an inversion and describes both cherubim and seraphim as many-eyed and six-winged – though according to Professor M. Plumley, this could be just an accident of Bohairic grammar.[8] The Coptic repeats *zu gar ei* (For you are the one) and it explains why the faces of the seraphim were covered. The common form of the sanctus pericope which they represent has the following characteristics:
1   It is introduced by Ephesians 1:21.
2   Beside God stand:

> (i)   (Dan 7:10) armies of angels and archangels (Coptic: Commanders).
> (ii)   the two most honourable living creatures, the cherubim (Greek).
> (iii) The seraphim (Greek).
> or, (iv) the two most honourable living creatures, the seraphim and cherubim (Coptic).

The term 'two most honourable living creatures' needs some explanation. It is taken from the LXX version of Habakkuk 3:2. The LXX version differs considerably from the Massoretic text. (There also exists a Greek translation of the text called the Barbarini version.) Whereas Habakkuk 3:2 in the Hebrew reads:

O Lord I have heard your report and your work, O Lord, I fear. In the midst of the years renew it; in the midst of the years make it known.

(RSV)

the LXX reads:

O Lord I have heard your report and was afraid; and I saw your work and was amazed. In the midst of two living creatures [en mesō duo zōōn] you shall be acknowledged.

The explanation for this difference would seem to be that 'two living creatures' is a corruption of *sanim ḥayyhu* into *sᵉne ḥayym*.[9] Rudolph suggests that it may have arisen through the influence of Exodus 25:22 and that, in connection with Isaiah 1:3, it may have given rise to the tradition of the ox and ass at the crib.[10] The same Greek term, *zōa*, is also used in the LXX to render the *ḥayyôt* of Ezekiel.

The term is used as part of the Egyptian sanctus, though in Serapion we find 'the two most honourable seraphim'. As has been noted, Gregory Dix speculated that behind this term we have an early Alexandrine theology as represented by Origen, where two honourable creatures = seraphim = the Son and the Holy Spirit. According to Dix this is the meaning in Serapion, though in St Mark, although the term has been retained, the identification has been given up.[11]

While undoubtedly the reference to honourable creatures suggests that Alexandria associated Habakkuk 3:2 with Isaiah 6:3, there is little justification for seeing the theology of Origen behind it. Clement of Alexandria could say of the Christian gnostic:

He is inseparable from the commandment and from hope, and is ever giving thanks to God, like the living creatures figuratively spoken of by Isaiah.[12]

Similarly Athanasius identifies the honourable living creatures with the seraphim.[13] However, neither give the slightest hint that there is any connection between the seraphim and the Son and Holy Spirit. They simply link Habakkuk 3:2 with the seraphim of Isaiah, which is the natural interpretation of the reference in Serapion. At a later date, Cyril of Alexandria in his commentary on Habakkuk identifies the two living creatures with the cherubim.[14] It could well be that this dual identification amongst influential Egyptian theologians could account for the vague reference in St Mark. The Coptic version could, grammatically, identify the two living creatures as both seraphim and cherubim. This dual identification is born out by a text attributed spuriously to St John Chrysostom, entitled 'The Four Living Creatures'. According to this work, the four living creatures of Ezekiel are the two seraphim and two cherubim.[15] All one may conclude is that in Egyptian theology Habakkuk 3:2 was associated with Isaiah 6:3, and in the liturgy of Alexandria and of Thmuis, Habakkuk 3:2 is used in the sanctus pericope alongside Ephesians 1:21, Daniel 7:10 and Isaiah 6:3.

3   The sanctus is specifically made into the song of the church on earth.

4   The sanctus is part of the intercessions. It has been assumed by many scholars, including Coquin, that the intercessions at the beginning of the anaphora of St Mark are a later interpolation, and that originally the sanctus followed a thanksgiving for creation and redemption, giving an *oratio theologica* not unlike, for example, Addai and Mari. The Strasbourg Papyrus at least confirms that the intercessions were placed after the reference to oblation at an early date, giving us the thought sequence:

We offer ... And we pray and beseech you for.[16]

Contextually the sanctus of St Mark is within the intercessions and is used as a spring-board to continue the intercessions, namely the first epiklesis. Whereas the Syro-Byzantine anaphora continues after the sanctus with a pick up on the word 'holy', in St Mark it is the word 'full' which is the pick-up word:

Full in truth are heaven and earth of your glory through our Lord and God and Saviour Jesus Christ: fill, O God, this sacrifice also with a blessing from you through the descent of your Holy Spirit.

This Egyptian peculiarity is also found in an inscription which, according to Baumstark, preserves part of an old Egyptian eucharistic prayer, though the title theotokos is clearly a much later addition:[17]

Master, Lord God of Abraham [?] who shines brightly, having no part in darkness, where dwells the fullness of your godhead, to whom armies above, archangels and angels, minister and unceasingly honour you, singing with a thrice-holy voice and saying: Holy, holy, holy are you Lord, heaven and earth are full of your glory ... for they are full of your greatness, all compassionate Lord, for being invisible in the heavens, in the richness of your powers, you condescended to live among mortals, made flesh from the Virgin theotokos, Mary.

This inscription preserves the literary link, though unlike the Egyptian anaphora, there is no intercessory link.

Although Bernard Botte questioned the authorship of the collection of prayers attributed to Serapion, G. J. Cuming rightly warns that it is premature to speak of 'Pseudo-Serapion'.[18] Serapion was bishop of Thmuis in the Nile delta, c. 340–60, and a friend of St Athanasius. The anaphora in this collection of prayers has a structural similarity to St Mark, though it has some characteristics which are Syro-Byzantine. It opens with a hymn of praise to the Father as the creator God, and gives praise for the Son. There is no reference to oblation or Malachi 1:11 at this point as in 'Strasbourg' and St Mark, but the opening praise passes to intercession: 'We pray you: Make us living men.' It prays for the Holy Spirit, and then introduces the sanctus pericope with the petition 'May the Lord Jesus, speak in us, and Holy Spirit, and hymn you through us.' As with St Mark, the sanctus pericope opens with Ephesians 1:21, and then Daniel 7:10. However, there then comes the angelology of Colossians 1:16, more familiar in the Syro-Byzantine family. The biblical order is preserved, as in Greek James, AC 8 and Byzantine Basil, though since 'Powers' occurs in the Ephesians quotation, Serapion does not need to add it to the Colossians quotation. Serapion does not mention the cherubim, but the 'two most honourable seraphim' illustrates the linking of Habakkuk 3:2 with Isaiah 6:3. This link, together with the strange petition which introduces the pericope, might suggest to the speculative mind Origen's theology equating seraphim with the Son and Spirit. However, the text does not actually make this equation and is perfectly consistent with the understanding found in Clement and Athanasius that the two living creatures were the seraphim. The thought of the Thmuis eucharistic prayer seems to be:

Christ and the Holy Spirit speak in us, so that we, like the living creatures [seraphim] who stand beside you, may praise you with the Holy, holy, holy.

Serapion, like Cyril of Jerusalem, keeps the LXX reading of 'face'. The text suggests that it was the priest rather than the congregation who recited the sanctus. Like St Mark, the post-sanctus continues the intercession with an epiklesis. The verbal pick up is on the word 'full', but the word 'sabaoth' is also brought into play. Lord Sabaoth in the sanctus is rendered in the post-sanctus in terms of the LXX of 2 Samuel 6:2, Lord of Powers, and God is asked to fill the sacrifice with his power (*tēs sēs dunameōs*).

Amongst the various fragments, the Deir Bala'izah Papyrus confirms that the general pattern of St Mark's anaphora was also known in Upper Egypt. The fragment preserves a remnant of the intercessions, followed by Ephesians 1:21, a fragmentary sanctus pericope and an epiklesis

which uses part of the *Didache*.[19] The reference to seraphim or
cherubim is missing but, whatever they were, they 'stand in a circle'.
The sanctus is recited by the celebrant. After the *Didache* material,
with the petition 'so gather the catholic church', the fragment leads into
the institution narrative.

The Manchester papyrus (Greek) and the British Museum Tablet
(Coptic) are textually very similar, preserving a post-sanctus epiklesis
as far as the second epiklesis.[20] The transition from sanctus to epiklesis
to institution narrative is extremely brief.

The Louvain text preserved a post-sanctus epiklesis and institution
narrative; the post-sanctus picked up on the word 'glory', made a
reference to Christ, and offered the bread and wine. However, the
sections of the anaphora of the Barcelona papyrus which have so far
been published appear to be the Greek version of the same or similar
anaphora.[21] After a thanksgiving to God as creator, the sanctus is
introduced in a manner different from that so far encountered in the
Egyptian texts:

It is he that sits upon the chariot of the cherubim and the seraphim in front of
him, before whom stand a thousand thousand and myriad myriads of angels,
archangels, thrones and dominions, hymning and glorifying. With whom we
also hymn and sing.

Here we do not find the hitherto invariable use of Ephesians 1:21, but
an allusion to 1 Chronicles 28:18 and Ecclesiasticus 49:8, to the Chariot
of the cherubim (*merkāvāh* influence?) with the seraphim in front, and
Daniel 7:10 is applied to angels, archangels, thrones and dominions.
The pick up is on the word 'glory'. However, in the Coptic version of
the Louvian Papyrus, after the note of offering, an intercessory note is
introduced by an epiklesis. With these two fragments, therefore, we
have evidence of a rather different Egyptian pattern, where the sanctus
is within a thanksgiving addressed to God the Father.

With the exception of the Louvain and Barcelona fragments, we find
in the peculiarly Egyptian anaphoral pattern a distinctive sanctus
pericope which is rather different from that encountered in the East
Syrian and Syro-Byzantine traditions. It has the following characteristics:

1 If the Strasbourg Papyrus is a complete anaphora representative of the
  old indigenous Egyptian anaphora, then we must conclude that the
  sanctus and its epiklesis (together with the institution narrative, anamnesis and second epiklesis) is a later development.
2 When the sanctus was introduced into this tradition, it was added after

the intercessions, introduced with Ephesians 1:21, and generally included reference to Daniel 7:10, Habakkuk 3:2 and Isaiah 6:3. Colossians 1:16, utilised by some Syro-Byzantine eucharistic prayers, is found only in Serapion (and part in the Barcelona fragment), coming in Serapion as an unnecessary repetition. Serapion, who seems to have been influenced in places by Syro-Byzantine usage, may have been influenced by that anaphoral tradition at this point.

3 The sanctus is the song of the Christian assembly (cf. *Sharar*, Cyril of Jerusalem, and the anaphoras of Theodore and Gregory), even though in the early texts it was recited by the priest. (It is possible that the anaphora of Gregory has been expanded before the recitation of the sanctus to accord with Egyptian custom.) Despite the use of Ephesians 1:21, it was addressed to God the Father.

4 In the anaphoral texts which have survived, although textually the sanctus is a hymn of praise, *contextually* it occurs within the intercessions and is used as a spring-board to further intercession, namely an epiklesis. The epiklesis is wedded to the sanctus with a carefully constructed verbal link; we have in fact a sanctus–epiklesis unit.

The most puzzling question is that of the possible source of this unit. The development from the Strasbourg Papyrus to the *textus receptus* of St Mark could easily be explained by borrowing from the Syro-Byzantine pattern and, more particularly, from Egyptian Basil or *Apostolic Tradition* – the latter also being influential in Egypt.[22] However, the sanctus–epiklesis unit, with its introduction from Ephesians 1:21, has no convincing parallel in the Syro-Byzantine tradition, nor could *Apostolic Tradition* have been an inspiration since it has no sanctus. The textual evidence suggests that this unit was an indigenous literary development which was firmly established by the time of Serapion's eucharistic prayer in the mid-fourth century.

Louis Bouyer, in looking for Jewish parallels, pointed to the *qeduššah d^e 'amidah*, since this *qeduššah* occurs in a series of *berakot* which include intercessory material.[23] However, this *qeduššah* is not preceded by intercession, and there are no convincing verbal parallels.

There is, however, some similarity to be found in Jewish and Gnostic ideas associated with the power of the divine name and expressed in the Egyptian Greek magical papyri. E. E. Urbach observes:

The power manifested in sorcery and also the means employed in connection with it are called *dunamis*. The fame of the God of Israel, as the God of power and might is extensively used in magical papyri and invocations.[24]

Both Irenaeus and Origen bear witness to the fact that Sabaoth was regarded by some Gnostic groups as a name employed in incantations,[25] and Scholem has drawn attention to the importance of 'the name of the Dynamis' or 'Great Power', which was interchangeable with 'The Great Glory' in some of the *Hekhalot* literature.[26] In the Gnostic work from Nag Hammadi, *On the Origin of the World*, we learn, concerning Sabaoth, son of Yaldabaoth, that:

Moreover when Sabaoth received light, he received a great authority against all of the powers of Chaos. Since that day, he has been called 'the lord of the powers'.[27]

In *The Discourse of the Eighth and Ninth (Heavens)*, we find a prayer:

O my father, I call upon you who rule over the kingdom of power ...
Lord, grant us a wisdom from your power that reaches us.[28]

In a Greek and Coptic exorcism spell found amongst the Greek magical papyri, which date from the third century CE, we find the following petition:

Hail, God of Abraham; hail, God of Isaac; hail, God of Jacob; Jesus Christ, the Holy Spirit, the Son of the Father, who is above the Seven, who is within the Seven. Bring Iao Sabaoth; may your power issue forth from him, NN, until you drive away the unclean daimon Satan, who is in him.[29]

In Kropps' collection of magical papyri there is a petition reminiscent of the epiklesis connected to the sanctus, though here simply connected with the names of God, and especially Sabaoth:

That you vouchsafe today
To leave (whatsoever) place where you are
And come down upon the cup of water
which stands before me.
May you fill it for me with light like that of the sun and moon,
seven times greater ...
Yea, come! For (I adjure) you by the great true name of the Father,
whose name is Aio, Sabaoth.[30]

The Prayer of Jacob is a Jewish magical text from Egypt, which Charlesworth dates between the first and fourth centuries CE, but which he notes has much in common with second-century Egyptian Greek papyri. It contains a lengthy prayer which includes the petition:

He who has the secret name Sabaoth
God of gods: amen, amen
... Fill me with wisdom.[31]

It is not being suggested that any of these are genuine parallels, and even less the source of the sanctus–epiklesis unit in the Egyptian anaphora. However, there is a marked similarity in *function*. In the Egyptian anaphora the sanctus – the name of Lord Sabaoth – is recited, and then he is asked to fill the bread and wine with power (Serapion) or his blessing (St Mark). All that can be concluded is that whereas in the Syro-Byzantine and East Syrian traditions the sanctus is used in a manner akin to that of the Jewish *qeduššah dᵉ Yoṣer*, praise of God's majesty, in the Egyptian anaphora it has similarities with the ideas regarding the divine Name and especially Sabaoth which were current in Jewish and Gnostic groups in the second to the fourth centuries. It was regarded as an acclamation which could be used for petition, and its function in Egypt as represented by Serapion and St Mark is quite unlike that of Syria or, for that matter, its use in the West.

ROME AND MILAN

The Roman *canon missae*, which eventually became the sole eucharistic prayer of the Western Catholic Church, and which still survives as Eucharistic Prayer 1 of the Missal of Pope Paul VI, presents itself as something of an enigma.[32] Its origin, development and final shaping remain intractable questions, as does also its relationship with other regional uses in Italy, and with the Gallican rite. Much of it has parallels in the fourth-century writings of St Ambrose;[33] its Cyprianic theology of sacrifice together with its Old Latin institution narrative and its vocabulary point to North African influence.[34] Many scholars have suggested the long pontificate of Pope Damasus (366–84) as the probable time when the early Latin canon was redacted in its essentials, the final redaction being in the pontificate of Gregory the Great (590–604).

In contrast to the Eastern anaphoras which are fixed compositions, the Roman *canon missae* has three variable parts – the *praefatio* or (Proper) Preface, the *Communicantes* and *Hanc igitur*. The first of these, the preface, introduces the sanctus. In general the Roman prefaces introduce the sanctus in four ways:

1 The so-called *praefatio communis* or *Cottidiana*, beginning *Per quem*:

> Through whom the angels praise, the dominions adore, the powers fear your majesty; the heaven of heavens and virtues and the blessed seraphim together proclaim with exultation.[35] With whom we beseech you, bid that our voices be admitted with suppliant thanksgiving, saying, Holy ...

2 The most common variant is that which begins *Et ideo*:

> And therefore with angels and archangels, with thrones and dominions, and
> with the whole host of the heavenly army, we sing the hymn of your glory
> endlessly [*sine fine*] saying, Holy ...

There are slight variants in the introduction of this form.

3 *Quapropter [unde] profusis*:

> Wherefore with exceeding joy the whole round world exults. The supernal
> virtues also and the angelic powers sing together the hymn of your glory
> endlessly saying, Holy ...

4 *Quem [quam] laudant*:

> Which the angels and archangels, cherubim and also the seraphim praise,
> who cease not daily to cry out, with one voice, saying, Holy ...

Again there are some slight variants in the introduction to this form.

These forms occur in the prefaces of the Verona (but not 4), Gelasian
and Gregorian Sacramentaries.[36] However, the great problem is the
question of the antiquity of the anaphoral sanctus in the Roman canon.

Among the earliest witnesses to Western liturgical usage, it is
significant that Ambrose, in *De Sacramentis*, gives no hint of the
sanctus, and Jerome, Ambrosiaster, Gaudentius of Brescia and Augustine, while commenting upon Isaiah 6:3, give no indication that it had a
liturgical context.[37]

The Roman canon itself makes little attempt to connect the sanctus
with what follows. The paragraph immediately after the sanctus
begins: 'Therefore, most merciful Father, through Jesus Christ your
Son, our Lord, we humbly pray and beseech you' (*Te igitur, clemen-
tissime Pater, per Iesum Christum filium tuum dominum nostrum
supplices rogamus et petimus*). It is difficult to see what 'Therefore',
igitur, refers to. B. Botte and C. Mohrmann suggested that it represented nothing stronger than the Greek *de*, and made no attempt to give
it any representation in their French translation.[38] However, it does
have some sense if it refers back to the preface. E. C. Ratcliff and G. G.
Willis have argued that if the sanctus with its introduction is regarded as
a later intrusion, then *te igitur* will be seen to carry on the thought of the
preface.[39] The thought is, whatever the variable preface, 'It is meet and
right to give you thanks through Christ. Therefore through Christ we
ask you to accept our thanksgiving.' Thus, the sanctus with its
introduction breaks the flow and logic of the Roman canon, suggesting
that it might be an intrusion.

This supposition finds some support from what are known as the Mai fragments. These two fragments (published by Cardinal Mai in 1828) present us with two portions of early Italian prayers which correspond structurally with the beginning of the *Canon missae*.[40] These are Arian fragments, and demonstrate the existence of written prefaces in North Italy at the beginning of the fourth century. The second, longer formula, after giving thanks and praise to the Father for the gift of the Son and for redemption through him, includes two phrases reminiscent of the *te igitur* and another paragraph of the canon, *supplices te*, but there is no trace of the sanctus. Indeed, the ending 'through Jesus Christ our Lord, through whom we ask and beseech', seems deliberately to exclude the sanctus, which the *canon missae* introduces 'through Jesus Christ our Lord, through whom angels praise'. Many of the prefaces given in the Sacramentaries simply end with 'through' or 'through Christ [our] Lord'. It is not clear, therefore, whether this abbreviation led originally in all cases into the sanctus, or whether, like the Mai fragments, there was no sanctus.

According to the *Liber Pontificalis*, the sanctus was introduced as early as Xystus I (*c*. 117–*c*.127).[41] Most commentators are of the opinion that this is most unlikely, and see it as evidence for the sixth century when the *Liber Pontificalis* was written, rather than for the second century. However, Gamber made the suggestion that this might really be applicable to Xystus III, which would not be implausible.[42] More importance is attached to the reference to the sanctus in the *Libellus* on the Holy Spirit attributed to Ambrose. In a thorough discussion of this text, Lucien Chavoutier drew attention to the statement that the people join with the priest in the sanctus in almost all of the Churches of the East, and some of the West.[43] Chavoutier dates the document *c*.400 CE with North Italy as its provenance. He suggests that this passage should be interpreted as affirming that by *c*.400 all the Eastern churches had the sanctus as part of the eucharistic prayer, but only certain Western churches used it. He further surmises that the Western churches which were in the process of adopting the sanctus as part of the anaphora were those of North Italy and Rome, on the grounds that the writer knew the Old Latin translation of *doxa* ('glory') by *maiestas* rather than *gloria*, and the Old Latin was localised in North Italy.[44]

A. H. Couratin questioned whether this is what the text actually implies. What the text seems to say is that almost everywhere in the East, and in a number of places in the West, the people join in reciting the sanctus with the celebrant. This may well mean that the almost universal custom (by c.400) in the East of the sanctus being a congregational chant was also becoming the custom in the West. The *Libellus* may therefore simply bear witness to the sanctus in the West being recited by the priest alone.[45] The *Libellus*, then, would not rule out the sanctus being part of the anaphora well before c.400, but said only by the priest.

P.-M. Gy has also suggested an earlier date than the sixth century witness of the *Liber Pontificalis*.[46] If certain of the prefaces of the Verona and Gelasian Sacramentaries which presuppose the sanctus can be attributed to St Gelasius and St Leo, then clearly the sanctus was an established element in the canon when they composed their prefaces. Basing his case on the work of A. P. Lang,[47] Gy concluded:

One is able to suppose then that the sanctus entered the Roman Canon before [the time] of St Leo. But its adoption could not be much older since in the first third of the century the Church of Africa, whose bonds with the Apostolic See were very close, completely ignored it.[48]

The conclusion to the common preface, so Gy concludes, is probably contemporary with the insertion of the sanctus into the Roman canon, making its appearance towards the end of the fourth century.

In summary, therefore, it would seem from internal and external evidence that the sanctus in the Roman canon represents a later addition, and the studies of Chavoutier and Gy point to the end of the fourth or early fifth century for its introduction. Although the preface could be altered to introduce it, the post-sanctus *te igitur* seems to have been left unmodified. There is no literary link as in the Syro-Byzantine and Egyptian anaphoras, nor is there a logical development of thought as in Addai and Mari. It may well be that the sanctus was inserted because it was by that time a universal feature in the East. It might be the case that in some places and on some occasions the sanctus formed part of the eucharistic prayer at an earlier date, and gradually became a regular feature of the anaphora at every celebration, but such a conjecture cannot be proven. If the sanctus at Rome was borrowed from the East, is there an Eastern model? According to Gy, we must look to Jerusalem and to Greek Chrysostom.[49] The result of the Roman adoption of the sanctus results in an anaphoral structure of praise–sanctus–oblation or intercession. The preface and sanctus are akin to the *oratio theologica* and sanctus of the Syro-Byzantine and East Syrian traditions, but the canon does not continue the element of praise after the sanctus.

The angelology of the common preface raises one or two interesting points. Archangels and cherubim are absent. Furthermore, there is a problem over the precise meaning of *caeli caelorumque virtutes*, which we have translated as 'the heaven of heavens and virtues'. On the grounds that *caeli caelorumque* is not an angelic class, Capelle suggested that *caeli* belonged with 'powers', and *caelorumque* with 'virtues'.[50] M.-F. Lacan drew attention to the term *caeli* in the Vulgate, and concluded that the term designated all the heavenly armies.[51] However, as Gy observes, in St James we find the expression 'the heavens and the heaven of heavens and all their powers' which seems to be repeated here in the Roman common preface.[52] Also, each group of celestial beings is given a particular function of praise in a manner found in St Gregory.

In the other forms we meet a very restrained angelology, never reaching the complicated systematic hierarchy of St James or AC 8. The *Quem laudant* form is close to Greek Chrysostom; 'the whole host of the heavenly army' echoes the 'unnumbered armies' (*anarithmoi stratiai*) and 'eternal armies' (*stratiōn aiōniōn*) of AC 8. Archangels make an appearance only in 2 and 4. Daniel 7:10 does not feature at all.

In a recent article Jean Magne, concerned with showing that many early hymns and prayers were addressed to Christ as God, including the anaphoral sanctus in some cases, has suggested that the *quem laudant* form, together with a Gallican introduction, *cui merito*, indicate that the sanctus was originally addressed to Christ in the Western tradition.[53] However, since the *quem laudant* form is not found in the early Roman prefaces, it may well be that this form was imported into Roman use from a tradition where the anaphora, or parts of it, were addressed to Christ. Gy points out that those prefaces which may be attributed to St Leo place the sanctus in a trinitarian setting, after the manner of Greek Chrysostom.[54] Indeed, if the Roman sanctus is a later fourth-century addition to the eucharistic prayer, it was inserted at a time when anaphoras seem to have been concerned with a trinitarian context.[55]

The rite of Milan as witnessed by St Ambrose had much in common with the Roman rite, though it also had its own distinctive elements.[56] In the rite which developed, as witnessed by the Sacramentary of Bergamo (tenth century), the canon is practically that of Rome, though the book contains 203 prefaces.[57] A. A. King divided them into five groups – in the form of collects, narratives relating to the lives of saints, oratorical prefaces, antithetical prefaces where two subjects are opposed to each other in a series of antitheses, and prefaces with parallels between persons.[58] Tradition ascribes the authorship of the early Milanese prefaces to Eusebius, Bishop of Milan (451–65), and this has been corroborated in the study of Paredi.[59] Eusebius was a Greek from

Syria, and Gregory Dix suggested that he may have been responsible for the Western preface and sanctus.[60] This would seem rather too late a date for the Roman preface, and it is probable that the sanctus was in use before Eusebius' episcopate.[61] Syrian influence might, however, account for the expansion at Milan of the common preface:

Through whom the angels praise, ARCHANGELS VENERATE, THRONES, dominions, virtues, PRINCIPALITIES AND powers adore your majesty, WHOM CHERUBIM and seraphim together proclaim with exultation.

It increases the classes of celestial beings to nine, as in some of the Eastern rites, though not in the same sequence which would suggest a specific source. In addition to the four introductions encountered in the Roman rite (though the *quem laudant* form is often made explicitly trinitarian) there are a number of variants. As in the Roman canon, there is no pick up after the sanctus, the *te igitur* following immediately – though in the rite for Holy Saturday a *vere sanctus* (Truly holy) similar to the Gallican and Spanish usage is provided. Overall, however, the function of the sanctus, with its lack of logic within the total anaphora, is identical to Rome.

SPAIN AND GAUL

There is an undoubted link between the two non-Roman Western rites – the Spanish Visigothic or Mozarabic rite, and the Gallican (and Celtic) rite. In respect to the eucharistic prayer, they seem little more than variations of a single rite, often with the same technical terms, phrases and formulae. It has been argued that the Spanish rite is derived from the Gallican, though the view at present seems to favour the Spanish rite as being the primary source.[62]

Though the Spanish rite may be the source of the Gallican, its own origins are uncertain. It has been argued that it was derived from the Roman rite, and Coebergh has shown that material from the Verona Sacramentary has been used in the Spanish rite.[63] There is, however, also evidence of North African derivation.[64] It may be that the indigenous rite which ultimately developed stemmed from both Roman and African sources.

No evidence exists for written eucharistic texts in Spain before the fifth century.[65] However, Ferotin believed that some of the texts in the *Liber Mozarabicus Sacramentorum* went back to 400 CE, on the grounds that the feasts of certain saints such as Jerome, Augustine and Martin appear in some rare manuscripts and are described as 'newcomers'.[66] A number of *inlationes* (corresponding to the Roman prefaces) reflect the circumstances of the fifth and sixth centuries, and there are feasts in honour of important sixth- and seventh-century Spanish bishops.[67] Ferotin concluded that many of the texts were gathered together and revised during the sixth and seventh centuries, this process of revision being associated with the great sees of Toledo and Braga.[68] However, although Ferotin is probably correct to regard the collection as containing some quite early texts, it is almost impossible to identify which ones they might be, or whether an early text had been revised. A further complication is that at certain stages of its history, the rite has been quite deliberately 'Syrianised'.

In the *Liber Mozarabicus Sacramentorum* and the *Liber Ordinum*[69] the eucharistic prayer consists of a series of variable prayers introduced by a fixed dialogue, surrounding a sanctus and a fixed institution narrative. The use of the sanctus in the eucharistic prayer in Spain seems to be first attested to in the *Exposito fidei catholicae* of pseudo-Athanasius, probably dating from the middle of the fifth century.[70]

By far the majority of *inlationes* conclude with what appears to be a standard conventional introduction to the sanctus. The most common begins 'To him rightly' or 'To him rightly all the angels' (*Cui merito, cui merito omnes angeli*), though the full formulae do vary:

To him rightly all the angels and archangels, thrones, dominions do not cease to cry out and to say ...

To him rightly all the angels and archangels do not cease daily to cry out, saying in one voice ...

Sometimes the introduction is preceded by 'Through whom' or 'Grant this through him.' Alongside these we also find more elaborate forms, such as that for Pentecost:

O flame that in burning confers fruitfulness, whom every intellectual creature, vivified by it, confesses to be the Lord Omnipotent; participating in whose fire in more abundant measure the Cherubim and Seraphim, magnifying the equality of the Holiness Divine and the Omnipotence of the Trinity; never resting and never wearying in their office, amidst the song of choirs of the celestial host, of crying aloud with everlasting jubilation, adore and glorify, saying: Holy ...[71]

This is an example of that elaborate style which Edmund Bishop contrasted with the sobriety of the Roman rite.[72] What is of interest is that despite the florid form of some of the *inlationes*, they are not consciously concerned with enumerating a celestial hierarchy as in the angelology of some of the Eastern prayers.

Jean Magne has suggested that the form *cui merito* refers back to Christ in the formula 'through Christ our Lord' which preceeds the sanctus introduction.[73] Was, therefore, the Spanish (and Gallican) rite also once addressed to Christ? It is interesting that the opening dialogue in the Spanish rite includes the priest's exhortation, 'To Our God and Lord Jesus Christ the Son of God, who is in heaven, let us offer [*referamus*] fitting praise and fitting thanksgiving', to which the people reply 'It is fitting and right.' Ferotin believed that the exhortation was originally addressed to the Father, but this address to Christ could be a sign of antiquity, though it could equally be of Syrian influence.[74]

In summary, therefore, the introduction to the sanctus in the Spanish rite is usually short, with a very brief angelology – though the *inlationes* themselves can be quite long. The main conclusion to be drawn, however, is that when these *inlationes* were edited, the sanctus and benedictus were regular chants in the rite. The majority of post-sanctus prayers begin with 'Truly holy, truly blessed', indicating that sanctus and benedictus were at this time wedded together.[75] The sanctus was an accepted invariable in the eucharistic prayer, and the *inlationes* wend their way towards it, even if it has little contextual logic. The 'Truly holy' pick up echoes the Syro-Byzantine use, and perhaps reflects Eastern influence. If the *Libellus* of Pseudo-Ambrose is to be interpreted as Chavoutier suggests, then perhaps Spain was one of the Western areas which adopted the sanctus before Rome. Parts of the eucharistic prayer including the sanctus might have been addressed to Christ, but firm evidence is lacking.

The *Te Deum* which is regarded as a canticle of Morning Prayer, and which contains the sanctus, was subjected to a detailed study by Paul Cagin who showed that it has much in common with a Spanish *inlatio*, and the sanctus also corresponds to the Spanish form.[76] He suggested that it was originally an *inlatio* used at Easter. The study of E. Kahler concurred with this.[77] He argued that the first part of the *Te Deum* was an *inlatio* concerned with the mass of the Easter Vigil, and the Christological part has parallels with Spanish and Gallican post-sanctus prayers. He concluded that the *Te Deum* in its original form ended with Psalm 27:9, and was the core of a mass for the Easter Vigil which had been worked up into artistic form by the hand of a master.

There are a number of theories of the original of the Gallican rite,[78] but the strongest is that it was basically Roman with influence from the

Spanish and Milanese rites, and later, the East.[79] One of the problems of assessing this rite is that the evidence which survives bears witness to an increasing Romanisation which resulted in its total replacement by the latter.[80] There are the masses of Mone, *c*.650 CE; the *Missale Gothicum* of the seventh century; the *Missale Gallicum vetus* and *Missale Francorum*, though these are of the eighth century; and some fragments. There is also the *Expositio Missae Gallicanae*, wrongly attributed to St Germanus of Paris. All these are relatively late, though we may reasonably assume that the masses of Mone give us an insight into late sixth- and early seventh-century Gallican usage. The use of the sanctus is attested by Caesarius of Arles and the Council of Vaison in the sixth century.[81]

In the Gallican anaphora we find the same structure as the Spanish rite, namely, three fixed points around which are arranged variable prayers. The opening prayer is the *contestatio*, corresponding to the *inlatio* and preface.

In the masses of Mone there are seven mass formularies, 'purely Gallican in character, without any discernible traces of Roman influence.'[82] The seventh is for the feast of St Germanus of Auxerre, but the first six seem to be a selection for Sunday use. Each of the Sunday formulas has two *contestationes*, and the sixth has an additional two. Thus there are fifteen *contestationes*. Of these, eight have the incipit indicating the following introduction to the sanctus:

'To him rightly all the angels do not cease to cry out saying'
which is almost identical to the most common form in the Spanish prayers. Three have the slight variant, 'Rightly to you.' This standard introduction indicates that the sanctus was, by this time, a *sine qua non* of the anaphora. This is further illustrated by two *contestationes* concerned with the histories and legends of saints – Elias and St Germanus. After a lengthy account of Elias' ascent to heaven in a fiery chariot, where he joins the angels who praise the King seated on his throne, the sanctus is simply introduced by 'Rightly'. Likewise it is St Germanus' merits and the angelic praise which again introduce the conventional 'To him rightly.'

In some of the *contestationes*, such as the first one in mass 1, a further contextual introduction has been created. It mentions that through Christ all things sing the song of God's melody, and asks that God will hear our singing and be pleased with our praises. Mass 4, and the alternative in mass 5, have long *contestationes*. The first of these exalts God who is above every virtue and power, who heaven and earth, angels and archangels, thrones and dominions, cherubim and seraphim proclaim with incessant voices; the second of these places the stars, sea, earth and depths (inferno) with the cherubim and seraphim.

Most of the masses have a post-sanctus. Some of these pick up on both the sanctus and benedictus as in the Spanish rite, or even just on the benedictus. Some, however, have no verbal link at all (for example, mass 3).

The conclusion to be drawn from the masses of Mone is similar to that for the Spanish rite. Normally the sanctus was introduced by a fixed formula; it could be given a context in the *contestatio*, but a context was not necessary. The sanctus was simply a necessary and expected part of the anaphora, but not essential to the thought expressed in the *contestatio*; it was simply a convention to conclude the *contestatio*. There seems to have been no great concern with including an elaborate angelology. Where this occurs, it is exceptional.

In contrast to the Syro-Byzantine and East Syrian eucharistic prayers, the sanctus in the Egyptian and Western tradition seems to have a far less logical context. In the former two traditions, for all their variations, the sanctus is in a context of praise and seems to be a logical part of the *oratio theologica*. In contrast, in Egypt in the type of anaphora represented by St Mark and Serapion, it has an entirely different function, being within the intercessions and being a springboard for further intercession in the first epiklesis. In the West, most of the evidence points to the sanctus being a late comer, borrowed from Eastern usage. It is used as a climax to the preface which praises God for some work of Christ, or the life of a saint, and takes on the role of a formal conclusion to the preface. There is little indication that the sanctus is integral to the thought of the preface. In Rome (and Milan) there was no attempt to give the sanctus a verbal link with what followed.

The angelology of the Eastern rites tended to reflect certain geographical links. Edessa and Antioch made use of Daniel 7:10 and cherubim, as well as Isaiah 6:3, Cappadocia and Jerusalem used Colossians 1:16, 'powers' from Ephesians 1:21, as well as archangels, angels and cherubim. In Egypt we find Ephesians 1:21 used as a standard introduction, together with Daniel 7:10, Habakkuk 3:2 and Isaiah 6:3. The fragments of Louvain/Barcelona, however, give a different tradition where Ecclesiasticus 49:8 was used. A complex angelology is not a sign of later expansion. Cyril of Jerusalem knew a complex angelology, whereas the later Western angelologies and East Syrian anaphoras had a simple, non-hierarchical angelology.

Perhaps the firmest conclusion to be drawn is that the sanctus is most integrated in the anaphoras of the Syro-Byzantine and East Syrian families, and it is in these areas that it has its earliest attestations. This may not be insignificant in relation to the problem of the origin of the anaphoral sanctus.

6

✠

The possible origins of the sanctus in the eucharistic prayer and its literary forms

SOME IDEAS ON ANAPHORAL EVOLUTION

ULTIMATELY the question of the origin of the sanctus cannot be divorced from the question of the origin or origins of the eucharistic prayer in which it is found.

In recent literature, a large body of opinion has regarded the Jewish table prayers called the Birkat ha-mazon (BHM) as being an important element in the evolution of the eucharistic prayer. Beginning with W. O. E. Oesterley and F. Gavin, and furthered by Gregory Dix and J.-P. Audet, the Jewish *berakot* came under careful scrutiny in the search for links with Christian prayers.[1] Whereas Audet appealed to the *berakot* as a literary genre, it was Dix who drew attention to the *berakot* of the *qiddus* and of the BHM. Dix did not himself pursue the inquiry, but in passing he emphasised the second pericope of the BHM as a possible key to understanding the development of the eucharistic prayer.[2] This insight has in more recent years been developed in different ways by a number of scholars.

Whether the Last Supper was a Passover meal, an anticipated Passover meal or *haburah*, the BHM was the traditional grace after meals and, it is suggested, may well have been the prayer used by Jesus before the distribution of the cup. This grace, which goes back in form to the time of the Book of Jubilees,[3] consisted then of three *berakot* giving three themes – blessing for creation, giving thanks for redemption, and supplication.[4] There is, however, no *qedussah* and no logical context for it, and there is no evidence that any Jewish meal prayer ever contained it.[5] The inference must be that, if the BHM is the key to the origin of the eucharistic prayer, the sanctus is a component added to the earlier structure at a later date.

Louis Bouyer has argued that the BHM, which Jesus pronounced at the end of the meal,[6] can be schematised as DEF (blessing for creation, thanksgiving for redemption, and supplication). However, quite apart from the brevity of this grace, Bouyer noted that in comparison with the classical anaphoras, an institution narrative with anamnesis/oblation, intercessions and the sanctus have been subsequently developed or added. He thus turned to the Synagogue *berakot* – both of the *shema* and *'amidah* (all twenty-one or twenty-two *berakot*!). Placed altogether he schematised these as ABC, corresponding (but not in length of material!) with the DEF sequence of BHM. He suggested that the Christian anaphora could be explained by a gradual synthesis of the two groups of *berakot* – AD, BE, CF. This, he believed, happened as the meal disappeared and the rite of bread and wine became fused with the readings and prayers of the Morning Service. The sanctus of the anaphora was thus borrowed from the Synagogue *berakot*. Although he offered no dating, he argued (on very different grounds from Dix) that we first see this development in Egypt. Accepting the views of Bousset and Goodenough, he regarded AC 7 as 'Alexandrine' and attempted, mainly on the basis of the absence of the benedictus, to see some correlation between the sanctus in AC 7 and its form in the Egyptian anaphoras. AC 8 then represents an Antiochene introduction of this adapted Synagogue *qeduššah* into the Syro-Byzantine anaphora. The ultimate source is the Synagogue and, by implication, *qeduššah d^e 'amidah*.

Bouyer's arguments are open to serious questions at a number of points. To begin with, it seems unnecessarily complex, and vague, to make the comparisons with Jewish *berakot* so wide without proper reference to their context and sequence. Furthermore, as has been noted, the most recent views concerning AC 7 place this collection in the orbit of Antioch, not Egypt.

Critical of Bouyer's wide appeal to all the Synagogue *berakot*, Louis Ligier followed both Dix and Bouyer in regarding the BHM as the correct starting-point. Ligier's main concern was to explain why the institution narrative with anamnesis/oblation came to be included in the eucharistic prayer. His earlier work was concerned with considering the embolisms which were inserted into the Jewish liturgy of Yom Kippur, and in the BHM for Hannukah and Purim, and to establish the antiquity of such embolisms. His conclusion was that these date back at least to the second century CE, and at that time could be inserted in either the second or third pericope of the BHM.[7]

Ligier, accepting that Jesus 'consecrated the sacramental cup at the moment of the birkat ha-mazon',[8] believed that Jesus could have added his own thanksgiving to the Father for his redemptive mission, and that it is easy to see how the Church could choose this pericope of thanksgiving for the eucharistic embolism – the institution narrative. The preponderant influence of the BHM is seen in *Didache* 10. However, a transference had apparently taken place. *Didache* 10 commences at once with thanksgiving for redemption, and then returns to give thanks (*not bless*) for creation. In Addai and Mari (shorn of its sanctus!) Ligier believed that the three *gehanata* recalled the three pericopes of the BHM, and that *Sharar* gave us an institution narrative within the third pericope, the supplication, as an embolism. On the other hand, the two primary movements of thanksgiving and supplication are found in the *Apostolic Tradition*, where the institution narrative has been inserted in the thanksgiving section.

As for the sanctus, it was not part of the BHM and, it may be presumed, was still not in use when *Didache* 10 and the *Apostolic Tradition* were composed; Ligier was content to follow Ratcliff in regarding the sanctus in Addai and Mari (and *Sharar*) as a later intrusion into the earlier text. However, in explaining where the sanctus has come from, Ligier pointed to the *qeduššah* of *Yoṣer* and the *'amidah*.[9]

Strangely, in the same paper, Ligier suggested that in St James and St Basil the sanctus was an original component; in these, he argued, the first part of the eucharistic prayer testified to an intention to glorify God, in contrast to the thanksgiving orientation formulated by the opening dialogue.

Ligier offers no dates for this supposed development, other than that it took place between the inclusion of an institution narrative and the attainment of the final structural form in the fifth century.[10]

Ligier's own lines of enquiry have been further explored in a cautious and precise manner by the American liturgist, T. J. Talley. In his paper read to the International Societas Liturgica, and subsequently expanded in *Worship* 1976, Talley made two preliminary observations.[11] First, although Audet was right to draw attention to Jewish *berakot* as the source of Christian euchology, particularly the eucharistic prayer, his description of a *berakah* was artificial and required careful qualification.[12] Following on from this, Talley pointed out that to regard *eulogein* as synonymous with *eucharistein* could no longer be sustained.[13] He suggested that in the institution narrative of Paul and Luke, the reference to *eulogein* referred to a simple benediction, but that *eucharistein* referred probably to the BHM and particularly to its second pericope which begins *nodeh lekah*, 'we give you thanks'.[14]

Noting the three pericopes of the BHM, each one ending with a *chatimah* or short benediction formula, and noting the themes of blessing God, giving thanks for redemption, and supplication, Talley agreed that the three pericopes were found in *Didache* 10. However, *berak* disappears to be replaced by *eucharistein*; the *chatimot* are replaced by *doxo*logies; and the tripartite scheme of blessing God, thanksgiving for redemption, and supplication becomes bipartite – thanskgiving for redemption and for food, and supplication. This bipartite schema, Talley suggested, formed the core of the Christian eucharistic prayer. Thus in Hippolytus and Epiphanius, although we find one continuous prayer in place of a series of pericopes, they nevertheless give us the scheme of thanksgiving for redemption and supplication.[15] He also suggested influence of the BHM upon the anaphora of Addai and Mari.[16]

In this particular paper Talley dealt with the sanctus only indirectly:

It is quite possible that the Jewish use of kedushah (sanctus) in the Synagogue liturgy influenced the Christian adoption of that hymn, and perhaps at an earlier date than has been supposed, but that usage (from both the Jewish and Christian sides) is too clouded by uncertainty to justify seeking the roots of the anaphora itself in the berakoth and kedushah before shema.[17]

Here Talley hinted that the Synagogue might be the source of the anaphoral sanctus, but not the source of its introductory preface of praise. Since, however, the BHM is the starting point, it follows that the sanctus must represent a later insertion after the time of *Apostolic Tradition*.

In subsequent papers Talley has expanded, qualified and revised some of the earlier suggestions. Thus, for example, he notes a tripartite pattern of eucharistic prayers such as Addai and Mari which became standard at Antioch, and another and possibly earlier pattern in which the first two sections (of the BHM) are elided into a thanksgiving and supplication (*Apostolic Tradition*). Talley saw this bipartite structure in the Egyptian Strasbourg Papyrus (regarded as a complete eucharistic prayer) and the Roman Canon.[18] However, in papers published in 1982 and 1984, Talley hinted that in Addai and Mari it is possible to see a bipartite nucleus beginning after the sanctus (thanksgiving–supplication) to which was added or restored 'the original threefold pattern by the addition, from the daily office, of an opening Praise of the Creator hymned by the heavenly choirs'.[19] Appealing to Auf der Maur's study of the paschal homilies of Asterios, where the sanctus is used at the Easter Vigil, Talley thought it likely that the sanctus entered the eucharistic prayer from the 'Christian Synagogue' rather than directly from the Synagogue in Judaism. However, he allowed the possibility that Macomber's reconstruction of the 'original text' of Addai and Mari (which contains the sanctus) may very well present to us the earliest appearance of the sanctus in a Christian eucharistic prayer.[20]

The Dutch liturgist, Herman Wegman, in a paper which he described as somewhat premature,[21] outlined a hypothetical genealogy of the eucharistic prayer, again starting from the BHM. Wegman traced a link between the BHM through *Didache* 10 to Strasbourg Papyrus and Addai and Mari (minus sanctus!). The *Apostolic Tradition* represents a different branch: 'This enigma remains without solution: one has no idea how Hippolytus arrived at this structure.'[22] However, the sanctus, when and where it appears, is 'a later interpolation'.[23] The Spanish liturgist José Sánchez Caro builds on the work of Bouyer, Ligier, Talley and Giraudo,[24] and again emphasises the BHM as the foundation for the eucharistic prayer. The sanctus he regards as a later addition, borrowed from the Synagogue *qeduššah d[e] Yoṣer*.[25]

The views of these scholars serve to illustrate an emerging consensus amongst some leading Continental and North American liturgists; they also illustrate that one's theory of anaphoral origins in turn determines the explanation for the origin of the sanctus. Where the BHM is regarded *a priori* as the basic nucleus, it must follow that the sanctus is a secondary addition to an archetypal structure.

Although this approach to the origin of the eucharistic prayer is widely espoused, there are reasons for questioning its methodology and its concentration on a single archetypal structure. Recently Paul Bradshaw has pin-pointed the problem:

In spite of the transformation which has taken place in New Testament studies in recent years in recognizing the fundamental pluriformity of early Christianity, there has still been a residual tendency in liturgical scholarship to look for the most ancient stratum in those elements which are common to all, or nearly all, later texts, rather than in those which are distinctive of individual traditions, and in particular to seek to trace the evolution of all eucharistic prayers from a single root. Though this frequently runs into difficulties in explaining the diversity of later prayer-texts, and especially such things as the variation in the position which the narrative of institution occupies, and the existence of some prayers which seemingly have a bipartite structure and others which have a tripartite structure, yet there is not much sign of a willingness to abandon it altogether.[26]

Although Ligier argued strongly in favour of regarding the BHM as the archetype for understanding anaphoral development, he acknowledged his difficulty over the total evidence before him. He asked:

Does this mean that in the first two centuries our eucharistic prayer was *always* modelled after the pattern of this Jewish meal prayer?[27]

Then, with reference to the prayers in the Apocryphal Acts:

The structure of these celebrations and the style of these prayers show no apparent contact with the Birkat ha-mazon; and if they still suggest the Didache at all, it is not in virtue of their liturgical structure, but on account of a few theological ideas.[28]

Then, turning to the anaphoras of the Twelve Apostles, Greek Chrysostom, Addai and Mari and the Strasbourg Papyrus, he noted:

In short, these four liturgical documents, whose opening thanksgiving is concluded by a doxology or a *qanona*, each constitute a complete and closed euchologia which does not demand to be prolonged by anything at all, either a *Sanctus* or a narrative.[29]

Here the inference is that the *oratio theologica* or 'preface' of these anaphoras serves perfectly well as an anaphora, and could have existed as such in isolation from any other element.

The late G. J. Cuming took up these remarks, suggesting that one could add to the list the opening sections of Egyptian Basil and St James. He suggested that the argument could be applied also to the first eighteen lines of AC 8 and Serapion.[30]

A danger in Cuming's line of argument is that it tends to ignore other known factors in the development of some anaphoras. AC 8, for example, is a cumbersome piece of work, and its first eighteen lines wending towards the sanctus, but then embarking upon salvation history, are better explained as the exuberant work of the compiler than as a fragment of an earlier eucharistic prayer.[31] Much more important, however, is Cuming's observation on Ligier's comments:

Ligier's suggestion implies a certain method of construction. The anaphora will originally have ended with a doxology or the sanctus, and successive sections would then be added on at the end of the prayer, or slotted in at appropriate points. Does this seem a probable, or even possible, method of developing an anaphora?[32]

Cuming himself illustrated how, if Strasbourg Papyrus is a complete anaphora, it was extended by adding large chunks of material onto the end to give the present structure of St Mark.[33]

Cuming's suggestions have in turn been tested by another English liturgist, John Fenwick, in his work on the anaphoras of St Basil and their influence on the Jerusalem liturgy of St James.[34] Fenwick accepted that Cyril of Jerusalem knew a two-part anaphora, of thanksgiving for creation with the sanctus, and supplication with epiklesis and intercessions. It shows no affinities with the BHM. Fenwick has convincingly demonstrated that the anaphora of St James was derived from this earlier structure by slotting in material from the Egyptian form of St Basil.

Fenwick's findings regarding the Jerusalem anaphora are important not only in terms of theories of anaphoral development, but also with regard to the place of the sanctus in this development. At Jerusalem the sanctus was part of the eucharistic prayer *before* the introduction of an institution narrative and anamnesis, or even a thanksgiving for redemption. Furthermore, as has been argued earlier, the sanctus known to Cyril (and preserved in St James) is so integrated into the whole opening of the prayer that it is difficult to see how it could not have been part of the Jerusalem anaphora from whenever that form was first used. To regard this section in the same way as Talley has suggested for Addai and Mari – a borrowing from Christian Morning Prayer – would leave us with a nucleus for the Jerusalem anaphora of an epiklesis and intercessions, analogous to some Gnostic prayers but certainly not to the BHM.

Undoubtedly the BHM was an ancient established grace, though the prayer fragment from the Synagogue at Dura-Europos may suggest that some Jewish groups used other forms of meal grace.[35] The BHM may have been used at the Last Supper, but perhaps Jesus deliberately avoided it. Allan Bouley writes:

The brief blessing over bread was perhaps unspecific enough to be serviceable, but using the unaltered birkat ha-mazon would have confusedly linked Jesus' covenant up with food, land, city and probably the Passover of the former covenant, whereas the meaning of all these was being changed in the very celebration of the supper.[36]

The BHM belongs to that group of Jewish prayers which the Jewish liturgist Joseph Heinemann classed as 'Statutory Prayers'. The rules for these Statutory prayers were not laid down until the third-century CE Rabbis, the Amoreans, but they were merely making standard one type of a hitherto variety of prayer forms.[37] In another category which he designated 'Private and Non-Statutory Prayer', Heinemann turned to consider the Lord's Prayer and the implications of Jesus' teaching on prayer. Heinemann suggested that here, particularly in the teaching of

Matthew 6:5–6, Jesus espoused the tradition of Private and Non-Statutory rather than the forms which became Statutory.[38] Amongst the additional styles which are characteristic of private prayer, Heinemann included the formulae 'I thank you' and 'We give you thanks', which are commonly found at the beginning of a prayer of thanksgiving.[39] One wonders whether this is the origin of the Christian preference for *eucharistein* rather than specifically the second pericope of the BHM. In any case, the recent surveys by James H. Charlesworth suggest that a wide variety of prayer forms influenced the composition, themes and structures of Christian prayers.[40] Given the diverse groups which made up the early Christian Churches,[41] and the freedom of the celebrant to compose his own eucharistic prayer,[42] the prayer models upon which different celebrants drew may have varied widely. Such freedom and diversity (quite apart from whether or not Jesus used his own forms) might better explain the differences between *Apostolic Tradition*, Addai and Mari, Strasbourg Papyrus and the Gnostic eucharistic prayers. From this diversity there came gradual standardisation by amalgamation, addition, and slotting in blocks of material as Fenwick has demonstrated.[43]

Although this alternative 'English' view of anaphoral development will be less satisfying to the systematic and tidy mind, it may in the end provide a better framework for understanding and explaining anaphoral growth. It may also provide a more promising framework for considering the possible origin of the sanctus.

The Synagogue (Jewish or Christian)?

We have seen that although Ligier, Talley and Sánchez Caro saw no need to appeal to the Synagogue to explain the origin of the eucharistic prayer, they suggested the Synagogue as a possible source for the anaphoral sanctus. However, anticipating in some respects the work of Bouyer, C. P. Price investigated the similarities between certain anaphoras and the Synagogue *berakot* in an article in 1961.[44] The *shema* itself, and *Gu'ellah*, had, in his opinion, no great influence; however, the other *berakot* had, particularly upon AC 8 and Serapion. The *Yoṣer* with *qeduššah* had an influence on the preface and sanctus, and the *'amidah* on the intercessions.[45] With regard to the anaphoral sanctus, Price saw no need to appeal to *qeduššah dᵉ sidra*, and he eliminated *qeduššah dᵉ 'amidah* on the grounds that it had no angelology. He therefore settled for the *qeduššah dᵉ Yoṣer*.[46] He was to conclude that later anaphoras are the fusion of morning prayers rooted in the

Synagogue liturgy but not followed exactly, and a eucharistic nucleus of which Hippolytus is an example.[47]

One of the weaknesses of Price's paper is that the parallels he adduced were widely scattered in different anaphoras of different date and provenance, and the themes themselves are common religious imagery. The actual verbal similarity in any one anaphora is minimal. The most convincing parallels are to be found in AC 8, but we know that the redactor reused themes and phrases from the Synagogue prayers of AC 7. The greatest problem is that *Yoṣer* blesses God as Creator of the Luminaries (as a morning hymn) and *not directly* for creation, whereas the Christian anaphoras praise God for his name, or the Being of God, or his general creating activity, and not specifically for light.

A more interesting case for the influence of the Morning Synagogue *berakot* on anaphoral formation has been made by Jacob Vellian in relation to Addai and Mari.[48] Although his comparison requires qualification,[49] it is as convincing as the comparison of Addai and Mari with the BHM. *Yoṣer* is centred on the commemoration of the luminaries, includes praise of the Name, and *qeduššah*. The first part of Addai and Mari has the same general focus (though by no means identical) to which is added a general commemoration of the economy of Christ. *Ahabah* is an anamnesis of God's gifts such as the Torah and the Land; it also contains a petition for peace and the coming of God's kingdom. The second part of Addai and Mari has a similar content.

It has to be admitted that Vellian's comparison is no more conclusive than Sánchez Caro's comparison with the BHM. In the former there is no parallel to the epiklesis, and in the latter no parallel to the sanctus. But Vellian's comparison is *no less* convincing, and remains a viable explanation.

Talley, we have noted, suggested that rather than direct borrowing, the explanation may be that borrowing took place from a Christian adaptation of the Synagogue Morning *berakot*. This is an attractive suggestion, but difficult to demonstrate. Apart from AC 7, we have no early Christian adaptations of Synagogue prayers. Furthermore, the compiler of AC used the material in Book 8 in a manner which suggests that the sanctus was already a recognised part of some anaphoras and was *different* from its use in the Synagogue prayers.[50] If borrowing took place from this source, it was certainly in a very general way rather than a simple appropriation of the *qeduššah*. Borrowing from this source would also seem to presuppose either the existence in the anaphora of a thanksgiving for creation, or the borrowing and remodelling of the *Yoṣer*. Yet, as we have suggested, such a borrowing is difficult to apply to the anaphora of Jerusalem, which seems to presuppose the sanctus as an integral part of its opening prayer of praise.

Merkāvāh mysticism?

Another possible origin may have been the very same diffuse tradition which led to the use of the *qeduššah* in the Synagogue *berakot* – *merkāvāh* mysticism. Amongst the diverse strands which made up the early Church, Revelation 4 and 5 bear witness to the fact that *merkāvāh* mysticism was one of them. How widespread this tendency was and how typical we do not know. Its continued influence is found in the *Passio* of Perpetua, and in Aphrahat; furthermore, many of the Pseudepigraphal books which show *merkāvāh* influence were preserved and copied by Christian groups. Could it be, therefore, that amongst such groups the sanctus came to play an important part in their eucharistic prayers? Cuming's suggestion of a thanksgiving terminating in sanctus does have a parallel with the *Hekhalot* hymns which are a product of this same diffuse movement. It is also strange that, although the Book of Revelation was late in being accepted in the Syriac-speaking Church, the phraseology of the hymns of Revelation 4 and 5 is echoed in the first *gehanta* of Addai and Mari. Furthermore, we have noted earlier the parallel ideas between the second part of the *berakot* in *Ma'aśeh Merkāvāh* and the opening praise section of Addai and Mari. In this context it is perhaps no accident that Addai and Mari is the eucharistic prayer from the area of Edessa and Nisibis, influenced in a variety of ways by the Jewish region of Adiabene.[51] It was within these Babylonian Jewish communities that the *merkāvāh* tradition was steadily developed. J. Neusner, though acknowledging that the evidence is suggestive rather than uncontestible proof, writes:

Nonetheless, this much is certain: in the light of the findings of Scholem and others on the existence of a mystical tradition as evidenced by Hillel and, more immediately in the second century, by Hananiah the nephew of R. Joshua, and also possibly by Yosi of Huzal (if the Mishnaic reading is accepted), Jewish mysticism was studied in Babylonian Jewish academies at the time of R. Judah the Prince, and, specifically, speculation on Ezekiel's vision was carried on. That a whole wall in the Dura Synagogue was apparently devoted to the prophet Ezekiel further strengthens my conviction that Babylonian Jewry did cultivate the traditions of its own prophet in indigenous academies.[52]

It would have been quite natural, given the realised eschatology of Christianity, to include *qeduššah* in some of their prayers, including some eucharistic prayers. Such an inclination may have been stronger in the East Syrian communities. In Egyptian Basil, which would seem to have a Cappadocian origin, there is a definite reference to the person of God sitting on the throne of Glory, adored by every heavenly power – the very subject-matter of *merkāvāh* mysticism. Perhaps, therefore, the same mystical tradition which gave rise on the one hand to the Synagogue *qeduššot*, and on the other to the *Hekhalot* hymns, was also the stimulus which led some Christian groups to use a version of Isaiah 6:3 with an angelology in eucharistic prayers.[53]

Imaginative developments from biblical phraseology?

Perhaps, however, the origin could be far less sophisticated. Could the sanctus in the eucharistic prayer be the result of some biblically minded and enterprising celebrant who simply decided to include it?

In at least three of the prayers which are regarded as relatively early – Strasbourg Papyrus, Cyril of Jerusalem and Egyptian Basil – the thanksgiving is concerned with creation. The first of these has, of course, no sanctus. Its opening thanksgiving or blessing, albeit lacunose, has the following in the Greek text:

se
eulogein   nuktōr te
kai m[e]th′ [hē]meran   (soi tō poiēsanti ton ou]
ran[on kai] panta ta en [autō, gēn kai ta en tē gē, tha]
la[ossas]kai [pot]am[o]us k[ai panta ta] e[n au tois].[54]

The language has in fact been culled from scripture: Genesis 1 suggests the morning and night; the description of God who made heaven and earth, the sea and all that is in them, may have been lifted from Acts 4:24, but also perhaps from Exodus 20:11, or Psalm 146:6. To this has been added Genesis 1:26, and possibly a link to Christ via Psalm 104:24 and John 1:9.

A similar number of biblical phrases and words underlie the opening praise of Egyptian Basil (though this may have been influenced by an Egyptian anaphoral tradition)[55] and Cyril of Jerusalem, and the later St James, though these latter two may have been influenced by Psalm 148 where creation itself hymns God. In Basil, and more particularly in Cyril, the sanctus is included as a natural progression of thought. The sanctus is not simply an appendage.

However, instead of the language about creation being culled from a variety of biblical sources as outlined above, nearly all the language is found in the opening of Ezra's prayer in Nehemiah 9:6ff., though there it leads into a reference to the worship of the heavenly host. The LXX has:

su ei autos Kurios monos, su epoiēsas ton ouranon kai ton ouranon tou ouranou, kai pasan tēn stasin autōn, tēn gēn kai panta hosa estin en autē, tas thalassas kai panta ta en autais. kai su zōopoieis ta panta, kai soi proskunousin ai stratiai tōn ouranōn.[56]

Not only does this text provide the basic phraseology used in Strasbourg Papyrus, it also provides an even better basis for Egyptian Basil where 'you are adored by every holy power' (*ho para pasēs hagias dunaméos proskumoumenos*) echoes the last words of Nehemiah 9:6, and 'the heavens and the heaven of heavens' (*hoi ouranoi kai hoi ouranoi tōn ouranōn*) in St James finds a perfect parallel in this text rather than in 1 Kings 8:27. Any Christian celebrant with a good knowledge of the Bible and a little imagination could easily have seen a connection between Nehemiah 9:6 and Colossians 1:16, and the mention of angelic beings and the worship of the heavenly host would readily suggest Isaiah 6:3. An awareness of Synagogue usage or *merkāvāh* would have provided further incentive, if any was needed, but a knowledge of John 12:41 would have sufficed for a creative mind to have acted independently.

Again, in the prayer contained in the Martyrdom of Polycarp, the opening sections has the following:

O Lord God Almighty, Father of Thy beloved and blessed child Jesus Christ, through whom we have received our knowledge of Thee, God of Angels and Powers and of all creation [ho Theos (ho) angelōn kai dunameōn kai pasēs ktiseōs] and of the whole race of the righteous who live in Thy Presence.

Allan Bouley comments that the language of much of this prayer indicates most strongly its relation to early liturgical prayer and to the eucharistic prayer in particular. It may, he suggests, reflect the type of eucharistic prayer extemporised by Polycarp.[57] Yet any celebrant using similar phraseology had, with the reference to 'God of Angels and Powers', a ready-made cue for the sanctus.

The thought in Addai and Mari is different: the Name is praised, and there is a reference to creation and salvation, and then the adoration of God by the angelic host. In the Gospel of Bartholomew (4:49) we find a prayer slightly reminiscent of Addai and Mari:

O Lord Jesus Christ, the great and glorious Name. All the choirs of the angels praise you, O Master, and I that am unworthy with my lips . . . do praise you, O Master.

There is no sanctus, but any prayer with similar phraseology could easily have suggested to an imaginative celebrant the inclusion of the sanctus. This, however, seems more feasible where a variety of models for eucharistic prayers is envisaged rather than simply the BHM model.

Although the three possible sources for the sanctus offered above are suggested independently of any particular theory of anaphoral origins, it would appear to me that its inclusion is easier to explain and understand where a variety of models is accepted. At the same time, however, it may be that the sanctus originated in a different way in different places; for example, perhaps the East Syrian rite developed it under the influence of *merkāvāh*, whereas elsewhere biblical phraseology, or Nehemiah 9:6, was the inspiration. Elsewhere, perhaps, there was a more conscious reflection of the Synagogue *qeduššot*, or more precisely, that of the *Yoṣer*. Although it can only be speculation, a possible difference in origin may account for why in some places the sanctus seems to have been addressed to Christ as God, reflecting the 'Higher Christology' which came from the Johannine community, where the Son is one with the Father.[58]

As far as the place of origin is concerned, in the Egyptian and Roman traditions, the sanctus would seem to be a later addition to the sense of the anaphora, though the Egyptian unique use remains an enigma. Our examples of eucharistic prayers where the sanctus seems to be an integral part of the prayer are Jerusalem, Cappadocia or North Syria, and Edessa. It may have been integral to the anaphora at Antioch, but our information here is too sparse. The evidence points to the Syrian part of the Church, and those later anaphoras which stem from that area. Once included, it presumably became a popular congregational acclamation and gradually came to feature in all anaphoras as part of the initial praise of God – even when, as in the case of the Roman canon, it had no logical context. Egypt, however, developed its own unique supplicatory use of the sanctus.

Appendix: The literary forms of the sanctus

In considering the context, function and origin of the sanctus, only indirectly has the actual form been mentioned. There is good reason: many manuscripts give only the opening words – 'Holy, holy, holy' – the rest of the formula being assumed. Where the full formula is given, it often reflects elaboration, and its antiquity is difficult to establish.

In the Synagogue *qeduššot* (but not *qeduššah dᵉ sidra* where the Targum version is included) the unaltered text of Isaiah 6:3 is given: 'Holy, holy, holy, is the Lord of Hosts; the whole earth is full of his glory.' This is not the case with the sanctus in the eucharistic prayer. In the evidence considered in previous chapters, the earliest form quoted would seem to be that found in Asterios. In Homily XV only the first line of the sanctus is given, representing the LXX version, though Ezekiel 3:12 is linked with it. In Homily XXIX the form is

Hagios, hagios, hagios kurios sabaōth (Holy, holy, holy, is the Lord Sabaoth)
plērēs ho ouranos kai hē gē tēs doxēs autou (Full is the heaven and the earth of his glory).

In comparison with the biblical text, 'heaven and' has been added, and 'whole' has been omitted. This expansion and omission is the hallmark of nearly all forms of the anaphoral sanctus in subsequent early documents. Ezekiel 3:12 is also found quoted in association with the sanctus in Asterios. Such a link is also found in AC 7, and its continued association with the sanctus by some groups may be suggested by a sermon of John Chrysostom:

I mounted to the heavens and gave you as proof the chorus of angels as they sang: 'Glory to God in the highest, and on earth peace, good will among men.' Again, you heard the seraphim as they shuddered and cried out in astonishment: 'Holy, holy, holy, the Lord God of hosts, all the earth is filled with his glory.' And I also gave you the cherubim who exclaimed: 'Blessed be his glory in his dwelling.'[59]

The link between these two passages was still known when Dionysius the Areopagite was writing.[60]

Cyril of Jerusalem gives only the first line, and there is no change here from the LXX. His mention of 'hymns' in the plural might imply that some other chant was associated with Isaiah 6:3 – perhaps Ezekiel 3:12, or even the benedictus – but the fact remains that he does not actually quote any other chant. In Serapion we have:

Hagios, hagios, hagios kurios sabaōth
plērēs ho ouranos kai hē gē tēs doxēs sou.

Here in the second line 'his' has been changed to 'your', addressing the sanctus directly to God. There is no suggestion that either Ezekiel 3:12 or any other chant was attached to the sanctus here. In AC 8 the form is as in Asterios, to which has been appended Romans 1:25:

eulogētos eis tous aiōnas. amēn (Blessed be he for ever. Amen).

The benedictus also occurs in this rite, but after the anaphora and before communion.

In Addai and Mari, the Mar Esa'ya text gives only the incipit, but the text of Theodore in the same manuscript gives the following:

qaddis qaddis qaddis marya hiltana
da-mlen smaya w'ar'a men tesbᵉhateh

The words in italics are identical to the form found in the fourth-century 'History of John the Son of Zebedee', which may reflect a liturgical sanctus. There is therefore good reason to believe that although the Mar Esa'ya

manuscript itself dates from the tenth or eleventh century, the form of the
sanctus it gives has changed little, if at all, from the third or fourth century. In
the Syriac of this text, however, the first line gives an interpretation of *kurios
sabaōth*; *kurios* is rendered as 'Lord', but *sabaōth* is rendered by an adjective,
'strong', 'powerful'. The second line is introduced as a relative clause. In
English it may be rendered as:

Holy, holy, holy, [is the] Powerful Lord of whose glories heaven and earth are full.

As far as later texts of the sanctus are concerned, each anaphoral family
developed its own particular variation. It is useful to consider each of the two
lines of the sanctus in turn.

Line 1

In the Greek liturgies of the Syro-Byzantine and Egyptian families the first line
is that of the LXX. An exception is the sanctus inscription described by
Baumstark where we find:

Hagios, hagios, hagios ei kurie (Holy, holy, holy, are you Lord).

However, as Baumstark observed, this is in any case an adaptation of the
anaphoral sanctus.[61]

The Coptic translation follows the Greek form, but the Ethiopic (chapter 7)
appears to qualify Lord of Hosts with 'perfect'.[62] The Syriac anaphoras have
the form already encountered in the Mar Esa'ya text, but adding 'God' to
'Powerful Lord'. The Maronite rite (chapter 7), perhaps under Latin influence, adds 'Sabaoth', giving 'Holy, holy, holy, [is the] Powerful Lord God
Sabaoth.' This rite also addresses the whole sanctus in the second person
singular rather than in the third person. The Armenian rite (chapter 7) adds
'God'. The Roman rite has:

Sanctus, sanctus, sanctus, Dominus Deus Sabaoth
(Holy, holy, holy [is the] Lord God of Sabaoth)

thus following the Syriac and Armenian in adding 'God', but retaining the
'Sabaoth' as in the Greek tradition. The non-Roman Western rites have the
same, though Pseudo-Ambrose gives a literal translation of the biblical version,
without the addition 'God'.

Line 2

The second line is far more variable. The 'whole' earth has, as noted, been
dropped, and 'heaven' or 'heavens'[63] has been added. The Egyptian Greek (and
Coptic) anaphoras have the form: *plērēs ho ouranos kai hē gē tēs hagias sou
doxēs* (Full are the heaven and the earth of your holy glory). In comparison
with Serapion, *doxēs sou* has been inverted, and *hagias* has been added. The
Syro-Byzantine Greek anaphoras have the same as Serapion. However, as

noted above, Asterios and AC 8 retain the third person, 'his glory', as is the case in most Syriac formulae. In Syriac James, as given by Rucker, the form is:

qaddis qaddis qaddis marya hiltana hu da-mlen 'nun smaya w'ar'a men tesbᵉhateh.

Other versions add to *tesbᵉhateh* the words *w'yqara d-rabuteh* – 'and the honour of whose majesty' – giving 'of whose glories and the honour of whose majesty heaven and earth are full'. The later manuscripts of the East Syrian rite also extend this line: 'glories and the nature of his being and of the excellence of his glorious splendour'. The Armenian has 'Heaven and earth are full of your glory', reflecting Syro-Byzantine Greek usage, though some versions omit 'and earth'.[64]

Translation of the Ethiopic rite has caused confusion. Harden rendered the line as follows:

Right [or wholly] full are the heaven and the earth of the holiness of your glory.

Harden noted that the word translated 'right' or 'wholly' is an addition and seems problematical. He suggested that originally it may have been an abbreviation coming after the sanctus incipit, meaning 'etc.', and later, when the sanctus was written in full, was incorporated into the text.[65] Hammerschmidt, in his magisterial study of the Ethiopic anaphoras, argued that it represented the Hebrew word 'whole' and that the Ethiopic rite had reintroduced the word from the biblical text, 'the whole earth'.[66] In a subsequent study, however, he conceded that, analogous to usage elsewhere in the anaphora of the 318 Orthodox Fathers, the word actually belongs to the first line, qualifying God in the sense of 'the complete One'.[67] Indeed, Daoud had already adopted this view on his English translation:

Holy, holy, holy, *perfect* Lord of Hosts
Heaven and earth are full of the holiness of your glory.[68]

Without parallel in the early literature is a Coptic fragment of a preface and sanctus published by Crum which uses the version of Rev 4:8.[69]

In Western use, the Roman sanctus has *pleni sunt caeli et terra gloria tuae* (heaven and earth are full of your glory), as in the Syro-Byzantine rites. The Mozarabic rite has an addition – 'full of the glory of your majesty'. The *Te Deum* has *maiestatis gloriae tuae* – 'the majesty of your glory'.

In summary, therefore, the first line in some traditions has been interpreted rather than simply translated or transliterated. In the second line in every tradition 'heaven' has been added. Heaven is mentioned in the Targum version, and Eric Werner quotes a midrashic passage where Isaiah 6:3 is linked with Jeremiah 23:24.[70] Nevertheless, although there may be a Jewish precedent, it is probably more likely that the addition is a deliberate Christian addition made in the interests of Christology. The 'glory' which Isaiah saw, according to John 12:41, was Christ, and both in his pre-existence and after the ascension Christians believed that the glory was in heaven. The change from 'his glory' to 'your glory' seems to be stylistic, addressing it directly to God. In the Syriac traditions further elaboration has taken place. Only in one instance does it seem that a relatively early anaphora made use of Revelation 4:8.

What of the benedictus which came to be attached to the sanctus in all traditions other than the Egyptian and Ethiopic? It is an adaptation of Matthew 21:9. The absence in the Egyptian rite has been seen by many to point beyond any doubt to the use of the benedictus as a much later development, and to regard Egypt as preserving the earlier usage. This view is perhaps less certain when the peculiar Egyptian use of the sanctus is taken into account; the sanctus–epiklesis unit hardly allows for anything to follow the sanctus other than petition.[71]

The benedictus would seem to be a Syrian development, but the precise date is impossible to pin-point. The early evidence poses three questions:

1 Since Asterios associates Ezekiel 3:12 with Isaiah 6:3 as in Jewish usage, did the benedictus replace an earlier use of Ezekiel 3:12, perhaps for Christological reasons?
2 In AC 8 the benedictus is found after the *Sancta sanctis* as a pre-communion acclamation; it is also found before the communion in *Testamentum Domini* and in the Byzantine rite. Was this its original place from which it was introduced into the anaphora?
3 In AC 8 the sanctus is followed by Romans 1:25. Does this represent an interim development from Ezekiel 3:12 to Matthew 21:9?

In considering the use of Romans 1:25 in AC 8, few commentators seem to have asked whether this might represent the compiler's Arian sympathies. Since the benedictus is addressed to Christ, it would hardly have fitted the compiler's anaphora which is so clearly addressed to the Father and where, in the sanctus, the Son is deliberately subordinated. Far from representing an interim stage, this may simply be theological substitution and the opposite of a once universal stage of development. Of more significance, perhaps, is the fact that Asterios' discussion of the sanctus takes place in Homily XVI in connection with Psalm 8:3b and Matthew 21:9. At Easter, Matthew 21:9 would have been an appropriate chant, and one may conjecture that perhaps at Easter it replaced Ezekiel 3:12 – if this latter was ever used with the anaphoral sanctus – or simply became an Easter embolism. That its use was once restricted to festivals is suggested by a rubric in the East Syrian Mar Esay'ya manuscript.[72] Or it may have been a deliberate Christian counterpart to Ezekiel 3:12, added in the interests of Christology, originating perhaps in those Syrian areas in close contact with Jews. However, the evidence is so meagre that no firm conclusion can be reached.

As an addition to the sanctus it took various forms in the different traditions. In the Greek Syro-Byzantine liturgies we find two forms of the chant. In the Byzantine tradition:

1 *Hosanna en tois hupsistois* (Hosanna in the Highest).
2 *Eulogēmenos he erchomenos en onomati kuriou* (Blessed is the one who comes in the Name of the Lord).

3 *Hosanna en tois hupsistois* (Hosanna in the Highest).

In St. Gregory of Nazianzen (Greek and Coptic) we find an addition in line 2:

Blessed is the one who *came and* [elthōn kai] comes in the Name of the Lord.

This is also found in the Syriac anaphoras of this family. The change seems to have been made in the interests of Christology (perhaps influenced by Rev.4:8) to identify the coming Christ with Jesus. In the Armenian rite, in line 1, 'Hosanna' is replaced by 'Blessing', and in line 2, 'Blessed are you who came and will come in the Name of the Lord.'

The East Syrian rite follows the West Syrian form, though in the Mar Esa'ya text line 3 is rendered 'Hosanna to the Son of David.' In some other manuscripts it has been expanded to:

Hosanna in the Highest. Hosanna to the Son of David.
Blessed is he who came and comes in the Name of the Lord.
Hosanna in the Highest.

In the West, the benedictus is first mentioned by Caesarius of Arles in the sixth century and as part of the Roman rite in the seventh century. The Roman form is simply the Latin of the Byzantine Greek form. In line 1 the Mozarabic rite has 'Hosanna to the Son of David.' Although this has similarities with the East Syrian form, it is probably to be explained as a literal use of Matthew 21:9. The vast majority of Mozarabic and Gallacan post-sanctus prayers pick up from the language of both the sanctus and benedictus – Truly holy, truly blessed – indicating that at the time of their composition or revision, the benedictus was an invariable part of the eucharistic prayer in these regions.

Part III

7

Developments in East and West to the Reformation

THE JACOBITE AND MARONITE EUCHARISTIC PRAYERS

THE Syriac anaphoras which are in use, or were once used, in the Jacobite and Maronite Churches number over eighty. The most complete list we have is that of A. Raes, who listed eighty.[1] A. Vööbus has subsequently discovered a previously unknown anaphora attributed to Johannan of Qartamin, and there is every possibility that the list will be further extended.[2] A large number of these anaphoras were published in Latin translation by Renaudot, and critical texts of some are available in the series *Anaphorae Syriacae*.[3] The majority remain unpublished, and some are contained in manuscripts not readily accessible to Western scholars. Here reference has been made to the works listed above, and Cambridge University Library manuscripts Add 2887 (which contains thirty-nine anaphoras) and Add 2917, together with Hayek's translation of some of the Maronite texts.[4]

One of the greatest problems in any assessment of these anaphoras is that of origin and date. They range from the sixth and seventh centuries to at least the fifteenth century. The attribution of some of them gives us a date *terminus post quem*, but others are obviously pseudepigraphal, and the date is uncertain. H. Fuchs has attempted a classification of some of the anaphoras, dividing them into six groups, within two broad divisions:

1 Texts with non-Syrian ascriptions. This group includes: pseudepigraphal anaphoras which are definitely translations from the Greek, *c*. sixth to seventh century (anaphoras such as Timothy of Alexandria, Severus of Antioch and John of Bostra);[5] probable translations from the Greek but without external distinguishing marks from the text, dating perhaps

from the seventh century (such as Caelestine of Rome, Eustathius of Antioch and Julius of Rome);[6] and late original Syriac texts with pseudepigraphal names belonging to the second millennium (such as John Chrysostom, John the Evangelist and Dioscorus of Alexandria).[7]

2 Texts with Syrian names. These include: texts belonging to the second millennium, mainly twelfth–fifteenth century (including John Bar Susa [b.1072], Dionysius Bar Salibi [b.1171], Michael the Patriarch [1199] and Ignatius Behnan [1454]);[8] pseudepigraphal texts whose alleged names belong to the first millennium (for example, Moses Bar Kepha [903], Marutha of Tagrit [649] and Philoxenus of Mabbourg [523];[9] and the rest of the anaphoras of the first millennium (such as Cyriacus of Tagrit [+817] and James of Serug [+517]).[10]

As Fuchs himself points out,[11] the original inspiration or models for the earlier anaphoras were the Greek anaphoras of St James and, to a lesser degree, St Basil and St John Chrysostom. Certain themes were developed, abbreviated or omitted by each subsequent author, and as the number of anaphoras grew, so the new anaphoras in turn provided new models for further compositions. The anaphoras are, therefore, the result of a growing number of possible permutations, though many of the authors made their own distinctive contribution. In comparison with the three Greek basic models, and the first of Fuch's groups which he believed were originally composed in Greek, the many later anaphoras bear witness to a high degree of abbreviation of ideas and themes, though some also represent extensive expansions such as Eustathius, Patriarch of the 318 Fathers. The recent study by Stevenson also suggests that one characteristic of these anaphoras is to play down the concept of offering in the anamnesis.[12]

In addition to being inspirations for new compositions, the anaphoras of James, Basil and John Chrysostom were translated into Syriac, and St James and *Twelve Apostles* have already been considered. St James the Less seems to be later abbreviation of St James. Syriac Basil is from the Byzantine form, though the recent study by Fenwick suggests that the intercessions of Syriac Basil are nearer to Egyptian Basil than to the Byzantine forms.[13] The opening praise section is practically the same as the Byzantine version, *until* the transition to angelology. At this point we find the following (from Cambridge University Library MSS Add. 2887 and 2917):

The divine beings exalt you in their ranks and the heavenly things hymn your glory in their habitations [2887 only]. And Angels and Archangels worship you; Thrones and Dominions praise you. Powers and Heavenly Armies extol

[2917: hallow] you. Before you stand the two honourable creatures who surround the holy throne of your glory, having many faces and many eyes and six wings, the seraphim and cherubim [2917: cherubim and seraphim]. With two of their wings they cover their faces, so that they do not gaze on the mystery of your divinity which is invisible. And with two their feet lest they are burnt from the flames of your terrible might, of whom all the creation perceivable to the mind and perceptable to the senses drink from the heat of your vehemence, a small portion and feeble flash which is poured out. And with two they fly and call one to another in never-silent mouths and in sonorous voices, doxologies which do not cease, the hymn of victory and of our salvation, crying out, calling and saying ...

In this expansion (or re-write!) we encounter the two honourable creatures associated with the Egyptian tradition (and the hiding from the divinity recalls Coptic Cyril). However, we also encounter some of the characteristics of the development of the sanctus introduction of this large family of eucharistic prayers:

1 The separate *activity* of the celestial beings is described – for example, 'Angels and Archangels *worship*' (cf. Greek Gregory of Nazianzen).
2 Mention is made of avoiding the divine gaze.
3 There is an interest in flames and fire.

The dependence of the Syriac anaphoras upon the Greek anaphoras of James, Chrysostom and Basil is well illustrated by the anaphoras of Severus of Antioch and Timothy of Alexandria, where the angelology of James is retained, but expanded. Severus has:

What thoughts can we conceive or what virtue of speeches can we attain whereby to glorify you, king of kings and God of all; who, when you had constituted the powers endowed with intellect and made the sensible creation, also made man from what is visible and invisible to attain every excellence and the divine likeness so that nothing out of all things made should not be a partaker of your grace, so that the very dust might become happy in the contemplation of your glory, and might share in the happiness of angels, and through all your works we might marvel and with profound silence honour you. For also both the congregations of angels and the first rank of the archangels, and the pre-eminent ones of the stable thrones and the jurisdiction of the Authorities, the greatness of the Powers, the sublimity of the Dominions, the Spirits of the just, the Church of the First Born which are written in heaven, with the many-eyed cherubim and the six-winged seraphim, endowed with knowledge and trembling before your invisible and incomprehensible Godhead, turning one to the other and absorbed in the invisible and incomprehensible sight, crying out, calling and saying ...

Timothy of Alexandria is considerably longer, having three sections of initial praise, each beginning 'Truly'. The third section leads directly into the sanctus:

Truly Lord it is fitting that we should praise and glorify and exalt you, for you are praised and glorified and exalted by mouths which are never silent and by ineffable voices, angels, archangels, principalities, authorities, thrones, dominions, powers which are above the world, heavenly armies, spirits of the prophets and the righteous, spirits of the martyrs and apostles, the cherubim with many eyes and six-winged seraphim, and each of these having six wings, and with two wings they cover their face because of your invisible and incomprehensible divinity, with two the feet and with two they fly one to the other singing the triumphant hymn of magnificent praise, calling out and saying ...

Similar echoes of James are found in some of the shorter anaphoras such as St Mark and St John the Evangelist.

The vast number of these anaphoras makes it extremely difficult to systematise them in any accurate manner. For example, where a compiler produced a short anaphora, the corresponding *oratio theologica* is also shortened, sometimes to a bare minimum. In this category are anaphoras such as Thomas the Apostle, Xystus and Abraham the Hunter. The latter has:

Truly it is right and just to praise the Trinity and exalt and glorify the secrecy of your majesty. With angels and archangels we also in sublime voice cry out and say ...

However, it is possible to delineate certain characteristics, developments and peculiarities of this large group of anaphoras.
1   The anaphoras invariably begin with the assertion that praise and worship are due to God who is creator, Lord of the invisible and visible creation, of heaven and earth. Ignatius Bar Wahib has:

Glory befits you and to you is due worship from all the heavenly ranks and earthly orders, with everything which your Being created, sentient and insentient.

2   Following St James which has 'you are hymned by the heavens and the heaven of heavens', several of the anaphoras include this (Clement II, Gregory John) or elaborate it. Thus Cyril of Jerusalem has 'the heavens which are the seat of your majesty'; Clement II, 'The heaven of heavens and everything in them'; Moses Bar Cepha, 'For you, Lord are in the heavens and the heaven of heavens.'

3   As in St James, there is a concern in some anaphoras with listing the physical universe. Clement I:

The sun and moon in their courses venerate, the stars in their splendour proclaim you; the sound of the thunder trembles at your command; the movement of the air signifies your virtue; the water in the clouds knows your will.

John Bar Madani mentions 'orbs with the luminaries of heaven'. Dionysius the Areopagite, Gregory John and Marutha of Tagrit show a similar concern.

4   Again apparently with St James as the model, some anaphoras have ecclesiological lists and concepts forming part of the lead up to the sanctus. Hebrews 12:22 occurs, for example, in Severus, Cyril of Jerusalem, Caelestine of Rome and Cyriacus of Tagrit. Timothy of Alexandria includes the spirits of the prophets and the righteous, spirits of the martyrs and apostles. Cyril of Jerusalem has an interesting list: God is praised

In the mouths of the children of the Church, the movements of the prophets, the company of the apostles, in the sufferings of the martyrs, in the witness of the confessors, in the theology of the teachers, in the godly stations of the ascetics, in the assemblies of the just, in the condition and state of the faithful.

Xystus includes 'your entire faithful people'. Marutha of Tagrit includes 'the theatres of martyrs' and 'congregations of anchorites'.

5   A few of the anaphoras specifically mention the creation of man (cf. Greek John Chrysostom and Gregory of Nazianzen). Severus asserts that God created man 'so that the very dust might become happy in the contemplation of your glory, and might share in the happiness of angels' – a remarkably modern scientific sentiment.[14]

6   The opening praise usually has a trinitarian reference, often specifically mentioning the Father, Son and Spirit. In some anaphoras doctrinal statements are introduced together with specialised theological language. In Timothy of Alexandria, God is described with the negative epithets found in Greek Chrysostom. Clement I can qualify the Trinity as 'one nature on high, one substance, who in three persons is adored'. St John Chrysostom (again quite different from the Greek anaphora) has 'the one majesty of the Trinity, or equal substance, adored in three persons'. In John Bostra we find 'God in the beginning one and who is one nature and one substance, and who is immutable, who is known in three hypostases'. The phraseology of some of the anaphoras seems to have been culled from Pseudo-Dionysius; thus in St

Ignatius, God is described as being sublime and immaterial, the great Beauty.[15] Dioscorus of Jazirat and John Bar Madani also echo this source.

7   As might be expected in such a vast family of eucharistic prayers, the angelology ranges from no mention at all (Ignatius the Maphrain) to repetition of that of James or Basil, to incredible speculative detail and vast numbers of celestial classes. In Julius only the seraphim are mentioned, and Abraham the Hunter and St Peter II only mention angels and archangels. Anaphoras such as St Mark, St John the Evangelist, Severus, Timothy of Alexandria, Moses Bar Cepha, the Holy Roman Church and Cyril of Hah include the classes found in St James without much enlargement. Ignatius Bar Wahib outlines an ascending hierarchy, each order serving the order above it.

As in Syriac Basil, there is a tendency to describe the activity or functions of the various celestial groups, or to give them further qualifying descriptions. God is lauded in the chants of angels and in the sounds of joy of the archangels (Cyril of Jerusalem); by congregations of angels, and stations of archangels, and bands of chief-ones (Clement II); by ardent bands of strong cherubim, terrible orders of holy seraphim (Eustathius of Antioch); and by thrones who sing, dominions who exalt, powers who extol (Dioscorus of Alexandria I).

There is also a marked tendency towards what may be described as esoteric and ethereal angelology, with an emphasis on the image of fire and on non-matter. This speculation on the nature of angels is already to be found in the writings of Gregory of Nazianzen.[16] It is explained at length by Pseudo-Dionysius, particularly the element of fire:

I think, then, the similitude of fire denotes the likeness of the Heavenly Minds to God in the highest degree ... It is both uncontrollable and invisible, self-subduing all things, and bringing under its own energy anything in which it may happen to be.[17]

An expression of this thought is found in Syriac John Chrysostom:

For those who praise you are innumerable; infinite powers of light, the yoked cherubim, and seraphim glorifying, thousands and multitudes without number, myriads and companies without calculation. Extending rows of consuming fire. Marvellous powers of burning coal, ordered legions who stand firm; the chariot of the cherubim, the movements of wheels which are infinite; cohorts of archangels, troops of seraphim who by the sound of their wings move the threshold; a glorious sound of many voices which from the midst of the burning coals of fire is audible in its movements; thousand thousands who stand before you and myriad of myriads who glorify your Being; with one clear voice and one loving harmony, with sweet song and ethereal tongue, they cry out the one to the other and raise their voices in eternal praise, calling and saying ...

In Gregory of Nazianzen we encounter intelligent spirits of immutable fire and winged flames; Caelestine includes fervent ardourous congregations of flame, flames of fiery ardour, and intellectual spirits. Other images include fiery beings (Dionysius Bar Salibi, John Sabae); armies of fire (James of Serug I); bands of legions of fire (Gregory of Nazianzen); substances made from fires which do not burn (Clement II); and the chariot of fire (Clement I). Dionysius the Areopagite lists forces of exalted ones from intelligence, radiant ones who are from the perfect light, and speechless ones from their silence unceasingly sing words of glory. Peter I gives 'companies of immaterial power'; John Bar Madani, 'simple substances and immaterial carbons from fire'; Philoxenus of Mabbourg II lists orders of fire and spirit, numerous flaming troops, principal substances, supernal orders, honourable and awesome persons of fire.

In a few anaphoras there is a concern to emphasise the sounds made by the heavenly company. Ignatius includes unceasing doxologies, sweet and pleasant citeras, and unending celebrations. In some there is also a stress on the non-fleshly and incorporeal nature of the agents of praise – for example, Ignatius, James of Serug II. Two anaphoras, Clement I and St Basil, mention the two honourable living creatures. In Basil they seem (as in Coptic Cyril) to be identified with the cherubim and seraphim. In Clement I, however, they are the living creatures with four faces from Ezekiel.

A number of these anaphoras omit all reference to the cherubim and seraphim (for example, John Sabae and Gregory John). Several, such as Cyril of Jazirat and Xystus, omit the cherubim. Many simply restate the description of these beings found in St James. However, in line with the tendency to elaborate, these two classes of beings are also developed in several anaphoras. Thus, for example, the cherubim become 'many-eyed and abundantly wise' (Caelestine of Rome), 'with many eyes and swift movement' (Dionysius the Areopagite). The *merkāvāh*, the chariot, is introduced in connection with the cherubim in several anaphoras (for example, Dioscorus of Jazirat and Cyril of Hah). In Dioscorus of Jazirat they beat their wings. A similar elaboration takes place with the seraphim. According to Cyril of Hah, their place is at the footstool of God. They are not burnt up by God's devouring fire (Dionysius the Aeropagite, Clement I and Timothy of Alexandria).

Merkāvāh echoes also occur in other ways. The *galgal* of Ezekiel are found in Clement II, Gregory of Nazianzen, John Chrysostom, James of Serug I and Cyriacus of Tagrit. Indeed, the latter actually describes the 'thrice-holy' as 'the mystical *qeduššah*'. Although it is possible that this *merkāvāh* element was the result of Jewish *hekhalot* influence, at this late date it could be more easily accounted for by a combination of the Pseudepigrapha such as Enoch, and the imagination of the individual authors.

8   The immediate conclusion of these anaphoras is usually that of Syriac James. However, the description of praise which the seraphim or all the heavenly beings recite varies considerably. For example, Peter I has:

... unceasingly extol with voices of jubilation and from returning, with effusion of understanding, and fear, and with wisdom, distinct varied sanctifications, voices extolling, calling out, shouting and saying ...

9   The function of the sanctus also varies in this large family of anaphoras. In so far as James has a dominating influence, it is the hymn of all creation, or the hymn of the angelic hierarchy, or the seraphim. In such anaphoras we have a continuation of the functions found in James, Basil and Greek Chrysostom. However, in a number of anaphoras we find (as in Greek Gregory of Nazianzen) a deliberate petition that the sanctus will be, or a statement that it is, also the praise of mankind, the church or the present worshippers. Thus in Jacob Baradeus there is a blending of our voices with the praise of the heavenly host:

Blend also now our hymns and imperfect glories with the glories of the watchers and angels who unceasingly glorify you: And mix our songs and feeble psalms with virtuous songs of fires and spirits who praise you without intermission. And unite our weak sounds with the clear sounds of the cherubim who fearfully bless you. And mingle our wretched voices of sanctification with the sweet sanctifications of the seraphim who have six wings, who sanctify you thrice.

Cyril of Hah explicitly unites the praise of the congregation with that of the seraphim;

And with them we also cry out the mystical *qeduššah* and say and glorify ...

And John Bar Susa includes a note of unworthiness, as does John Maron (influence of *Sharar*?):

And we also, Lord, in spite of our weaknesses and our sins, we are admitted by your grace to say with them ...

Here the idea is made explicit that the sanctus is now the praise of the Church which, through grace, is admitted to join the angelic chorus.

Of the many anaphoras considered in this section, many have their own peculiar features and phrases. In conclusion, attention is drawn to three in particular:

1 Ignatius Bar Wahib utilises the second line of the sanctus in its opening *oratio theologica*:

> You are the Lord of whom heaven and earth and all that is in them is full of your glory.

2 Dioscorus of Jazirat includes what appears to be a deliberate echo of Jewish *berakah* formulae:

> Holy creator of creatures: holy are you who bestows wisdom to children. Blessed is your honour from your habitation feared by all things: Blessed is your virtue, whose power is in all things.

The angelology of the sanctus, together with the Jewish echo, is continued in the post-sanctus:

> Holy are you, holy are you: Blessed is your honour out of this place: holy are you three and one, who are blessed, sanctified and glorified by cherubim, seraphim and thrones; who are honoured, praised and exalted by virtues, powers and dominions; who are extolled, glorified and celebrated by principalities, archangels and angels.

Here Ezekiel 3:12 is used.

3 The theme of the sanctus is continued also in the post-sanctus of John Maron:

> Holy, holy, holy, are you, Father, Son and Holy Spirit; the voices of the seraphim proclaim, Lord, the holiness of your trinity, and the assemblies of the cherubim bless your hiddenness; the armies of angels praise your marvellous essence. Glory to you who honours the human race through grace, and mingles the voices of the earth with those of heaven.

All too often the vast number of Syriac anaphoras of the Jacobite and Maronite anaphoras are mentioned in passing and are simply classed as 'West Syrian' in structure, as though they were a homogeneous group. Although it is true that their basic inspiration seems to have been James, Basil and Greek Chrysostom, they in fact reflect a great diversity, and this is amply illustrated by the manner in which the sanctus is introduced.

ARMENIAN EUCHARISTIC PRAYERS

Although the Armenian tradition traces its Christian origin to the apostles Thaddeus and Bartholomew,[18] the great missionary of Armenia was St Gregor Partev, or Gregory the Illuminator (c. 240–332 CE), and probably by 301 CE Christianity was the prevailing religion in Armenia.[19] Gregory was from Caesarea in Cappadocia,[20] but the evidence suggests that some areas of Armenia were influenced by Greek-speaking Christianity, and others by Syriac-speaking Christianity. V. K. Sarkissian writes:

Up to the end of the fourth century the Christian worship was conducted in Armenia either in Greek or Syriac, according to the knowledge of the clergy and the area of influence of these two languages and cultures in Armenia. In fact, the expansion of Christianity into Armenia was the result of a twofold activity carried on simultaneously by Syrian missionaries from Edessa and Nisibis (S-W of Armenia) and by Greek missionaries from Cappadocia, namely from Caesarea, Sebastia and Melitene (N-W of Armenia).[21]

Only in the fifth century, with the creation of an alphabet, could translations be made into Armenian and with them new 'indigenous' compilations. Later, Armenia was influenced by Byzantium, and later still by the Roman rite.[22]

The Armenian Church today uses a liturgy with a single anaphora, attributed to St Athanasius of Alexandria. According to Salaville, the rite is a compilation from the Greek St James and Greek St John Chrysostom, while A. A. King describes it as a local modification of St Basil with Latin interpolations.[23] Regarding the anaphora, King is nearer the mark in that Byzantine Basil seems to have been a prime inspiration. However, the background is rather more complex than either Salaville or King imply, since the manuscripts indicate that at one time several anaphoras were in use in various parts of Armenia, representing both Greek and Syriac influence. The following anaphoras are found in translation:

St John Chrysostom (Byzantine)
St Basil (Byzantine)
St James (Syriac)
St Ignatius (Syriac)
The Roman canon (Latin)

In addition there are four other anaphoras:

St Gregory the Illuminator
St Gregory of Nazianzen

St Cyril of Alexandria
St Isaac the Parthian

Of these, Gregory the Illuminator seems to be a pre-Byzantine version of Basil, and A. Renoux has called it 'the ancient Armenian anaphora of St Basil'.[24] If this really is associated with St Gregory, it may indeed confirm that the texts of St Basil do represent the early anaphora of Caesarea. Apart from the name, Gregory of Nazianzen and Cyril of Alexandria have nothing in common with the Greek and Syriac anaphoras of those names, and together with Isaac (Sahak) seem to represent independent Armenian compilations.

In our consideration of the sanctus in this tradition, we shall consider Gregory the Illuminator, and the four indigenous Armenian anaphoras – Athanasius, Gregory, Cyril and Isaac.[25] All reflect the Syro-Byzantine structures and seem to have been inspired mainly by St Basil.

Gregory the Illuminator seems to be a pre-Byzantine version of St Basil, and the sanctus forms part of the *oratio theologica*, praising God for his Being. After the mention of God's throne, the transition is made to the heavenly host and their chant. There are some differences between the manuscripts,[26] though not of any great significant. There are some differences from the pre-Basil Egyptian and Byzantine versions, but often this seems to be mainly a matter of translation and of no theological significance.[27] The order of the angelic beings is, interestingly, that of Byzantine Basil and Greek James rather than that of Egyptian Basil and Syriac James.

In the other four eucharistic prayers, the opening praise leading to the sanctus is generally inspired by one or more aspects of St Basil/St Gregory. With the exception of Athanasius, they show an interest in the divine attributes which are multiplied, and in the case of Isaac, the post-sanctus anthropological theme of Basil is developed in the pre-sanctus. Thus, for example, Isaac includes amongst its attributes of God, Lord and Father of Truth, producer of creatures, provider and caretaker of men, fount of goodness, giver of uncorruption, bestower of felicities, vivifier, life-giver, greatly glorious Lord of glory, and of all exaltations above, producer of all, receiver of the total, complete protector of all, and maker of all visible and invisible things.

The context and function of the sanctus in these prayers fall into three categories.

As part of the Oratio theologica

Following the pattern of Gregory the Illuminator, Gregory of Nazianzen uses the sanctus as the heavenly praise of the Being of God. After a
list of divine attributes, the heavenly chant is introduced:

Truly worthy in fear, with faith, with holy heart and with glorification to bow
down, heavenly God, uncreate, self-existing, ternary power, light unapproa-
ched, maker of light and of all creation visible and invisible, heavenly and
earthly, and all sea creatures [lit. fishes]. Myriad troops of angels bless you,
celestial powers, with spiritual song, cherubim and six-winged seraphim, who
terrified in fear of the divinity of your glory, flapping with wings cover you on
all sides and always stand with thrice-holy voices of holy speech, they say, call,
cry and say [aloud] triumphant blessings saying, calling, crying out and
saying . . .

As response to the redemption of mankind

In Athanasius the sanctus is recited by redeemed mankind together
with the celestial host, as a result of God's salvation. The Father, by his
immaterial and fellow creator Word 'removed the hindrance of the
curse'. He 'made the Church his own people' and from the Virgin 'as a
divine architect, framed a new work, making earth into heaven'. He
became man for our salvation and 'granted to us to join the spiritual
choirs of the inhabiters of heaven'.

Isaac is a much longer anaphora, and the *oratio theologica* develops
into a rehearsal of creation and the Fall. While the themes have a
parallel in the *oratio theologica* and post-sanctus of Basil and James,
Isaac follows the pattern of AC 8 in placing all these *before* the sanctus.
Whereas AC 8 tends to be rather pedestrian in its language, Isaac is
more poetic. After recalling the rejection from the Orchard (Paradise),
the prayer continues:

Although to some extent threatening fury, you counselled, being beneficent,
yet again by reason of your kindness, you raised him to heavenly and infinite
kingship. And now who is capable to say in word your overflow of kindness or
to glory your divinity with praises and spiritual songs? To whom angels,
archangels, thrones, dominions, principalities, authorities, powers bow down,
whom terrified, the cherubim bless, the seraphim murmur, because with terror,
with fear, with two wings they cover their faces, afraid by the great power of the
splendour of your light, and with two wings in flight with great fear they fill the
orderly blessings with calling, they cry out with thoughtful theology and

restlessly with voices one to another together with us saying [aloud] triumphant blessings, calling, crying out and saying ...

Once again we have the idea hinted at in Addai and Mari, and found in some of the Syrian anaphoras, that the restoration of mankind now allows his participation in the sanctus. The 'angelic' or eschatological status of the Christian is recognised in the prayer.

In the context of petition to join the angels in this chant

The anaphora of Cyril opens with a long list of ascriptions of God – beginningless God, uncreate, timeless, infinite, unknowable, unsearchable, greatness, measureless, eternal, permanent, ever-flowing, form without quality, deathless, fount of deathlessness, giver of good, holy Father. The Son and the Holy Spirit are then also given ascriptions. The prayer continues:

To you alone is due the thrice-holy of the dominions and it is truly fit to send up in songs of glorification which you alone in the divine kind have wonderfully made heaven and earth and all that is in them creation visible and invisible. Because wholly ineffable in word, they glorify your glorified divinity with knowable and unknowable thought. Make worthy, Lord, by your mercy, our unworthiness according to the angel classes of blessing, to sing to you triumphant songs, which, terrified, in the burning irradiant light of your divinity, wing-covered, with fine turns they sing to you songs of holy speech.

Here, as with Greek Gregory of Nazianzen and some Jacobite anaphoras, petition is made for worthiness to join in the sanctus.

In comparison with the longer Jacobite anaphoras, the angelology of these 'indigenous' Armenian anaphoras is very restrained. There is no attempt to elaborate on the function of the various groups, other than in Isaac where the cherubim 'bless' and the seraphim 'murmur'. Gregory the Illuminator reproduces the list of Byzantine Basil; Isaac has the same categories, though alters the sequence slightly. Gregory of Nazianzen mentions only angels, powers, cherubim and seraphim; and Athanasius, only inhabitants of heaven, spiritual choirs, seraphim and cherubim. Cyril simply mentions angelic orders and dominions. The themes of God's light (fire) and the fear of the heavenly beings are mentioned, but again on a more restrained note than in the Jacobite anaphoras.

Other than Gregory of Nazianzen, the Armenian anaphoras have the usual Syro-Byzantine post-sanctus link; Gregory introduces the post-sanctus with, 'In the beginning, Creator most blessed and dwelling in holiness.'

Although quite a distinct tradition, the Armenian sanctus is utilised in a similar manner to the Jacobite/Maronite eucharistic prayers – as the heavenly praise of God, as our praise, or requesting that it may be our praise.

THE ETHIOPIAN EUCHARISTIC PRAYERS

The origins of Christianity in Ethiopia are obscure. Rufinus of Aquileia relates that Athanasius consecrated Frumentius and sent him to Ethiopia as a missionary.[28] Certainly the first origins seem to have been Egyptian, and this is reflected in the use of two anaphoras, that of the Apostles, and that of Our Lord Jesus Christ. The first is a version of the Egyptian Sinados or Church Order (Hippolytus), and the second is based on the *Testamentum Domini*. These may be dated fourth and fifth centuries respectively, at the earliest, and seem to be the 'original' Ethopian anaphoras. However, other anaphoras came into existence. In his important study of this tradition, E. Hammerschmidt lists a further eighteen anaphoras.[29] Not all of these anaphoras were in use everywhere in the Ethiopic Church. For example, the shorter St Cyril which Hammerschmidt lists is found only in one manuscript, and St Mark, a translation from the Coptic (Cyril), seems to be a very late translation and its use does not seem to have been widespread.[30] There are clear signs of West Syrian influence is some of these prayers, and as in that tradition, we are dealing with obvious pseudonyms.

The eighteen additional anaphoras are classed by Hammerschmidt into two groups. The first is translations. In this group belong St Basil, St James and St Mark, together with Gregory of Alexandria, Cyril I and II which Hammerschmidt regards as 'very independent' developments of Greek/Coptic counterparts, with the emphasis very much on the 'independent'.[31] In addition he also suggests that the anaphora of the 318 Orthodox perhaps reflects a Greek origin, at least in the epiklesis, and James of Serug and Dioscorus as having foreign texts as their models.[32]

In the second group Hammerschmidt places anaphoras which he regards as indigenous Ethiopic compositions. Here he includes such anaphoras as Athanasius, Epiphanius, Gregory of Armenia, Mary Gregory (and its alternative) and John the Evangelist.[33] Athanasius is distinguished on account of its personification of the Sabbath, an Ethiopian feature which Hammerschmidt suggests was perhaps borrowed from the Falashas.[34] Mary Gregory is rhymed, suggesting a late date of composition.[35]

Although Hammerschmidt offers this grouping, he does not offer any precise dating; indeed, there seems to be no clear guide for attempting such dating, other than he notes that the anaphora of Mary was in use by the fifteenth century.[36] He also observes that Mary Cyriacos reflects a time when Islam was a threat to the Ethiopian Church.[37] He urges the need for a great deal of comparison with other Ethiopian literature, including critical texts of the bible.[38]

It was from a comparison with other Ethiopian literature that a somewhat controversial suggestion has been made more recently by Getatchew Haile.[39] He suggests that in the writings of Emperor Zar'a Ya'Eqob (1434–68 CE), in particular in MasEhafa bErhan, MasEhafa milad and Ta'ammEra Maryam, we find evidence of religious controversy, particularly over the Trinity. The dissidents composed their own liturgical books, including anaphoras based on what they believed about the Trinity, and the Church may have responded in the same way by composing anaphoras against dissident doctrine.[40] Haile examines some readings in Vat. MSS 15 and 18 of Mary Cyriacos and the 318 Orthodox, and finds expressed in them the Trinitarian understanding of the dissidents. Abba Giyorgis was approached to compose anaphoras against the dissidents, and Haile suggests that the anaphora of Athanasius was one of his compositions. Until this time, so Haile suggests, only the anaphora of the Apostles and the anaphora of Our Lord Jesus Christ were recognised by the Ethiopic Church. Some of the new compositions of the Church were never accepted and went into oblivion, such as that of Mary.[41] Fifteen anaphoras (Hammerschmidt's second category), therefore, are seen as creations of the fifteenth-century religious controversies. Later, dissidents and Churchmen were brought together against outside threats, and the dissident anaphoras were accepted and purged of their dissident theology – hence the change in the text of Mary Cyriacos and 318 Orthodox in Vat. MS 16, which gives the present readings of those anaphoras.

Haile's view seems to overlook the fact that while this may account for some of the indigenous anaphoras, it does not account for the Syro-Byzantine and Greek influence on some of the other anaphoras, which suggests a date or dates c. seventh to eleventh centuries CE. However, whether or not the anaphoras which are pure Geez creations are the result of religious dispute, Haile is probably correct in his view that they belong to the second millennium, and quite possibly as late as the fifteenth century CE.

In what is rather an understatement, Bouley observes:

The later Ethiopian anaphoras display a considerable amount of structural vagueness: traditional parts of the anaphora may practically disappear, or the order of parts may be arranged differently from one anaphora to another.[42]

'Freedom' is a keynote in the Ethiopic anaphoras. Some show a Syro-Byzantine pattern, others reflect the Egyptian pattern, and still others have a quite independent arrangement. For example, Mary Cyriacos is in part addressed to the Virgin Mary and has the Nicene Creed within it, and in the 318 Orthodox, the dialogue which normally opens an anaphora occurs within the prayer.

The sanctus occurs – as one would expect – in the anaphoras of Basil, James and Mark; they are translations, and no change of function has taken place.

Of the other anaphoras, it is not absolutely clear whether all contain a sanctus. The reason is that the manuscripts often omit the sanctus, or its diaconal introduction, but this itself does not mean that the sanctus was not inserted at some point when the anaphora was recited. Thus in Harden's version of Our Lord Jesus Christ there is no sanctus, but in Mercer's text there is. Hammerschmidt suggested that in Harden's manuscript it was omitted as something self-evident, and should come (as in Mercer's and the version of Daoud-Hazen) after the deacon's introduction 'Answer ye', between 'prepared for Thee a holy people' and 'He stretched forth His hands to the passion',[43] very similar to that of the Apostles. It should be noted that in the anaphora of Our Lord Jesus Christ, an adaptation of Rev. 4:8 occurs in the opening dialogue:

Priest: That which is holy 'for' the holy.
People: Holy, holy, holy, O Lord, God of gods, who wast and art for ever in heaven and earth.

In Dioscorus the sanctus is also missing from the text. In Harden's translation we find:

> By the devil was He tempted; by the power of His Godhead
> He destroyed the chiefs of darkness.
> The deacon saith: Answer ye.
> The priest saith: Holy, holy, holy is God in his Trinity.
> Though He was King, He showed His humility as a servant.[44]

Following Rodwell's translation, where another 'Answer ye' follows the words 'as a servant', Hammerschmidt suggested that the sanctus followed this.[45] However, since 'Holy, holy, holy, is God in His Trinity' seems to reflect the Syro-Byzantine pick-up from the sanctus, it would seem that a sanctus was inserted between 'Answer ye' and 'Holy,

holy, holy is God in His Trinity', as in Daoud-Hazen.[46] Harden
suggested that the sanctus was missing from Epiphanius,[47] but it is in
Euringer's translation, and in that of Daoud-Hazen.[48] Both Harden and
Hammerschmidt agree that it is missing from the 318 Orthodox, but it
is present in the text of Daoud-Hazen.[49]

The sanctus in the anaphora of the Apostles has already been
considered in another context.[50] In comparison with the *Apostolic
Tradition*, it is an insertion and has no proper context. This is also true
of Our Lord Jesus Christ; and it has been given no logical context in
Dioscorus and the 318 Orthodox. This is quite remarkable in the latter,
since elsewhere in the anaphora there are references to the throne of
God and to angels. Later the anaphora mentions the angels and
archangels who prostrate themselves before the Lord, and the seraphim
and cherubim who shout and say 'Holy God, holy mighty, holy living,
immortal, who yet died for the love of man' – a version of the liturgical
trisagion which in the Eastern rites occurs outside the anaphora.

The 318 Orthodox anaphora (and Epiphanius) makes great use of
Ezekiel 1, Revelation and Ethiopic Enoch. However, its almost
hekhalot-type passages have not been used to give the sanctus a context.
The conclusion would seem to be that when these eucharistic prayers
were composed, the sanctus was a congregational chant which came
somewhere, but a logical introduction to it was not necessary.

The lack of any set pattern to the Ethiopic anaphoras results in at
least three different positions for the sanctus:

In the Oratio theologica

As in the majority of Syro-Byzantine anaphoras, the sanctus is used as a
response to God for himself, his Being. This is so in John the Evangelist
and Mary Cyriacos (addressed to the Trinity), Gregory of Armenia
(addressed to God's Name), St Cyril I and II, Epiphanius and, without
any logical introduction, 318 Orthodox (God the Creator). In Epiphanius, after a lengthy description of creation in language reminiscent
of the books of Enoch and Jubilees (both part of the Ethiopic Old
Testament canon), the sanctus is introduced thus:

He alone putteth on the power of the highest heaven and is adorned with glory
and honour. The fiery cherubim and the seraphim dressed in light hallow him
with ceaseless words and a mouth which does not keep silent and a tongue which
does not tire; and all say together with one voice answering: Holy, holy, holy,
perfect Lord of hosts, heaven and earth are full of the holiness of your glory.
Deacon: Answer ye
People: Holy ...[51]

In the Oratio christologica

This is most obvious in St John Chrysostom, where after praise of
God's essence, his work of mercy in his son is rehearsed:

He became perfect man without sin and He was manifested as a servant, but He
wrought as God. Even as he bare witness be ye preachers of His Gospel.
The deacon saith: Let us attend.
By His Father He was glorified and by His angels adored and by man praised
and by Himself was He sanctified, and heaven and earth are full of the holiness
of His glory.
The deacon saith: Answer ye.
Never, then, let us cease in our hearts to utter the holiness of His glory, and let
us cry, saying:
The people say: Holy ...[52]

In James of Serug the sanctus is again concerned with the Son. It
is within the christological section of Dioscorus and Gregory of
Alexandria that the sanctus is located. In neither is there an angelological introduction. Hammerschmidt actually states that it is missing from
the latter.[53] He is correct that there is not a normal (compared with
other traditions) introduction, but nevertheless it is introduced by the
Ascension;

And he rose on the third day, and ascended in glory to heaven.
The deacon saith: Answer ye.
(People: Holy ...)
He covered the heaven with his beauty, He filled the earth with His glory.[54]

The sanctus is intruded into the christological sections of the Apostles
and Our Lord Jesus Christ.

In the Oratio anthropologica

This is the position of the sanctus in the anaphora of St Athanasius.
This is a strange anaphora, and includes a personification of the
sabbath; since the Book of Jubilees is canonical scripture in the Ethiopic
Church, this is probably the inspiration rather than the Falashas as
Hammerschmidt suggested. The sanctus occurs in the section dealing
with the creation of Man, which mentions Adam and Eve. After stating
that Christian Man has three births – baptism, the body and blood of

Christ, and the remission of sins – the sanctus is introduced in the following manner:

And let all of us in purity wash our bodies in pure water and be in the likeness of the angels who glorify God with a voice of praise. In their several majesties, ranks, hosts, names and numbers, some encircle and some surround and some glorify – having each six-wings thus they say, Holy, holy, holy, perfect Lord of Hosts, heaven and earth are full of the holiness of your glory.
    And we also say, together with them ...[55]

Here again the idea is found that the redeemed community has, through Christ, become angel-like, and can join in with the song of the seraphim. The sanctus is sung to God because man has been born again by God's redemption.

The form of the introduction of the sanctus – where there is one – also presents us with a variety. That inserted into the Apostles is modelled loosely upon the Egyptian form in that it includes the honourable creatures, though they are identified with the cherubim and the seraphim,[56] and has the sanctus first recited by the priest and then by the people; and the post-sanctus picks up on 'full of the holiness of your glory'. Also, the benedictus is absent, though it occurs in the Apostles in the epiklesis. Missing, however, is the use of Ephesians 1:21 as an introduction.

Several of the anaphoras reflect the Egyptian practice of the priest reciting the sanctus which grammatically belongs to the heavenly host, and then the people reciting it. Hammerschmidt notes that in Gregory of Armenia an inversion has taken place, with the introduction of the people's sanctus coming first, though the sanctus itself is never actually recited at that point.[57] Hammerschmidt is probably right when he says 'The text suggests that the "composer" knew both kinds of introductions or at least the combination already existing and used it freely.'[58]

Four of the anaphoras have a very full angelology of the type found in the later Syro-Byzantine prayers – John the Evangelist, James of Serug, Gregory of Armenia and Cyril. It is perhaps significant that the first two and the last all have a typical Syro-Byzantine post-sanctus form. In John the Evangelist we find lofty ones each in his order, angels in rank, watchers in their brightness, cherubim in their majesty, and seraphim in their holiness. In Cyril we find seraphim, cherubim, angels according to their hosts, watchers according to their orders, chief of the watchers according to their rank, angels of fire and spiritual ones. Of particular note is the mention of the hosts of Michael and of Gabriel in James of Serug.

We have already noted the Egyptian flavour of the anaphora of the Apostles' interpolated sanctus; the celestial beings include those of Daniel 7:10, holy angels and archangels, and the honourable creatures who are the cherubim and seraphim. On the whole, however, the majority of the anaphoras are marked by a distinct lack of angelology introducing the sanctus. For example, Epiphanius has fiery cherubim and seraphim in light. No angelology introduces the sanctus in Our Lord Jesus Christ, Gregory of Alexandria and Dioscorus.

Although we have noted some Egyptian elements in the Ethiopic anaphoras, on the whole there is no attempt to follow the pattern completely. The sanctus in Ethiopia is not part of the intercessory material, nor does it lead into an epiklesis.

SOME LATER WESTERN DEVELOPMENTS

As long as the Gallican and Mozarabic rites persisted, the West continued to have a variety of introductions to the sanctus alongside the four Roman types of introduction. These simply perpetuated the formulae which we have already encountered in these traditions. Thus in the *inlatio* for the Ascension attributed to Ildephonse of Toledo (657–67), after a rehearsal of salvation history, the sanctus is introduced with 'To him rightly all angels and archangels' and so forth.[59] The seventh-century fragment of Bruyne in North France is a little more ambitious in its *contestatio*. It mentions Rafael, Racuel, Michael, Rumiel, Sultyel and Danaiel (*sic*), and with the twenty four elders and four living creatures of Revelation 4, leads into the sanctus.[60]

During the eighth century the Gallican rite was replaced by the Roman rite, and the Spanish rite was suppressed (other than in Toledo Cathedral) in the eleventh century,[61] thus leaving the West with only one Roman anaphora with its four introductions to the sanctus. The canon of the mass in the Stowe missal bears witness to the fusion of Gallican and Roman elements, though the Roman predominates. Interestingly, the Stowe sanctus is an example of the fusion or conflation. The introduction in the preface is normative, but the *form* of the sanctus itself has been expanded;

Holy, holy, holy, Lord God of Sabaoth. Heaven and the whole [*universa*] earth are full of your glory. Hosanna in the Highest. Blessed is he who comes in the name of the Lord. Hosanna in the Highest. Blessed is he who comes from heaven, to preserve the earth, who was made man, that he might kill the pleasures of the flesh, who was made a victim, that through his passion those

who believe he would give eternal life: through our Lord. We therefore pray
[*Te igitur*][62]

F. E. Brightman pointed out that this extended benedictus is really a
Gallican post-sanctus which has been added on. Also, *universa*,
perhaps suggested by the biblical version of Isaiah 6:3, has been
inserted.[63]

Although the introduction to the sanctus was standardised in the
West by the adoption of the Roman rite, nevertheless, the text of the
sanctus was at times expanded. A popular addition of feasts of the
Blessed Virgin Mary, was, instead of 'Blessed is He who comes',
'Blessed is the Son of Mary who comes.'[64] Another development was
the use of Greek texts and their chants, which included the sanctus.[65]

A far more dramatic development in the West was by means of
tropes. These were textual and/or musical additions to the plainchant,
though the precise definition has been disputed.[66] Tropes seem to have
made their appearance about eighty years after the Gregorian repertoire, in the middle of the ninth century. Four developments associated
with tropes can be delineated:

1 Melismas – first supplementing the jubilia of the Alleluia, and then the
  Gradual and Offertory.
2 Prosulas – the filling-words, such as in the Hosanna of the sanctus.
  (Historically, Hosanna belongs to benedictus, of course.)
3 Sequences.
4 Towards the end of the ninth century, the interpolation or farsing of
  texts of the Ordinary of the mass – kyries, Gloria, sanctus and Agnus
  Dei.[67]

However, according to the definition of Paul Evans, only the fourth
category can be termed tropes.[68]

By means of 'interpolation' and 'substitution' tropes,[69] the Ordinary
of the mass could be made into propers for each feast. Although at one
time it was argued that the development of tropes centred on the
monasteries of St Gall in Switzerland and St Martial in Southern
France, Eugenio Costa stresses that it is impossible to trace the
development to a particular school or place: France, Aquitaine, the
Rhine region, South Germany, North and South Italy, and later,
Scandinavia, constitute the ground where the techniques emerge.[70]

Some sanctus tropes are contained in the collection *Analecta Hymnica*,[71] and further edited texts can be expected.[72] In some cases they take
the form of hymns using the sanctus as a refrain; a few form an

introduction to the sanctus text; the majority make additions after each
'holy', and between 'your glory' and 'Hosanna'. Thus:

Sanctus O quam dulciter[73]

O how sweetly
the voices resound there
when all the Holy Ones
sing the praises of God
saying: sanctus.

Thus we also praise
the Lord on earth
whom the holy angels
praise in the highest
saying: sanctus.

You alone make
clean from unclean
cleanse us, as long as we are in the world
because you alone are: sanctus

Sanctus Pater cuncta creans[74]

Sanctus, Father causing all things
Sanctus, Life-giving Son
Sanctus, Sanctifying Spirit
        Dominus Deus–gloria tua
        One Divinity
        Of equal glory.
Hosanna in excelsis.
        Of whom are all things
        in heaven and earth
        air and sea.

Benedictus – nomine Domine
        Hear the prayers
        Of your humble people
Hosanna in excelsis.

Costa noted that the second part of the sanctus was the object of a
particular elaboration, analogous to the *prosulae ad Regnum* of the
Gloria:

One first placed the prosulas on the melismas corresponding to (Hosann-) *a*, or
to (ex) cel (sis); then one added the verbo-melodics interpolated between

Hosanna and excelsis. The musical composition then established itself a tendency to separate itself from the sanctus, becoming a separate piece, of definite and sealed form.[75]

The Hosanna for the Trinity is one such example.[76]

It is possible to regard these developments as an intrusion and a digression, though Guilo Cattin denies that they represent a 'malignant growth', but rather, 'the most meaningful response made by the musical and liturgical genius of new peoples in a new era'.[77] Certainly, within the confines of a single fixed canon, the sanctus tropes were in one sense a Western counterpart to the more elaborate material found in some of the Syriac Jacobite and Ethiopic anaphoras. Nevertheless, it also reflects an attitude which regarded the sanctus simply as a chant not necessarily tied to a particular anaphora's logic. The development of tropes coincides with the tendency found in missals to regard the canon as beginning with *Te igitur*, and isolating the sursum corda, preface, sanctus and benedictus as a pre-anaphoral unit. This in turn would influence the Reformation handling of the sanctus; oddly enough, although the era of tropes was over by the time of the Reformation (the development reached a peak in the thirteenth century and declined thereafter) some newer forms of sanctus tropes survived in one Reformation tradition to replace the liturgical sanctus itself.[78]

8

🙏

The Reformation rites

THE treatment of the sanctus by the sixteenth-century Reformers must be seen within a twofold context. First, when discussing tropes, we noted that medieval manuscripts regarded the canon as beginning with *Te igitur*, and the sursum corda, preface, sanctus and benedictus were regarded as a separate preliminary unit.[1] The result was that the sanctus and benedictus could be regarded as congregational and choir items. The Reformers never had reason to question this understanding, and their target was the canon of the mass, and not harmless chants. The sanctus, therefore, was an item which could either remain because it was of no doctrinal consequence, or could be replaced by something more useful and fitting.

Secondly, the foundation rites of the Reformation were the writings and recommendations of Martin Luther, and the rites prepared in Switzerland by Zwingli and Oecolampadius. This is not to deny the individual contributions by Bucer at Strasbourg, Calvin at Geneva, or Cranmer in England. However, they drew upon the experience and precedents set by the earlier Reformers.

LUTHERANISM

In his early writings, such as the *Babylonian Captivity of the Church*, 1520, *The Misuse of the Mass*, 1520, and *Receiving Both Kinds*, 1522, Luther suggested that since the stumbling block in the mass was the canon and anything which spoke of sacrifice, then priests should simply omit anything which referred to sacrifice.[2] The entire canon could be omitted and replaced with the words of institution, or a prayer shorn of any hint of offering. Thus, the sursum corda–preface–sanctus unit could remain intact, though not all proper prefaces were doctrinally acceptable. Much to Luther's annoyance, some German Reformers put his advice into practice.

During Luther's absence from Wittenberg in 1522, Karlstadt acted upon his advice in *Ordnung der Stadt Wittenberg*. The mass was in Latin still, and permission was given for the introit, kyrie, Gloria, collect, Epistle, Gradual, creed, offertory, preface and sanctus with variable *de tempore* prefaces.[3] After the sanctus the words of institution alone follow, the entire canon being omitted. The isolation of the sanctus from what followed is thus made more pronounced.

Two German vernacular reforms, again anticipating Luther, were composed by Kasper Kantz at Nordlingen, 1522, and Thomas Müntzer at Alstadt, 1524. Kantz gave the sursum corda, common preface, sanctus and benedictus.[4] Müntzer published an outline of his Reformed mass in 1523, retaining sursum corda, preface and sanctus.[5] In his 1524 text he gave the following preface and sanctus:

Truly it is meet and right and it is salutary that we should always and everywhere give you thanks, Lord, O holy Father, almighty, everlasting God. Because you conceived your holy manhood from the Virgin Mary by the overshadowing of the Holy Spirit, which she brought forth with chastity intact, the eternal Light of the world, Jesus Christ our Lord. Through whom the angels praise your majesty, and the ruling angels honour you; the angels of power are themselves seized with fear. With them the heavens and the heavenly virtues and the holy seraphim praise you unceasingly with one joyful voice. Grant us, O Lord, that our voice may ring out with theirs, so that we may praise you always in true confession, saying . . .[6]

Prefaces were also provided for the Passion, Christmas, Easter and Whitsun. Although Kantz had a prayer of consecration which included the institution narrative, and Müntzer had an introduction to the narrative, in both instances there was no obvious link with the sanctus and, as in Karlstadt's order, it appeared as the tail end of the preface, isolated from what followed.

Although Luther had urged priests to make their own reforms, he repudiated those made by Karlstadt and Müntzer, both of whom he regarded as dangerous fanatics. Nevertheless, because others were prepared to make reforms, Luther eventually felt compelled to offer advice himself. This he did in the Formula Missae (FM), 1523, and the Deutsche Messe (DM), 1526.[7]

In FM Luther retained the Latin sursum corda and preface. However, he suggested that the preface should then be followed by the words of institution, preferably intoned, and the sanctus and benedictus should be sung to accompany the elevation. Luther used the common preface, but since the sanctus was moved, the mention of angels and archangels was deleted.

In DM Luther believed that he was providing a vernacular mass rather than merely a German translation of the Latin idiom. Earlier, perhaps with the attempts of Kantz and Müntzer in mind, he had said:

I would gladly have a German mass today. I am also occupied with it. But I would very much like it to have a true German character. For to translate the Latin text and retain the Latin tongue or notes has my sanction, though it does not sound polished or well done. Both the text and notes, accent, melody and manner of rendering ought to grow out of the true mother tongue and its inflection, otherwise ... it becomes an imitation, in the manner of the apes.[8]

In DM the sursum corda and preface disappeared, being replaced by a brief paraphrase of the Lord's Prayer and a brief exhortation. It would seem that Luther regarded these as a German cultural equivalent, or interpretation, of the sursum corda and preface; like other Reformers,[9] he seemed to regard the sursum corda as an exhortation to the worshippers to lift their hearts and minds to heavenly things, and to give thanks for salvation. This, in the German idiom, could be achieved more effectively by a paraphrase of the Lord's Prayer and a brief exhortation. Then the words of institution were intoned as far as the words relating to the bread, followed by the *German* sanctus – a new paraphrase based upon Isaiah 6:1–9:

Isaiah 'twas the prophet who did see seated above the Lord in Majesty High on a lofty throne in splendour bright; the train of his robe filled the temple quite. Standing beside him were two seraphim; Six wings, six wings he saw on each of them. With twain they hid in awe their faces clear; With twain they hid their feet in rev'rent fear. And with the other twain they flew about: One to the other loudly raised the shout: Holy is God, the Lord of Sabaoth, Holy is God, the Lord of Sabaoth, Holy is God, the Lord of Sabaoth, Behold his glory filleth all the earth. The angels' cry made beams and lintels shake; The house also was filled with clouds of smoke.[10]

According to Y. Brilioth and L. D. Reed, this removal of the sanctus to a place after (or in the middle of) the words of institution was 'without doubt one of the least successful of Luther's suggestions for reform'.[11] However, in contrast to those Reformers who left the sanctus intact because they gave it no thought, there seems to have been a clear logic behind Luther's suggestions.

To begin with, since the sanctus was regarded as an anthem or chant prior to the canon, there was no reason why it should have been given a place in a reformed canon. Luther deliberately utilised it as an anthem sung as a conclusion to his new canon. The reason for this new position seems twofold. It came at the end of the words of institution during the elevation as a joyful response to the proclamation of the gospel, the testament of forgiveness; it was a thanksgiving – the sacrifice of praise which follows the proclamation of justification. But there appears to have been a second reason which is not immediately apparent.

The sanctus is from Isaiah 6, and Luther chose to use this version and its context rather than the context of the heavenly Jerusalem of Revelation 4. Luther seems to have seen a distinct parallel between Isaiah 6 and the eucharist, the sanctus as a true sacrifice of praise – something which men could render to God.[12] But there is a deeper significance. Isaiah was overawed by a sense of sin. One of the seraphim cleansed him by putting a burning coal on his lips and saying, 'Behold, this has touched your lips; your guilt is taken away, and your sin forgiven.' Then the prophet was sent out as the servant of God. For Luther, the gospel and the mass were for sinners because both were a declaration of sins forgiven. The bread and wine were the tokens or seals of that promise, and they touch the lips of the communicant as a declaration of forgiveness. After the communion, the Christian is sent out as a servant of God. Thus, the sanctus was a fitting conclusion to the proclamation of the testament of forgiveness, that is, the words of institution.

Although in DM Luther provided the German sanctus, he suggested other hymns which might be sung at that point in the service. It would be tempting for those who followed the DM to see any suitable hymn as an alternative to the sanctus at this point, and to omit the sanctus altogether.

Luther's FM and DM were recommendations, and not mandatory services. Taken with the less detailed recommendations found in his earlier writings, such as the *Babylonian Captivity* and the *Misuse of the Mass*, three possible treatments of the sanctus are found in the Lutheran Kirchenordnungen, stemming from Luther.

First was to leave the inherited medieval pattern intact, with sursum corda, preface and sanctus, in Latin or the vernacular, before a reformed canon. Amongst the Lutheran rites which retained this pattern are Brunswick 1528,[13] Pomerania 1535,[14] Osnabruck 1543,[15] Buxtehude 1552[16] and Saxony 1539.[17] The latter, for example, allows for the preface and sanctus in Latin, and the Lord's Prayer and Institution narrative in German.[18] The Danish masses of 1528, 1535 and 1539 also allow for the traditional pattern, either in Latin or Danish.[19] The rite prepared by Bucer and Melancthon for Archbishop Hermann von Wied of Cologne also retained the traditional pattern, though in the vernacular.[20] There is an interesting rubric regarding the singing of the sanctus:

After these things, Sanctus shall be sung; where clerks be, in Latin, but of the people in Douch, one side answering the other, thrice of both parts. As for that this is wont to be added, 'The Lord God of hosts' and Benedictus, it shall be sung communally of the whole congregation, and therefore in Douch.[21]

Where the mass was still said or sung in Latin, particularly in towns where there was a choir, the traditional pattern in Latin tended to survive. This was true in Sweden, where alongside the Swedish mass of Olavus Petri, the directions of Laurentius Petri for the Latin High mass assume the sursum corda, preface and sanctus will be sung as in the Roman mass.[22]

Second was to follow the pattern of FM, with sursum corda, preface, words of institution and sanctus. Amongst these are the rite of Andreas Dober 1525,[23] the Prussian rites of 1525 and 1524,[24] the Brandenburg–Nürnburg rite of 1533,[25] the 1543 Pfalz–Neuberg rite[26] and, when there was a choir, East Friesland 1535,[27] Wurttemberg 1536[28] and Wittenberg 1533.[29] Some of these, such as Dober's mass for Nürnburg, were in German rather than Latin.

The most distinctive rite which followed Luther's 1523 suggestions was the Swedish rite. In the 1531 vernacular mass of Olavus Petri, we find the following outline:

> Sursum corda
> Preface
> Institution
> Sanctus
> Lord's Prayer
> Agnus Dei
> Exhortation[30]

The provisions of Laurentius Petri allowed for many parts to be said or sung in Latin – presumably choirs had no music for the new vernacular texts for some time.[31]

Much more Catholic in tone was the Swedish mass of 1576, the 'Red Book' of King John III.[32] This was an attempt to reach some *rapprochement* with Rome, since John III's queen was a Catholic. There are three parts to the Liturgy, more expansive than comparable sections in other Lutheran orders: the Office of Preparation, the Offertory and the Eucharistic Prayer. According to the study of Sigtrygg Serenius, this order drew upon the medieval Swedish mass tradition, the German Lutheran Church orders, and the Church of England's Book of Common Prayer.[33] The rite has been variously assessed, from 'unlutheran' to a 'Liturgical masterpiece'.[34]

A full eucharistic prayer was provided, with eight proper prefaces, and a reworking of the portion of the Roman canon missae from the *Unde et memores* to the *Nobis quoque*. However, even so, the sanctus with its angelic introduction comes *after* the preface–institution as in FM. Yelverton wrote:

The common introduction is called the Laudes – in four different forms according to the day adopted from the medieval Missal. The Hymnus Trisagion which follows appears in two forms, the only difference between them being that Hosanna in the one is rendered as Salvation [Saliggor oss] in the other.[35]

The Communion Office of Charles IX, 1600, was described by Brilioth as bearing 'the stamp of the Reformed tradition'.[36] Here we find:

> Sursum corda
> Institution read
> Thanksgiving for redemption
> Institution with prayer (with the alternative Gospel Narratives)
> Sanctus read or sung, and the people and scholars sing it with the preacher.
> Lord's Prayer
> Communion

Despite the 'stamp of the Reformed tradition', the FM position of the sanctus was retained.

Third was to follow the pattern of DM, using the sanctus simply as a hymn, in Latin, the vernacular or in paraphrase, either during the institution narrative or after it; it could, however, be omitted in preference for another suitable hymn. Examples are the Wittenberg order of 1533,[37] Schwäbisch–Hall 1543 and Wurttemberg 1553.[38] In many Lutheran orders a latitude was allowed with either sursum corda, preface, sanctus and institution, or exhortation, institution, sanctus *or* hymn, or an amalgamation. An example of the latter is the Brandenburg–Nürnburg rite of 1533, where the vernacular exhortation and institution narrative are followed by either the Latin or German (paraphrase) sanctus. The 1540 order for Saxony actually provided for two different services for ferials and feasts.[39] The ferial usage was according to DM, but without mention of the sanctus; on feasts the minister intones the Latin prefaces and sanctus, followed by the Lord's Prayer and institution in German. In village churches there was provision for the Lord's Prayer, exhortation, institution and sanctus all in German. Indeed, it would seem that the pattern of DM came to prevail in village areas where there was no choir to sing the traditional chants. However, since DM gave the German sanctus as one chant amongst alternatives, it is hardly surprising that a few Lutheran orders simply make no mention of it. It is not mentioned for ferials in the Saxony order of 1540; it is not mentioned at all in the rite of Hess 1532;[40] and in Wurttemberg 1559 it appears to be covered by the rubric allowing 'another spiritual hymn' as an alternative to 'Gott sei gelobet' and 'Jesus Christus unser heiland'.[41]

An interesting development, or counterpart, to Luther's paraphrase is to be found in one or two Lutheran rites, the Danish being the prime example.

In Claus Mortengen's rite of 1528,[42] the sermon is followed by a psalm and an admonition to say the Lord's Prayer. Then the sanctus in Danish, with musical notation, is given, followed by the institution narrative. The sursum corda and preface occur in an appendix as optional. However, a Danish version of a sanctus trope, 'Tig ware laass' (from the sanctus–hosanna trope, 'Tibi laus'),[43] is provided *after* the institution narrative. The sanctus, therefore, occurs twice; once in its liturgical form, and then in a vernacular adaptation of a trope. In the 1535 Malmø mass, a sanctus paraphrase, 'Hellig er Gud Fader' (or another suitable hymn) was sung after the sermon and psalm as the bread and wine were prepared. This paraphrase was a translation of Nicolai Decius' hymn, 'Hyllich is Godt de vader', which was printed in 1531. In its German form it was included in the 1569 rite of Pomerania, placed after the institution narrative.[44] The Danish version is not mentioned in the 1537 Ordinance, drawn up by Bugenhagen, which omitted the sursum corda, preface and sanctus from the text, but offered them as optional for festivals. In the 1539 *Malmø Handbog* of Frands Vormordsen the sanctus in Latin or Danish comes after the sermon and psalm, and is optional; sursum corda and preface are sometimes used.[45] However, although the trope version is not mentioned in these later rites, it was included (though in a slightly different translation)[46] in the Psalmebog of 1528 and in successive Psalmebogen, and thus a dual use of the sanctus could still occur. What is strange is that the sanctus could be used before the institution, but shorn of sursum corda and preface. And just to add to the possible variations, Luther's paraphrase was included in Psalmebogen from 1533 to 1699.[47] The *Tibi laus* trope was also in use in Sweden, and was included in the Icelandic rite of 1594.[48]

THE REFORMED TRADITION

The eucharistic liturgies of the Reformed tradition had their origin in the early reforms of three cities – Strasbourg, Basle and Zurich. As H. O. Old has shown, the later eucharistic liturgies which emerged in various Reformed cities took their lead – and often their text – from these early liturgies.[49]

Strasbourg

The first reforms of the mass at Strasbourg were the work of Diobald Schwarz. On 16 February 1524 he celebrated mass in German in St John's Chapel in the Church of St Laurence.[50] Between the years 1524–5, nine or ten printed editions of the German mass appeared in Strasbourg, each differing slightly from the others, but all closely related in form and substance.[51] In Schwarz's first reform, the preface, proper preface, sanctus and benedictus were left intact. The Lavabo with its accompanying prayer followed, which was the custom at Strasbourg.[52] Then came a 'reformed canon' which included praise, intercession and an institution narrative. This sequence is found in successive orders, lettered by Hubert as A,A^1,A^2,A^3,A^4, B,C^1,C^2,C^3, D^1,D^2. In A, Schwarz had given a preface which concentrated on the salvation which came through the Cross, and the reversal of the disobedience of Adam, leading to:

Through Jesus Christ, our Lord, through whose majesty and
glory the angels and all the heavenly hosts praise you,
with whose exultant honour and praise we beseech you also
to hear our voices, as in humble confession we say:
    Sanctus
Holy, holy, (holy) Lord, God of hosts, heaven and earth are
full of your glory; O make us holy in the heights!
    (Benedictus)
Praise be to Him who comes in the name of the Lord; O
sanctify us in the heights![53]

This form remained almost without alteration until D^1 in 1525, when both contraction and expansion took place. The preface was shortened and fitted to an exhortation. The translation of the sanctus and benedictus was slightly altered, and the benedictus expanded almost to a Mozarabic form.[54] Liturgy E, dated May 1525, was lost; but by F, 1526, the sanctus had disappeared and the great Bucerian revisions never reintroduced it.[55] Here, therefore, the history of the sanctus between 1524 and 1526 is one of conservation, expansion and then abolition.

Basle

In 1523 Oecolampadius published *Das Testament Jesu Christi*.[56] Strictly speaking this was not so much a suggested reform of the mass as a devotional paraphrase for Maundy Thursday. The service was in German, and the preface and sanctus was followed by the Lord's Prayer and a canon. However, in his *Form und Gestalt*, 1525, the sursum corda, preface and sanctus entirely disappeared to be replaced by an exhortation and the Lord's Prayer.[57] Thus the sanctus ceased to be part of the Basle liturgy.

Zurich

Zwingli published his *De canone missae epicheiresis* in 1523.[58] The service was in Latin, and the sursum corda with preface were retained, the sanctus being introduced by the *praefatio communis* of the traditional Roman rite. The remainder of the canon (though for Zwingli only the post-sanctus was recognised as the canon) was replaced by four new Latin prayers. However, in the *Action oder Bruch des Nachtmahls*, 1525,[59] as with Oecolampadius, the sursum corda, preface, sanctus and new canon were replaced with an exhortation, Lord's Prayer, a prayer of approach and institution narrative. Again, therefore, the sanctus disappeared from the eucharistic liturgy, and it did not reappear in Bullinger's Agenda of 1532.[60]

Other Reformed rites

The Reformed rites of other cities were generally drawn up under the guidance of Bucer, Oecolampadius or Zwingli, and thus the rites of Berne, Memmingen, Augsburg, Ulm, Constance and Neuchâtel likewise dispensed with preface and sanctus.[61] Calvin's liturgies of Strasbourg and Geneva were based upon the rites of Basle, Strasbourg and Farel's rite published at Neuchâtel which was used in Geneva[62] and likewise had no sanctus. The nearest hint is the so-called 'Reformed sursum corda', found in Farel's exhortation which Calvin utilised:

Therefore, lift up your hearts on high, seeking the heavenly things in heaven, where Jesus Christ is seated at the right hand of the Father and do not fix your eyes on the visible signs which are corrupted through usage.[63]

This came at the end of the exhortation, and illustrates once again that the Reformers saw the sursum corda simply as an exhortation to the congregations which could be better achieved by a fuller exhortation to worthy communion. Calvin seems to have understood the sursum corda in this way.[64] The sanctus, however, found no place. This remained true of those rites which were either derived from Calvin, or were closely modelled on his Genevan rite – Pollain's *Liturgia Sacra*, John à Lasco's *Forma ac Ratio*, the Genevan liturgy associated with John Knox and its Puritan adaptations, the Pfalz liturgy of 1563 and Datheen's adaptation for the Dutch Reformed Church.[65]

THE CHURCH OF ENGLAND

Cranmer's first liturgical reform relating to the eucharist was the 1548 Order of the Communion. This was an English preparation for communion inserted within the structure of the Latin mass. Much of the material in this communion preparation was derived from the Consultation of Hermann von Wied, 1543. It will be recalled that this latter rite, prepared by Melancthon and Bucer, retained the traditional pattern of sursum corda, preface and sanctus.[66] The first English mass appeared in the Book of Common Prayer of 1549. Here Cranmer followed the pattern of the Latin mass closely, though the canon was entirely rewritten and transposed into a Protestant key.

The old pattern, as in Hermann's order, remained intact, though again it is clear that the sursum corda, preface, sanctus and benedictus were regarded as a unit quite separate from the canon. Cranmer provided a common preface and proper prefaces for Christmas, Easter, the Ascension, Whitsunday and the feast of the Trinity. There is, however, a common introduction to the sanctus:

Therefore with Angels and Archangels, and with all the holy companye of heaven, we laude and magnify thy glorious name, evermore praisyng thee and saying . . .

As with a number of German rites, Cranmer did not give a literal translation of the sanctus and benedictus:

Holy, holy, holy, Lorde God of Hostes: heauen and earth are full of thy glory; Osianna in the highest. Blessed is he that cometh in the name of the Lorde: Glory to thee, O Lorde in the highest.

The priest or deacon then addressed the congregation:

Let us praie for the whole state of Christes Churche.

The rubric before this refers to the sanctus, and directed:

This the clerkes shall also syng.

Thus sanctus and benedictus were retained as choir chants, though it is not clear whether the people were expected to join in.[67]

The 1549 Prayer Book was short lived, and its place was taken by a new Prayer Book in 1552. This book was far more Protestant in character than the previous book. In the Communion service, the sequence sursum corda, preface and sanctus was retained as a liturgical unit, but was now separated from the reformulated prayer corresponding to the canon. The unit now followed the confession, absolution and comfortable words of scripture, and was followed by the devotional prayer 'We do not presume' – later to be called the Prayer of Humble Access. Then came a prayer which contained the words of institution. Textual changes also took place. The 'company of heaven' was no longer 'holy', and the benedictus was omitted, though Cranmer's rendering of its second Hosanna was now appended to the sanctus:

Holye, holye, holye, Lorde God of hostes: heaven and y earthe are full of thy glory: glory be to thee, O Lord, most high.

This apparent departure from the pattern found in 1549 has been criticised by a number of scholars in much the same way as Luther's change. W. H. Frere, for example, comparing 1552 with that of 1549, wrote:

In 1552 this fine attempt [1549] at an English canon was broken into three pieces, and redistributed, after undergoing further modifications ... On one side the Prayer of Humble Access separates it from the Preface and *Sanctus*, with which it is intimately connected by right; and, on the other side, the whole act of Communion separates it from the Prayer of Oblation and the Lord's Prayer, which also are, when rightly placed, integral parts with it of one whole.[68]

However, Cranmer may well have deliberately placed the Prayer of Humble Access after the sanctus, because like Luther he looked carefully at Isaiah 6:1–9. Colin Buchanan writes:

The Benedictus qui venit was removed from the end of the Sanctus, and the whole biblical order of Isaiah 6 came to light. If we catch the vision of God and sing the angels' song, then if Isaiah is to be believed, we immediately express our own unworthiness. What could be more natural than the location of humble access at this point?[69]

This sequence remained in the subsequent Books of Common Prayer of 1559, 1604, 1625 and the revision of 1662. In the latter, the rubric is unclear as to whether the sanctus was to be recited by the congregation since it is attached to the preface recited by the priest.

It would be all too easy, on the basis of comparative liturgy, to view the Reformation handling of the sanctus as clumsy and inane. However, given sixteenth-century indifference to the sanctus as anything other than a pre-canon liturgical chant, it is quite remarkable that Luther and Cranmer fitted it into a theological context in their rites. Both actually made new positive theological use of the sanctus. In the actual reforms of this period, there is a noted tendency both to simplify the angelology, and to interpret or paraphrase the sanctus rather than give a literal word for word translation of it.

9

Protestant and Anglican liturgies, 1662–1960

THIS particular period is characterised by the recovery and repositioning of the sanctus in the Reformation churches, although the route and treatment differs between the various churches.

LUTHERANISM

For the most part, during the seventeenth and eighteenth centuries the patterns inherited from the sixteenth-century Lutheran rites were perpetuated in German agendas. Thus, for example, Coburg 1626 and Gotha 1645 omit the preface and sanctus; Magdeburg 1632, 1653 and 1740 require them on festivals; Mecklenburg 1650, and Brunswick–Lüneberg 1619 and 1643 permit their use.[1] However, the inroads of Pietism and Rationalism resulted in less frequent celebrations of the eucharist, and so the use of the sanctus became less common even in those areas whose agendas included it.

Of interest in this context was the Prussian Agenda of 1821, enforced by Frederick Wilhelm III of Prussia, following the union of Lutheran and Reformed Churches in 1817. This Agenda included a preface and sanctus, but in a position where they were used every Sunday even when there was no eucharist. The following order was given: hymn, invocation, versicle, confession of sins, declaration of grace, Gloria Patri (choir), kyrie (choir), Gloria in excelsis, salutation and collect, Epistle, Hallelujah, Gospel, Apostles' Creed, preface, sanctus, general prayer, Lord's Prayer and benediction. The sermon followed either the creed or the Lord's Prayer.[2]

The reintroduction of the sanctus in areas where it had fallen into disuse was stimulated by Wilhelm Lohe's *Agende für christliche Gemeinden*, 1844, in which he promoted a return to 'traditional' Lutheran forms. This Agenda provided the sursum corda, eight prefaces, and sanctus with benedictus. The benedictus allowed two expanded versions:

Blessed is Mary's Son who comes in the Name of the Lord.

Blessed is the Paschal Lamb who comes in the Name of the Lord.[3]

Much more recently, the 1955 *Agende für evangelisch-lutheranische Kirche und Gemeinden* provided alternative forms; either the 'traditional' Lutheran pattern of sursum corda, preface, sanctus and benedictus, followed by Lord's Prayer and institution narrative, or a eucharistic prayer beginning with sursum corda and including the institution narrative. On the other hand, the *Evangelisches Kirchengesangbuch*, Brunswick 1960, gives only the former pattern.

Outside Germany, Lutheran rites seem to have been less conservative. In Sweden, the Communion Office of Charles IX was revised in 1811.[4] Interestingly, this revised rite commenced with an anthem constructed from the sanctus and *Te Deum*. The anaphoral sanctus retained the Swedish position after the institution narrative, as it did also in the 1917 revision.[5] In 1942, however, this FM pattern was abandoned, and the sanctus followed the proper preface. The sanctus was in turn followed by a short prayer beginning 'Praise be unto thee, Lord of heaven and earth', described by Luther Reed as a prayer of 'humble access',[6] and then came the words of institution and the Lord's Prayer. In the Norwegian rite of 1685, all Latin was abolished, no sursum corda or sanctus were included, and the rite presupposed a communion psalm, exhortation, Lord's Prayer, institution narrative and communion.[7] The revision of 1889 restored the sursum corda, preface and sanctus as an *alternative* to the communion psalm. However, in the 1920 rite the sursum corda–sanctus unit was provided as the only form, giving a sequence of sursum corda, preface, sanctus, exhortation, thanksgiving, Agnus Dei, Lord's Prayer and institution narrative. The form of the sanctus was that of the biblical text of Isaiah 6:3 – 'The whole earth is full of His glory.'[8]

In the Danish Lutheran rite, the sanctus seems to have fallen into disuse in most places. Luther's German sanctus was omitted from the *Danmarks og Norges Kirke-Ritual*, 1685, and subsequently in the Gradual of Thomas Kingo, 1699. The hymn 'Dig vaere Loff' (Tibi Laus) was still in Kingo's Gradual with its tune, but not as an obligatory part of the liturgy. As a regular part of the Danish eucharistic liturgy, the sanctus was reintroduced into the text in the rite of 1912, though the version used was that of Revelation 4:8.[9]

The English-speaking Lutheran Churches in the United States have emerged from a complex linguistic background, and the differing Swedish, German, Norwegian, Danish and Finnish elements have each made some contribution.[10] The original groups from Europe used, of course, their own linguistic forms. The first liturgy compiled for Lutherans in the States was the German liturgy of Henry Muhlenburg, 1748, which had an abbreviated sanctus. After the sursum corda the biblical text of Isaiah 6:3 was used as a versicle and response.[11] As various Synods amalgamated, and as English became the mother tongue of succeeding generations, so the need was felt for an English liturgy. Many Lutheran groups therefore adopted a version of the 1888 Common Service which, with minor differences only, was reproduced in a number of Synodical Liturgies.[12] The Common Service provided for a hymn, sursum corda, preface, proper preface, sanctus and benedictus, possible use of an exhortation, Lord's Prayer and institution narrative. In *Service Book and Hymnal*, 1958, authorised by eight Lutheran bodies, a new development took place. In addition to the pattern of the Common Service, as a first alternative, a 'prayer of thanksgiving' followed immediately after the sanctus and benedictus, beginning 'Holy art thou, Almighty and Merciful God', and included the words of institution. The compilation of this prayer was the work of P. Z. Strodach and L. D. Reed, and was based upon a prayer compiled for the Lutherans in India, itself based on some classical anaphoras.[13]

REFORMED RITES

The earliest of the Reformed rites to re-introduce the sanctus into the eucharistic liturgy was that of Jean Frederic Ostervald, prepared for Neuchâtel and published in 1713.[14] Until this time Neuchâtel had used a rite derived from Farel's *La Maniere et fasson*. Ostervald had a keen interest in the Church of England even though he never himself visited England. Inevitably, therefore, the liturgy which he introduced was influenced by the Book of Common Prayer.

The eucharistic rite was contained in a separate section on the sacraments, and was a service quite distinct from the Morning Service. Bruno Bürki illustrates how this rite was a careful blending of elements from Calvin (and Farel) and the Anglican rite.[15] This is precisely what Ostervald achieved in his exhortation, which followed the institution narrative and was read from the pulpit. It concluded with a Reformed sursum corda (cf. Calvin–Farel), followed by preface, proper preface and the sanctus.[16] Proper prefaces were provided for Christmas,

Easter, Pentecost (two were provided, the first from the Roman missal, the second from the Anglican rite)[17] and for the September festivals. Bürki notes that there is no indication that the congregation could join in the sanctus.[18] He also suggests that Ostervald accentuated the fault of the Anglican rite which had already separated the sanctus from the Prayer of Consecration.[19] But here Bürki seems to have failed to see not only Cranmer's new use of the sanctus, but also that Ostervald was using it in a manner faithful to his Calvinist inheritance by extending the Reformed sursum corda.[20]

Further editions of Ostervald's liturgy were published in 1731, 1772, 1779 and 1873.[21] In 1853 an English translation was published for use by the French Reformed community in Charleston, South Carolina.[22]

Another pioneer in French Reformed circles was Eugène Bersier. Anglo-Swiss by birth, he spent his entire ministry at L'Eglise de l'Etoile in Paris;[23] like Ostervald, he was influenced by the Anglican rite. His liturgy, *Liturgie à l'usage des Eglises Réformées* was published in 1874.[24] It included sursum corda, proper preface, sanctus said by the minister and then repeated by the congregation, leading to a prayer for purity, petition for the Spirit, and the institution narrative. It included a Musical Supplement with settings by his sister-in-law; music for the sanctus was provided on pages 47–8 of this Supplement.

At a later date Bersier accepted an invitation by the General Synod of Nantes to prepare a liturgy to be considered for use in the Reformed Church of France. This was published in 1888 as *Projet de Révision de la Liturgie des Eglises Réformées de France*, though it was not considered until after his death.[25] The introduction gave a useful history of the French Reformed liturgy, and Bersier mentioned that only after the publication of his own rite did he become aware of Ostervald's work. However, in this *Projet* Bersier was too wise to promote his own liturgy in its entirety, and he made considerable use of the Genevan rites of 1743 and 1861. The sanctus was included, but its position was changed from that in his rite of 1874 and was now proposed as an alternative to the invitation to communion. The *Projet* was unsuccessful, and the 1897 *Liturgie des Eglises Réformées de France* had no sanctus.[26]

Neither Ostervald nor Bersier seems to have had much influence on other French rites at the time; the rites of Geneva of 1724, 1743, 1861 and 1875 which served for large numbers of French-speaking pastors reproduced a type of liturgy akin to Calvin's original forms – though with distinct changes in eucharistic theology.[27] The Vaud liturgy of 1899, though, had a eucharistic prayer, the conclusion of which seems to be a deliberate echo of the sanctus.[28]

It was with Richard Paquier and the 'Eglise et Liturgie' movement that the French Reformed (France and Switzerland) began to be influenced by traditions other then their own.[29] Paquier's liturgy of 1931 was inspired by the *Apostolic Tradition*, AC 8 and Justin Martyr, and included a eucharistic prayer, which Paquier divided into four parts – dialogue, preface, sanctus and consecration. The benedictus was reintroduced with the sanctus. A revised edition of this liturgy appeared in 1952. Bürki has examined a number of recent official revisions which show in varying degrees the influence of Paquier. Thus the Genevan liturgy of 1945 provided three traditional Calvinist eucharistic rites, and then a fourth based on that of 1931. After a lengthy preface giving thanks for creation and redemption through Christ, mention is made of the angelic hosts, and the congregation then sing the sanctus from their Psalter. It reappears in the 1950 draft liturgy for the Reformed Church of France, and in a Psalter version in the Berne rite of 1955.[30]

A similar mid-twentieth-century recovery of the sanctus is found in some German language Reformed rites such as that of Basle 1949, and the Dutch rite of 1955.

In the English-speaking Reformed tradition, an important development took place as a result of the influence of the Catholic Apostolic Church. This Church had its origins with Henry Drummond, John Cardale and Edward Irving. Although this new Church came from Reformed roots, it was entirely disowned by the Reformed tradition. Its liturgy, however, was to be extremely influential amongst certain Reformed groups.

In 1826 Henry Drummond, a wealthy banker, began a series of conferences at his home, Albury Park, Surrey. These conferences were concerned with Millenarianism. Edward Irving, a clergyman of the Church of Scotland and Minister of Regent Square Church, London, was a prominent member. In about 1830 in Scotland there were alleged instances of charismatic gifts and speaking in tongues, and Irving's London congregation became a centre of interest. When public worship in Irving's Church was interrupted by tongues, the Church of Scotland removed Irving from his ministry. However, Irving and his congregation continued in temporary accommodation and, through Drummond and Cardale, the Catholic Apostolic Church grew out of this charismatic congregation. Although nicknamed 'Irvingites', Irving himself played little part in its development; in 1843 he fell out with Cardale and, after returning to Scotland, died at the end of that year.

Drummond and Cardale had been recognised as 'Apostles', and instituted a complex hierarchy of ministry. The Catholic Apostolic

Church grew in numbers, and progressed from a Reformed congregation with charismatic utterances to a Church with a very Catholic-looking liturgy and a complex ceremonial.[31]

In its early years, when it was still recognisable as a Reformed schismatic group, the eucharist followed a nineteenth-century Reformed pattern.[32] In 1838 an outline 'Order for the Communion Service' was sent from Albury to all the Angels (bishops) of the churches. The eucharist began with the offertory, and had a confession, absolution and the Lord's Prayer; then a commemoration of the Living and the Departed; the thanksgiving over the bread was followed by the sanctus, the institution narrative and distribution of the bread; the thanksgiving over the cup was followed by the Gloria in excelsis, institution narrative and giving the cup. Between 1838 and 1842 the outline of the eucharist and other services were being developed.[33] In 1842 a printed liturgy appeared, which was subsequently expanded in various editions until 1880.

The eucharist was a full service of Word and sacrament, compiled from many sources – Anglican, Roman Catholic and Eastern – and included sursum corda, preface and sanctus; in 1847 the benedictus and hosannas were added. What is significant, however, is the shape and content of the anaphoral section. K. W. Stevenson observes:

Whereas revisions of our time all tend in the direction of the unity of the Eucharistic Prayer, the Catholic Apostolic Rite sees a great diversity in this part of the Rite.[34]

In fact, the anaphora is made up of ten sections – salutation and sursum corda, preface, sanctus and benedictus, Lord's Prayer, Consecration prayer, prayer of oblation, incense anthem, commemoration of the Living, commemoration of the Departed, and concluding prayer before communion.[35]

The liturgiographer and liturgist of the Catholic Apostolic Church was Cardale, and some of the rationale behind this compilation was revealed in his book *Readings upon the Liturgy and other Divine Offices of the Church*.[36] Cardale argued that thanksgiving and blessing are quite distinct acts; in thanksgiving God is praised for his mighty acts in the eucharistic prayer (preface–sanctus), but the bread and wine are blessed in the consecration. Thanksgiving, therefore, terminates with sanctus and benedictus; the Lord's Prayer separates the Thanksgiving from the prayer of consecration. In the definitive rite which was produced for the Church, there is a very lengthy preface as 'Thanksgiving' which, although taking thanksgiving seriously, perpetuates the medieval separation of the preface and sanctus from the business of consecration.

This arrangement of 'Thanksgiving' and 'Consecration' was to have an interesting influence upon the loose adaptations of this liturgy made by other Churches in the United States and the United Kingdom.

An immediate influence was on the Provisional Liturgy compiled for use in the German Reformed Church in the United States in 1857. The two leading members of the committee responsible for this liturgy were professors at the seminary in Mercersburg, Pennsylvania: Dr John William Nevin and Dr Philip Schaff.[37] Both held a high doctrine of the Church, ministry and sacraments, and their writings echo in some ways the English Tractarians. In 1854, Schaff visited England and wrote to his wife enthusiastically about the Irvingites. We may assume he returned to the States with a copy of the liturgy, because although a great many sources were used in the compilation of the Provisional Liturgy, the influence of the Catholic Apostolic rite on its eucharistic liturgy is unmistakable. Brenner has aptly remarked:

It is as though Schaff seated himself at an organ with the score of the Catholic Apostolic Liturgy before him and began to improvise.[38]

The anaphoral section of the Provisional Liturgy came after an exhortation, confession and absolution. Either consciously or unconsciously, Cardale's distinction between Thanksgiving and Blessing, or consecration was reflected in the rite. The sursum corda of the Provisional Liturgy is followed by a lengthy preface derived mainly from St James and the Catholic Apostolic Liturgy, ending with:

Thee, mighty God, heavenly King, we magnify and praise. With patriarchs and prophets, apostles and martyrs; with the holy Church throughout all the world; with the heavenly Jerusalem, the joyful assembly and congregation of the firstborn on high; with the innumerable company of angels round about Thy throne, the heavens, and all the powers therein; we worship and adore Thy glorious name, joining in the song of the Cherubim and Seraphim, and with united voice, saying . . .

The sanctus followed with benedictus, being the text of the Catholic Apostolic liturgy. However, this is then followed by the *recital* of the institution narrative (it is not a continuation of the prayer), followed in turn by an epikletic prayer. Thus the lengthy thanksgiving and sanctus represent the 'Thanksgiving'; the recital of the narrative and the separate epikletic prayer represent the consecration. The eucharistic prayer thus *terminates* with the sanctus and benedictus.

The influence of the Mercersburg liturgy upon the German Reformed Church and its repercussions with other Reformed groups in America is a story in its own right.[39] However, the major influence of the Mercersburg liturgy, together with its own inspiration, that of the Catholic Apostolic liturgy, was upon the liturgical forms of the Presbyterian Church in Scotland, England and Ireland.

As early as 1857, in *Presbyterian Liturgies with Specimens of Forms of Prayer for Public Worship*, A. Bonar had referred to the German Reformed liturgy just published in the United States. No sign of any dependence upon this work, or any other current or historic liturgies, is discernable in Robert Lee's *Order of Public Worship*, 1865. But quite different was the case with the *Euchologion* of the Church Service Society, 1867. In its introduction to the communion service, outlines were given of historic liturgies and of some 'Modern Services'. Amongst the latter were the Irvingite and the American German Reformed rites. One of the main authors of the *Euchologion*, George Sprott, later acknowledged that the eucharistic prayer was largely borrowed from the American (German) Reformed Church and that of the Catholic Apostolic Church.[40] However, in comparison with the sources, a number of changes had been made in the *Euchologion*. There was no sursum corda since it was not envisaged that a Scottish Presbyterian congregation would have the compilation in their hands, and would not, in any case, make responses. The prayer entitled 'The Eucharistic Prayer' duly begins 'It is very meet and right.' After a very long preface came the sanctus and benedictus, though the Catholic Apostolic/ Mercersburg form had been modified.

An asterisk by the first 'Holy' drew attention to a footnote: 'Anciently the people joined aloud in this hymn.' Then came a petition entitled 'The Invocation', which in fact was a Reformed epiklesis and oblation. However, although this section had its own title, it began with the words, 'And we most humbly beseech Thee', indicating that the invocation was a *continuation* of the eucharistic prayer. At the end of the invocation came the Lord's Prayer and institution narrative, with fraction and administration.

Here, then, was an attempt to reintegrate the various elements of the anaphora (though not the institution narrative) into one continuous prayer. The result is a lengthy thanksgiving for creation, restoration from the Fall, the work of Christ, the Holy Spirit and the sacraments, followed by the sanctus and benedictus, followed immediately by an epiklesis and anamnesis. The move from sanctus to epiklesis towards the end of the prayer echoes Egyptian usage, but it is, structurally, only a faint echo. The net result is a sanctus towards the end of the prayer, in contrast to a position at the beginning as found in most of the classical rites.

This part of the eucharistic rite remained virtually unchanged in subsequent editions of the *Euchologion* (the 1884 edition had the sequence anamnesis–epiklesis). Its impact upon the Church of Scotland is to be seen in *Prayers for Divine Service*, 1923 and 1929. These forms were mainly incorporated into the main eucharistic rite of *The Book of Common Order*, 1940. The institution was read as a warrant, followed by sursum corda, preface, proper preface, sanctus, benedictus and a pick up, 'verily holy, verily blessed', continuing with thanksgiving for the incarnation, anamnesis, epiklesis and self-oblation.

The Book of Common Order, 1940, was prepared for the United Church of Scotland which came about in 1929. Prior to this, the United Free Church of Scotland had had its own liturgical compositions, the *Book of Common Order*, 1923 and 1928. The United Free Church was itself a union in 1900 of the United Presbyterian Church and the Free Church of Scotland. The former had issued a liturgy under the title *Presbyterian Forms of Worship* 1891, 1892 and 1899; the latter Church had issued *A New Directory for the Public Worship of God*, 1898. In these rites we find a slightly different treatment of the sanctus.[41]

Presbyterian Forms of Worship contained two orders for the eucharist. In each case we have a lengthy eucharistic prayer (no sursum corda) (1891 edition, 43–5, 53–4) which *terminates* with the sanctus (Book of Common Prayer version), and in the first, with the benedictus also. A hymn follows the uncovering of the elements before the recital of the institution narrative. The first prayer, whether it ends in sanctus or whether the benedictus is also added, allows for congregational participation or response, for the sanctus is 'Doxology 17', and Hosanna is 'Sentence 90'. In both these prayers the tendency found in the Catholic Apostolic rite and the Mercersburg liturgy is used as a *fait accompli*: the eucharistic prayer *terminates* with the sanctus. While a 'Blessing' follows the first prayer, in the second the communion follows at once.

A New Directory for the Public Worship of God, 1898, provided a number of alternative prayers for various parts of the service. Prayer IV is a Thanksgiving and Consecration Prayer at the communion. The prayer ends with a doxology. However, a footnote allows that in place of the doxology, the eucharistic prayer may terminate with 'And now with angels and archangels', and so lead into the sanctus (Prayer Book version). Prayer V, reminiscent of the format of the *Euchologion*, has a eucharistic prayer ending: 'Blessing and honour and glory and power for ever and ever. With angels and archangels' and so leads into the sanctus, but it is immediately followed by a brief epiklesis entitled 'The Prayer of Consecration'.

The *Book of Common Order*, 1923, reproduced a shortened version of the *Euchologion*. The 1928 book contained three short orders for the communion. In the first, the sursum corda is followed by the institution narrative with a shortened exhortation. There follows a eucharistic prayer with a shortened introduction to the sanctus (Book of Common Prayer, no benedictus):

For Thou art from everlasting: Thou alone didst create the heavens and the earth and all that is therein. Thee all the hosts of heaven continually adore, crying aloud and singing unto Thee.

The second order has no sanctus, and the third has a compressed preface, sanctus without introduction, and a prayer adapted from the Book of Common Prayer 'Humble Access' prayer.

In all the denominational books of the Scottish Presbyterians we therefore find the reintroduction of the sanctus. Its use, however, differs. In some prayers it is recited by the minister alone, in others it is assumed that the congregation will join in. The most interesting point is the position of the sanctus in the earlier books. It comes either towards the end of the eucharistic prayer (*Euchologion*), or actually terminates the eucharistic prayer. Since it appears in the United Presbyterian book of 1891, we may assume that terminating the eucharistic prayer with the sanctus was an earlier established tradition amongst some ministers in this Church. J. M. Barkley has offered the following opinion:

The evidence for the United and Free Churches using the Sanctus as a conclusion to the eucharistic prayer is meagre, but I am inclined to think it was growing, if not absolutely common, practice otherwise it would not have been included in the 1891, 1892, 1898 and 1899 Books. There is also the fact that while men like my father used extempore prayer their prayers were full of Biblical quotations, especially the psalms, and also semi-liturgical language which was derived from Scripture.[42]

But certainly it is possible to detect the indirect influence of Cardale.

The Presbyterian Church of England was strongly connected with the United Presbyterian Church and the Free Church of Scotland. It is of little surprise, therefore, to find the same type of liturgical thinking. In 1894 there appeared the *Directory for the Public Worship of God*, compiled by a committee of the Synod of the Presbyterian Church of

England. For the Lord's Supper there was a series of instructions. Instruction 8 was the institution narrative read as a warrant; Instruction 9 was a eucharistic prayer 'which may conclude with this ancient doxology'. There followed the sanctus from the Book of Common Prayer. In the 1898 *Directory for Public Worship* there was no reference to the sanctus, but in the 1921 book of the same title two eucharistic prayers were provided, the second of which echoed the *Euchologion*, but ended:

Yielding ourselves unto Thee, a sacrifice of love, we worship and adore Thee. With angels and archangels, and with all the company of heaven, we laud and magnify Thy glorious Name; evermore praising Thee, and saying, Holy, holy, holy.

(BCP text)

This was followed by the fraction and narrative of institution.

This pattern was abandoned in *The Presbyterian Service Book*, 1948. On the other hand, the private compilation by Eric W. Philip, *Sacramental and Other Services*, 1927, provided three 'thanksgivings', A to C. Thanksgiving B ended with a sanctus:

For whose life and death of love, for whose rising again to be the living inspirer of our souls, we magnify and bless Thy holy name, evermore praising Thee and saying: Holy, holy, holy, Lord God Almighty: glory be to Thee for Thy great love. Amen.

The Presbyterian Church of Ireland revisions of the *Westminster Directory for the Public Worship of God* (1825, 1840, 1859, 1868 and 1887) make no reference to the sanctus; but both sanctus and benedictus appeared in the 1923 *A Book of Public Worship* and its revision in 1931, both showing the influence of the *Euchologion* which was also in use in Ireland. In the 1942 revision, the sanctus came nearer the beginning of the prayer with the preface considerably reduced in length. In all cases the text assumed that it would be recited by the minister.[43]

The English Congregational tradition had rejected set forms of the liturgy after the Westminster Directory of 1645, though apart from separate consecration of the bread and wine, the eucharist tended to follow the general outline of the Directory.[44] The sanctus made its re-entry into the Congregational tradition in the nineteenth-century adaptations of the Prayer Book.[45] The famous and influential *Devotional Services* of Dr John Hunter re-introduced the sanctus in the edition of 1895 and in the definitive edition of 1901. Dr W. E. Orchard, wearing his Presbyterian Church of England hat, compiled a liturgy c.1912 for St Paul's Church, Enfield, which had a Prayer of Thanksgiving (sursum corda, preface and sanctus) followed by a separate Prayer of Consecration.[46] When nominally a Congregationalist, his *Divine Service* of 1919 and 1926 both included sanctus and benedictus. In the 1919 edition, the Prayer Book sursum corda, preface, proper preface and sanctus occurred after the offertory and collects, followed by the Orate fratres, suscipiat Domine and benedictus, and then a eucharistic prayer based on St John's Gospel and 'Ancient Liturgies'.[47] In the 1926 edition, the Orate fratres and suscipiat Domine were placed before the offertory prayer, thus removing any interruption from the sursum corda through to the prayer of oblation.

Although the Congregational Union had issued a liturgy in 1847, it was not until 1920 that a further liturgy was issued on behalf of the denomination (as against the private publications of individuals), and one which contained a eucharistic liturgy. Heavily dependent upon the Prayer Book, it provided the sursum corda, preface and sanctus, followed by the institution narrative. However, these features disappeared in the *Manual for Ministers*, 1936, a book which gave liturgical expression to the excesses of Liberal Theology. With the Neo-Genevan books of 1948, 1951 and 1959 (revised 1969),[48] showing the influence of the eucharist of the 1940 Scottish *Book of Common Order* as well as that of the United Church of Canada's book, 1932, the sanctus reappeared as part of a eucharistic prayer. The 1959 book was published on behalf of the denomination, and accepted that preface and sanctus were a legitimate feature of the eucharistic prayer.

ANGLICANISM

No official revisions of the Anglican rite in England took place before the twentieth century; nevertheless, a number of unofficial and private liturgical revisions and even entire re-writings were attempted in the intervening period.

During the Commonwealth and Protectorate, Jeremy Taylor had compiled a liturgy which drew on that of St James and upon its sanctus, but was not connected with a prayer of consecration.[49] In 1696 Edward Stephens published a liturgy with two eucharistic rites, one for public use, and one for private use.[50] In the former, after the offertory (with sentences) came the Grace, sursum corda and a preface derived in large measure from the General Thanksgiving,[51] with the sanctus together with the 'worship of the lamb' from the Apocalypse, thus connecting

Isaiah 6:3 with Revelation 4:8–11 and 5:12–13. Patterned on the canon of 1549, this was followed by the intercessions and then consecration, though there was no attempt to link these prayers together into one continuous eucharistic prayer.

The second rite provided a similar link between the sanctus and Revelation, but the preface took the form of 'a turgid thanksgiving-series with responses',[52] leading up to 'Therefore with Angels and Archangels'.

Stephens published yet a third form, *A Compleat Form of Liturgy, or Divine Service, According to the Usage of the Most Ancient Christians* (second edition 1705), which appears to be a definitive revision. An offertory prayer led to the Grace, sursum corda and a preface covering seven pages with congregational responses. This extended preface actually developed into a Christology thanksgiving, thus giving the sanctus a new setting within Christology rather than praise of the Father.[53]

Early in the eighteenth century, two liturgies were published by Arian sympathisers, William Whiston and John Henley. Whiston followed the Prayer Book material fairly closely. Much more radical, however, was the eucharist of John Henley, *The Primitive Liturgy and Eucharist*, 1726.[54]Henley freely drew upon AC. The anaphora was divided into ten parts or paragraphs, each ending with an 'Amen' as the Roman canon missae. The 'preface' covered the first five paragraphs, thanking God for his own Being, as Creator of Christ, the heavenly bodies, the earth and finally man, and leading into the sanctus.[55] The thematic arrangement corresponds with the anaphora of AC 8.

For Catholic rather than Arian reasons, we find a similar use of material from the classical rites in the Non-jurors' liturgies of 1718 and 1734.[56] That of 1718 is more recognisably an enrichment of the Book of Common Prayer. After the offertory came a prayer of approach, the sursum corda, preface, proper preface and sanctus with benedictus from the 1549 Prayer Book. The post-sanctus was derived from that of St James, beginning 'Holiness is thy nature and being, O Eternal King; Holy is the only begotten Son.' In 1734, the Non-jurors departed further from the Church of England forms, and the anaphora was based directly upon that of St James and AC 8, the latter providing the form of the sanctus with Romans 1:25. As in Henley's rite, the benedictus occurs later in the service before communion, as in AC.

The eighteenth century also witnessed the emergence of two 'official' Anglican revisions: the 1764 Scottish Communion Office, and the 1789 rite of the American Episcopal Church.[57] Behind the former lie the

Prayer Books of 1549 and 1637, and the usage of the more moderate Non-jurors. It had precursors in the 'Wee Bookies' of 1722, 1735 and the recommendations of 1743.[58] The American rite was based in small part upon the 1764 Scottish Office, but is a more conservative revision of the English 1662 rite.

The 1764 rite removed the invitation, confession, absolution and comfortable words *and* Humble Access prayer to a place immediately before communion, thus restoring the sequence sursum corda, preface, sanctus, consecration and oblation, after which came the intercessions and Lord's Prayer. The preface–sanctus unit was thus reunited as part of a eucharistic prayer. Although 'Amen' still followed the sanctus, the Prayer of Consecration began 'All glory be to thee, Almighty God, our heavenly Father, for that thou of thy tender mercy', linking the Prayer of Consecration with the word 'glory' in the Cranmerian sanctus. At this point in the American book, however, the 1662 sequence was retained.

The 1662 pattern and that of 1764 represent the two patterns of handling the sanctus in subsequent Anglican revisions during this period. The '1662' pattern reappeared in the following revisions in the Anglican Communion: America 1789 and 1892; Canada 1918; Ireland 1920; and India, Pakistan, Burma and Ceylon 1960.[59] The '1764' pattern was given new impetus mainly through the work of Bishop W. H. Frere. In his influential book *Some Principles of Liturgical Reform*, 1911, Frere argued that the Prayer of Humble Access isolated the sanctus from the Prayer of Consecration, resulting in 'a very unsatisfactory pattern'.[60] Appealing to the Scottish example he suggested a simple rearrangement, linking the sursum corda, preface and sanctus, Prayer of Consecration and the Prayer of Oblation.[61] In the reformulations of a Prayer of Consecration leading to the Deposited Book of 1927–8, the Lower House of Canterbury on 19 February 1914 prescribed:

That the Prayer of Humble Access be removed from its present position and be placed immediately before the Communion of Priest and People; that the *Amen* at the end of the present Prayer of Consecration be omitted, and that the Prayer of Oblation follow at once (prefaced by the word *wherefore*), and then the Lord's Prayer.[62]

Although not necessarily following these particular directions of the Lower House of Canterbury Convocation, the removal of the Humble Access and the linking of the sanctus verbally to the Prayer of Consecration was adopted in the following Anglican revisions: Church of England 1928, America 1928, Scotland 1929, South Africa 1929,[63]

Canada 1959, Korea 1939, West Indies 1959, Madagascar 1945, Swahili, Hong Kong and Macao 1957, Japan 1957–9, India 1960, and Nyasaland and Northern Rhodesia (no date given).[64]

The sanctus, where the Prayer of Consecration was to follow directly, was normally linked to it with such words as 'All glory be to thee, Almighty God', 'All glory and thanksgiving' or 'Blessing and glory and thanksgiving.' The Japanese liturgy, almost certainly unconsciously, copied the idea found in Stephen's liturgy, with the sanctus followed by a reference to Revelation 4:11.

A slightly more subtle background lies behind the Ceylon rite of 1933–5, South India 1950–4 and India 1960. In 1920, J. C. Winslow and E. C. Ratcliff completed a liturgy for use in India which, they claimed, was more in keeping with Indian culture than the very Western European Book of Common Prayer.[65] The rite which they produced was inspired by the Liturgy of St James, and was authorised for use in 1920. This inspiration of the anaphora of St James lies behind the Ceylon rite. The Indian rites also drew on this source, but also on the Church of Scotland's *Book of Common Order* (itself inspired in part by St James).

Thus there was a strong move in many Provinces to reintegrate the sursum corda–sanctus unit with the Prayer of Consecration.

METHODISM

John Wesley combined the use of extempore prayer with a high esteem of the Book of Common Prayer. When forced into a position of ordaining a Superintendent and Elders for the United States, Wesley prepared an abridgement of the Book of Common Prayer.[66] In the Communion Service Wesley made minor changes, but the position of the prayers remained unchanged and thus the 1784 Abridgement followed Cranmer's arrangement.[67] A second edition appeared in 1786, and subsequent editions appeared under various titles in the eighteenth and nineteenth centuries in the Wesleyan Methodist tradition.[68] However, splits in the Methodist ranks quickly appeared after Wesley's death, and other Methodist groups tended to emphasise free prayer and despised liturgical forms. In the nineteenth century some of these groups did eventually issue forms of service for the guidance of the minister for occasions such as baptism, communion and weddings.[69] In his consideration of these rites, John Bowmer remarked that there was no provision for congregational responses, and so the sursum corda, preface and sanctus found no place in these rites.[70] When the full union of the Methodist Church in England took place in 1932, a new liturgy, *The Book of Offices*, was issued in 1936. Two orders for the communion were included. The sursum corda, preface and sanctus were included in both orders, but they perpetuated the legacy of Cranmer in keeping them as a separate unit. This was also true of American Methodism, which tended to follow Wesley's Abridgement.[71] There was no attempt at this time to reincorporate the unit into a eucharistic prayer.

10

The sanctus in some contemporary eucharistic prayers

SINCE 1960, most Western Churches have produced a mixture of revised, alternative and experimental eucharistic liturgies, with one or more eucharistic prayers. It is an impossible task to examine all these prayers (in the past twenty-five years more eucharistic prayers have been composed than in the whole previous history of the Church!). Some of these new prayers have been composed *without* using the sanctus, and this fact will be considered in the final chapter. In most new prayers, however, the sanctus finds a place. This chapter examines a selection from various traditions to see how it has been utilised, especially in those prayers where it has been given an unusual context.

THE ROMAN CATHOLIC RITE

Dated 20 March 1970, the Congregation for Divine Worship published the new Roman Missal together with an introduction, the *Institutio Generalis*. Whereas the Missal of Pius V of 1570 had conserved only the single Roman canon missae, and limited the number of proper prefaces,[1] the Missal of Paul VI, while giving a slight revision of the canon, provided three new eucharistic prayers entitled Eucharistic Prayer II, III and IV respectively; these new prayers had been published in 1968.[2] Eucharistic Prayer II was based upon the anaphora of *Apostolic Tradition*;[3] III, according to Bouyer, was based upon the Mozarabic and Gallican sources, though Wegman and Mazza feel that its structure is that of the Roman canon, with Antiochene and Alexandrine influence;[4] and IV was modelled upon the Coptic version of St Basil and, more loosely, on West Syrian forms.[5] A revised text of the Missal (but not affecting the eucharistic prayers) was published in 1975.

In November 1974 the Congregation for Divine Worship published five further eucharistic prayers – two on the theme of reconciliation, and three for use at eucharists with children.[6] These, together with the four prayers in the Missal, were composed in Latin, and National Bishops' Conferences and Synods were responsible for the vernacular translations and adaptations.[7] Subsequently national synods have been able to compose their own eucharistic prayers in the vernacular.[8]

Although the old Roman canon has retained its unique structure, Eucharistic Prayers II, III and IV have a common structure described as the *ingenium romanum*:

1 Opening doxology of praise to the Father
2 Statement of motives for thanksgiving
3 Sanctus – vere sanctus
4 Consecratory epiklesis
5 Institution narrative and acclamation
6 Anamnesis or memorial prayer with oblation
7 Communion epiklesis
8 Intercession
9 Closing doxology

Aidan Kavanagh has remarked that there is something here for everyone: proper prefaces of the Western tradition (not IV), a post-sanctus epiklesis as in the Egyptian tradition, and an epiklesis and intercession of the West Syrian tradition.[9] The resulting structure, however, is entirely new and without precedent.

Prayer IV, modelled upon St Basil, is not designed for use with a proper preface; it is a fixed prayer as in the Eastern tradition. Whereas the Western prefaces generally have a christological concern, the first part of this prayer is solely 'theological', praising the transcendent God for his Being. Although the prayer echoes Basil, here, in contrast to the latter's prolific angelology, angelology is kept to a minimum – perhaps as Mazza has suggested, because people today are so unreceptive towards angelology or, more simply, because philosophers have rejected any cosmological role for the angels.[10] This pruning of angelology – already encountered in many Protestant texts from the Reformation onwards – is a recurring factor in most modern eucharistic prayers.[11]

Eucharistic Prayers I, II and III are designed to be used with proper prefaces. Eighty-two proper prefaces are provided – fifty-one within the Order of the Mass, and the rest appearing in their proper places in the course of the missal.

Prayer II was based upon Hippolytus which is noted for its fixed thanksgiving and absence of the sanctus and intercessions. In the Latin text of Prayer II, the usual preface is based upon that of Hippolytus, but a sanctus has been inserted. The usual preface can, however, be replaced by any other proper preface which is appropriate, though this makes no difference to the modern 'interpolation' of a sanctus into the Hippolytus-based prayer. Eucharistic Prayer III has, as might be expected, regardless of whether Bouyer or the Wegman–Mazza view is correct, a sanctus and benedictus. Composition of Prayer II suggests that the compilers regarded the sanctus as a *sine qua non* for the modern Church.

In the Latin text of the preface, the transition to the sanctus is made with the traditional Roman formulae. However, in addition, new shorter angelological sections are provided, and an appendix contains twelve additional formulae which synods may use in translating into the vernacular.

It is interesting to observe that the English (ICEL) translations of the new proper prefaces discard the old Roman introductions with their angelology in preference for the formulae of the appendix with their simpler angelology. On the other hand, the 1970 Missal of the Nederlandse Commissie voor Liturgie opted for a more intermediate form.[12] For example, the preface for the Second Sunday in Advent:

1970 Latin Missal	ICEL
And therefore with angels and archangels, with thrones and dominions, and with the whole host of the heavenly army, we sing the hymn of your glory endlessly saying, Holy ...	And so, with all the choirs of angels in heaven we proclaim your glory and join in their unending hymn of praise.

Dutch 1970

Therefore with all the angels, powers and virtues ['machten en krachten'] with all who stand before your throne we praise and worship you and full of joy sing to you.

A certain latitude has been allowed, therefore, in translation and cultural adaptation.

The Dutch *Ordo Missae* of 1970 was remarkable because, alongside the official eucharistic prayers, it included twelve other 'indigenous' Dutch prayers compiled by members of the Dutch Commission which included the priest–poet Huub Oosterhuis, and the liturgist Herman

Wegman.[13] Some of the prayers presupposed the use of an authorised preface and sanctus; others provided new fixed prefaces. All the new compositions show a reluctance to use angelology as an introduction to the sanctus. Thus Prayer VIII:

Together with Him and with His Church from the whole world we want to thank you, and praise you and we sing to you.

Prayer XV:

We honour you in the Name of your whole church, with Mary, most blessed of women, with your disciples, martyrs and confessors,
with all who acknowledge you, we say ...

This latter introduction, uniting as it does the church on earth with the church triumphant, is reminiscent of the development found in some West Syrian anaphoras, though their exuberant angelology is not imitated in any sense at all. Prayer XII offered a variant version of the sanctus:

Holy, holy, holy, Lord of all Powers
Heaven and Earth are full of your glory.
Come to release us, You the Most High.
Blessed is he who comes in the name of the Lord.
Come to release us, You the Most High.

In this instance the Hosanna has been interpreted rather than merely transliterated.

The same tendency to play down the angelology is found in the eucharistic prayer of the Swiss Synod (particularly variable preface 4),[14] the two prayers for reconciliation and the ICEL English Eucharistic Prayer A.[15]

The Eucharistic Prayers for use with children reveal a more imaginative approach to the sanctus. The first has a long preface divided into three, interrupted by parts of the sanctus and benedictus as responses by the children. The second is characterised by many inserted responses, including Hosanna in the Highest, the sanctus and benedictus, and the benedictus on its own. The third prayer has sanctus and benedictus in the more traditional position.

Because the vernacular was adopted for the Vatican II reforms, each language-speaking area became responsible for translating and adapting the Latin original compositions. For the English-speaking world, a committee was appointed to standardise English translations, ICEL.[16] This was later broadened to an ecumenical group acting on behalf of all

English-speaking churches, ICET.[17] In the resulting text of the sanctus
and benedictus the following translation was adopted:

> Holy, holy, holy Lord, God of power and might,
> heaven and earth are full of your glory.
> Hosanna in the highest.
> Blessed is he who comes in the name of the Lord.
> Hosanna in the highest.

Two things should be noted here. First, on the grounds that the sense of
the LXX version of Isaiah 6:3 does not demand a comma after the third
holy, and the sanctus in the eucharistic prayer is addressed direct to
God (your glory in line 2), the first line becomes a vocative. Because of
the difficulty over the meaning of 'Sabaoth', this has been translated as
'God of power and might', suggested in part by 'pantocrator' of
Rev.4:8. Secondly, the Hosanna, which seems originally to have been
the introduction to the *benedictus*, has continued to be attached to the
sanctus.[18] These versions, therefore, are not only those of the English
Roman Catholic texts, but also of many English-speaking churches.

ANGLICAN RITES

Since 1960, a vast number of new liturgies have been compiled for use
within the Anglican Communion. Some of these have been experimental, some alternatives, and some are new definitive texts. Where the
English language has been utilised, or English versions have been
produced alongside vernacular liturgies, the language has been changed
from Authorised Version English, to Revised Standard Version
English, to Modern English and, for a number of texts, the ICET
versions. The majority of the new Anglican eucharistic liturgies have
been collected and edited by Colin Buchanan in **MAL**, **FAL** and
LAL.[19]

Overall there has been an almost uniform abandonment of the
Cranmerian 1662 utilisation of the preface–sanctus–Humble Access–
Prayer of Consecration sequence in favour of a unified eucharistic
prayer, although in many places the 1662 rite remains in use alongside
newer rites.[20]

In order to give some coherent unity in Anglicanism, a number of
guide documents have been produced, the most important being the
Lambeth Conference 1958, the Pan-Anglican Document and the
Second Pan-Anglican Document.[21] In addition there has been cross
fertilisation between Provinces and with other traditions.

Regarding the eucharistic prayer, Lambeth recommended the following:

The events for which thanksgiving is made in the Consecration Prayer are not confined to Calvary but include thanksgiving for all the principal 'mighty works of God', especially the resurrection and ascension of our Lord, and his return in glory.[22]

Perhaps inspired by the Eastern eucharist prayers, this recommendation involved what Frere had argued for, namely the reuniting of the sursum corda, preface and sanctus with the rest of the prayer. The Pan-Anglican Document of 1965 was vaguer on the content of the eucharistic prayer, but the Second Pan-Anglican Document was quite specific. Article 5, entitled 'The Thanksgiving over bread and wine' said:

The basic elements and progression of this eucharistic are:

(a) Sursum corda
(b) The proclamation and recital of the mighty acts of God in creation, redemption and sanctification
(c) The Narrative of the Institution
(d) The anamnesis of the work of Christ in Death, Resurrection and Ascension 'until he come'. It is recognized that this is the most difficult section of the prayer in view of the different doctrinal emphases which are expressed and recognised within the Anglican Communion. The whole concept of anamnesis is, however, so rich in meaning that it should not be impossible to express it in such a way that the needs of everyone are met. Whatever language is adopted should, however, avoid any idea of a propitiatory sacrifice or repetition of Christ's sacrifice. The 'once for all' character of his work must not be obscured.
(e) The prayer that through the sharing of the bread and wine and through the power of the Holy Spirit we may be made one with our Lord and so renewed in the Body of Christ.

The whole prayer is rightly set in the context of praise e.g., Sursum corda and sanctus.[23]

Here we shall consider the treatment of the sanctus in some of the more influential Anglican rites, and consider a more general overview of other recent Anglican revisions.

One of the most important rites, itself inspired by the CSI rite, was the Liturgy for Africa (LfA). Conceived in Kampala in April 1961, it was drafted there in April 1963 at a meeting with representatives of the Provinces of South Africa, West Africa, Central Africa, East Africa and

Uganda. The idea of a unitive liturgy arose in East Africa where the newly-formed Province united traditions of 1662 and the 1549/Roman use of Swahili. The Archbishop of Uganda, Dr Leslie Brown, was responsible for much of the work, submitting it to four members of the Church of England Liturgical Commission for comment. The definitive text was published in 1964.

The eucharistic prayer was entitled 'The Great Thanksgiving' and was drafted in AV language.[24] After sursum corda came a lengthy fixed preface based upon the CSI prayer, giving thanks through Christ for:

1 Creation and material things
2 The Incarnation and Resurrection
3 The Ascension and Heavenly Intercession
4 Sending the Holy Spirit and making a Royal priesthood.

This thanksgiving led to the sanctus:

Therefore with angels and archangels, with patriarchs and prophets, apostles and martyrs, and with all the holy company of heaven, we cry aloud with joy, evermore praising thee and saying . . .

Only the Prayer Book sanctus was included, with the pick up 'All glory to thee, O heavenly Father.'

Thus in LfA we encounter a fixed preface where the sanctus is a joyful hymn in response to *God's mighty Acts*, particularly in Christ and the Church. There is no proper preface. The angelology of Cranmer is left intact, but representatives of the Church triumphant are added.

The Alternative Services Book of the Church of England appeared in 1980, and the eucharistic liturgy in modern English – Rite A – provided four eucharistic prayers as well as a modernised form of 1662. The history behind the four eucharistic prayers is complex, and spans a period of some fifteen years.[25]

By the Prayer Book (Alternative and Other Services) Measure, 1965, the Church of England could authorise experimental services without Parliament's ratification. In the Alternative Services First Series, the 1662 text with some 1928 features, and many options, was authorised, following Frere's suggestion of reordering the preface, sanctus, prayer of consecration and oblation. However, in the same year, the Liturgical Commission also published as a report Alternative Services Second Series, which included a new eucharistic rite (Series 2). Although in AV/RSV language, it was very different from the Prayer Book. The Liturgical Commission explained some of the thinking behind the eucharistic prayer:

We have thought of the *Preface* and the *Prayer of Consecration* as two parts of one whole; and we have therefore removed the *Prayer of Humble Access* from its present position between them . . .

In the Preface, or first half of our Consecration Prayer, we have attempted to produce a *Thanksgiving* for the Creation of the World, the Redemption of Mankind, and the Sanctification of the People of God, through Christ. In order to mark the seasons of the Church's Year, we have provided short 'proper prefaces' to be inserted in the general thanksgiving. But we hope that we have written something which is of manageable length.[26]

Although there was considerable controversy over the anamnesis–oblation in the prayer,[27] the section from sursum corda to the sanctus of the revised authorised rite of 1967 hardly differed from that proposed in 1965.

The prayer included a lengthy fixed preface giving thanks for the same themes (though phrased differently) as LfA. However, after thanksgiving for the resurrection, there was provision for the insertion of proper prefaces for Christmas, Passiontide and Easter, and after thanksgiving for the Holy Spirit, a proper preface for use from Ascension to Pentecost. It thus combined a fixed 'Eastern'-type preface with the Western use of proper prefaces. The post-sanctus led immediately into a petition for 'consecration', without any literary link. The sanctus was the Prayer Book form, and the benedictus was included but, possibly influenced by convictions about AC 8, as an optional anthem immediately *after* the eucharistic prayer.

The prayer was inspired by the ancient anaphora contained in the *Apostolic Tradition*, and the account of the eucharist and writings of Justin Martyr. This explains partly the lengthy Christological fixed preface before the sanctus. Since, however, neither of these ancient sources include the sanctus, one had to be inserted and given a context. A former secretary to the Liturgical Commission, G. G. Willis, commented:

Perhaps the Commission thought it would be too shocking for words to an English Congregation if it were to behave in a really primitive fashion and excise the *Sanctus* . . . The Preface seems to be over-elaborate, and the insertions made into it at great festivals are clumsy, and tend to be tautologous, and the transition to the rest of the prayer is exceptionally abrupt.[28]

Willis also noted that the sanctus alone, without benedictus – after the Egyptian model – had been adopted.[29] However, much of this can be explained by the fact that the Commission at that time was influenced by the views of two of its members, E. C. Ratcliff and A. H. Couratin, both of whom at that time believed that the original form of *Apostolic Tradition* had included the sanctus as a terminating doxology.[30] Couratin explained the thought to me thus:

In the original draft, since Dialogue 41 (Justin) has no allusion to the sanctus, it was placed between eucharistia and anamnesis, because that is really the only place in which it had hope of being accepted. Ronald Jasper wanted it at the end, and even suggested that it should be sung twice, once after eucharistia and once after anamnesis. But it was pointed out to him that, if he could over the years convince the C of E that it ought to form the doxology of the Eucharistic Prayer, it would be very easy to move the paragraph to the end, and make it run: 'Through him therefore with angels and archangels, with Cherubim and Seraphim, and with all the company of heaven, we laud and magnify thy glorious name, evermore praising thee and saying: Holy, holy, holy, Lord God of Sabaoth, heaven and earth are full of thy glory, throughout all ages, world without end. Amen.' Meanwhile we introduced references to 'earth' and 'heaven' and 'the whole Church' into the ordinary doxology, to direct men's thoughts heavenward![31]

Indeed, the prayer ended with a reference to glory 'from the whole company of earth and heaven', and the sanctus would have been a fitting conclusion to the prayer.

In 1968, the text of Series 2 formed the basis for the modern English text included in *Modern Liturgical Texts*, which represented a stage towards the modern English Series 3 report of 1971 and the authorised text of 1973.[32] This latter included the ICET texts. Revised as GS 364 and GS 364A, the final definitive text became prayer 1 of the ASB.

The prayer was redrafted for the Series 3 report 1971 and Series 3 1973 – retained through to its ASB version – had a reminder of the original intention behind Series 2; the prayer did not terminate with the sanctus, but with another doxology after which the people responded:

Through him, and with him, and in him, in the power of the Holy Spirit, with all who stand before you in earth and heaven, we worship you, Father almighty, in songs of everlasting praise:
Blessing and honour and glory and power be yours for ever and ever. Amen.

Had the sanctus not already featured earlier in the prayer, it would have fitted neatly as a response to the doxology.

Although in modern English, and in places rephrased, together with provision for a proper preface in a single position before the introduction to the sanctus, the substance of the prayer remained unchanged in its scope of thanksgiving. From the 1978 redrafting onwards, benedictus could be used immediately after the sanctus. The sanctus in this prayer, from its Series 2 origins to its form as prayer 1 in the ASB, concludes a lengthy Christological thanksgiving.

The second prayer in the ASB is also descended from Series 2, and the differences between prayers 1 and 2 are found in the anamnesis. Prayer 3 was the result of initiatives taken by R. Beckwith and B. Brindly in November 1978.[33] It was based directly upon the *Apostolic Tradition* of Hippolytus, but like the Roman Catholic revision, the Church of England found it necessary to provide for a proper preface and sanctus with benedictus. Thus, after the barest reference to creation through the Word, the preface is a rehearsal of Christ's saving deeds. The sanctus is thus used as a response to the work of Christ.

Prayer 4 was based upon Series 1. Sanctus and benedictus come after a short preface with proper preface, though the Prayer Book initial thanksgiving has been expanded to include 'Creator of heaven and earth, through Jesus Christ our Lord.'

Unlike the Roman prefaces, there is no variety of introduction to the sanctus, but a standard introduction (partly, of course, because the proper prefaces are insertions and not complete independent prefaces as in the Roman rite). The angelology is simply that of the Prayer Book – angels, archangels and the whole company of heaven. An exception to this is for the feast of St Michael and All Angels, in which the cherubim and seraphim make an appearance.

The ECUSA revised Prayer Book was the culmination of some twenty years of revision. Two rites were provided for the eucharist: rite one in traditional (AV) English, with two eucharistic prayers reflecting the American 1928 Prayer Book, each retaining the Prayer Book sursum corda, short preface, proper prefaces (22) and sanctus with benedictus; and rite two in modern English, with four eucharistic prayers. Of these, A and B (cf. ASB prayer 4) have a brief preface (mentioning creation), proper prefaces and a common introduction to the sanctus:

Therefore we praise you, joining our voices with Angels and Archangels and with all the company of heaven, who for ever sing this hymn to proclaim the glory of your Name.

Prayer A has the pick up, 'Holy and gracious Father'; and prayer B, which is based on Hippolytus, continues 'We give thanks to you, O God.'[34] Prayer C, the 'Star-trek' prayer, was first published in 1970 for experimental use within the rite for an informal liturgy, and was the work of Captain Howard Galley of the Church Army.[35] After the sursum corda, it continues as a dialogue between celebrant and congregation, giving thanks to God as creator and redeemer, and leading to the sanctus. It is interesting that the use of modern cosmological terminology in this prayer coincides with its omission of any direct angelic (ancient cosmological?) reference.

Prayer D is 'A Common Eucharistic Prayer' compiled in 1975 by a group of liturgical scholars representing Lutheran, Episcopal, Methodist, Presbyterian and Roman Catholic traditions. It was based directly upon the Latin original of Eucharistic Prayer IV of the Roman Catholic rite, and upon the original underlying anaphora, Coptic St Basil. The sursum corda, fixed preface and sanctus are, apart from phrasing, those of the Roman prayer. The sanctus thus praises God the creator for his Being.

The American book also provides a further eucharistic order which gives only minimum directions for the celebration. The eucharistic prayer may be *ad hoc* or extempore, and may include sanctus and benedictus. If these latter are included, they are introduced with these or similar words:

And so we join the saints and angels in proclaiming your glory, as we sing [say].

Thus, apart from the responsorial preface of C and the fixed preface of D, the American full prayers retain the short preface form of the Prayer Book, with the sanctus close to the beginning of the prayer.

In those new Anglican rites which give a unified eucharistic prayer with the sanctus, there are in general three different treatments:

1 A *brief statement of praise*, provision for a proper preface, and an introduction to the sanctus, similar to 1662 – Eng 1, Scot R 1966, Wal 1966, Wal 1,2, Ire 1, Amer 1–1, Amer 2–2 (A and B).
2 A *lengthy fixed preface*, covering creation, redemption and the Holy Spirit – LfA 1964, Aus 2 1966, NZ 1966, Tan 1973–4, Scot 2 1982.
3 An *extended preface* with thanksgiving for creation, redemption and the Holy Spirit, with provision for insertions of a proper preface – Eng 2,3,A, EAUL, NUL 1965, Scot 1977.

Although these are three different approaches, the Western flavour prevails: thanksgiving is mainly christological and soteriological. God is praised for creation, but usually 'through Christ' or 'through the Word'. There is little extended praise of God as Father, or for creation. The exceptions are notable: Amer 2–2 (C), 'Star-trek', gives extended mention of creation; Aus 3(1969) gave thanks for creation and food;

Can 4(1) gives thanks for creation, the covenant, Abraham, Moses and the prophets; Can 4(4) is an expansion of 'Star-trek'; and NZ 1984 1 alternative and 2, deal with creation and Old Testament history. Overall, the sanctus is a hymn of praise for God's actions through Christ and the Holy Spirit.

With regard to angelology, there is a mixture of retaining Cranmer's list, expanding the list to include groups of the Church Triumphant – patriarchs, prophets, apostles, martyrs and the saints – or avoiding any explicit mention of angels at all. As to the form of the sanctus, English liturgies tend to use a modernised Prayer Book form, or the ICET form. There are some variations, but the boldest experiment with form comes from the New Zealand rite 2, a and b. The first has:

Holy God, Holy and merciful, Holy and just,
glory and goodness come from you.
Glory to you most high and gracious God.

The second has:

Holy, holy, holy,
God of mercy, giver of life;
earth and sea and sky
and all that lives,
declare your presence and your glory.

The benedictus is treated in four ways:

1 As in the Prayer Book – simply omitted
2 With the sanctus
3 Later as a communion anthem
4 With 2 and 3 as alternatives

THE REFORMED TRADITION

A particularly interesting experiment with the sanctus was made in the 1970 *An Order of Public Worship* of the Congregational Church in England and Wales. Starting work in 1964, the compilation was completed by 1967, but due to the publisher's delay, did not appear until 1970. It has been compiled in traditional language, but appeared at a date when most revisions were using modern English. The book therefore had an out-of-date appearance which detracted from its advanced liturgical thinking.

The order contained six eucharistic prayers. All commenced with the sursum corda, and all contained the sanctus (not benedictus); each had a preface and included thanksgiving for creation (except V) and redemption. Prayer III had proper prefaces for Christmas, Easter and Pentecost. However, a fascinating feature of Prayers IV, V and VI was that they all ended with the sanctus. The notes on the service explained:

In I, II and III, the Sanctus comes in the middle of the prayer – after the thanksgiving and before the prayer that God will transform what we are doing. In IV, V and VI the Sanctus comes at the end of the prayer as its climax, expressing the fact that in Christian worship Christ admits us to share in the eternal worship of heaven.[36]

Prayer III may be compared to the 1928 Prayer Book form of eucharistic prayer with sursum corda, brief preface and sanctus with a post-sanctus link, 'All glory be to Thee.' Prayer I and II both had a lengthy fixed preface, that of II deriving from the Statement of Faith of the United Reformed Church scheme of union. The sanctus in these two prayers comes in the middle of the prayer as praise for creation, salvation in Christ, the Holy Spirit and the Church.

In the other three prayers the Congregationalist Worship Committee achieved what the Church of England compilers had only half attempted – a eucharistic prayer which reached its climax, not with a doxology, but with the sanctus. It is true that there were Lutheran and Presbyterian precedents, as we have observed, but the Congregationalist prayers were the direct result of two distinct factors.

Firstly, the influence of English liturgical scholarship, following the hypothesis of E. C. Ratcliff concerning *Apostolic Tradition*.[37] This is related to the fact that one of the committee, Stuart Gibbons, had studied liturgy at Oxford under A. H. Couratin who at that time accepted and supported Ratcliff's hypothesis. A hint of this influence was to be seen in a paper which Gibbons read to the Church Order Group, in around 1960, entitled *The Eucharistic Prayer*. Gibbons observed that in Exodus 24, the making of the covenant, half the blood of the sacrifice was thrown on the altar and half on the congregation; the people were joined to God by the symbolism of the blood which was a sharing of life. After this the Elders were able to ascend the mountain, and they beheld God, ate and drank. Christ's death, the new covenant, has admitted Christians to eat and drink in the presence of the Holy God. The words of institution contain a promise:

This act of worship, this thank-offering of bread and wine, in this relationship of utter dependence and gratitude, is regarded by God as my body and blood.

From you, this is enough, in God's gracious design, to admit you poor, imperfect worshippers, into his sight, to stand in his presence.[38]

Gibbons had already pointed out that when Isaiah was admitted to the presence of God, he heard the sanctus; in the Book of Revelation the Church is admitted to God's presence and joins in the sanctus. The inference must be that the sanctus would form a fitting conclusion to the eucharistic prayer.[39] During the early 1960s, Gibbons was himself already using a eucharistic prayer which terminated with the sanctus, and he successfully persuaded the committee that they should adopt this pattern for some of the prayers. Gibbons explained:

It seemed to me that Ratcliff has made a good case for the hypothesis that this was the position in which the sanctus had come into liturgical use, but that as a hypothesis it provided no basis for an argument from history. However, I felt that the theological argument for a final sanctus is weighty if the biblical associations of the sanctus are given due emphasis. Isaiah's reaction to finding himself a spectator of the heavenly worship is that he is not fit to be there, and he has to be cleansed before he can serve. In Revelation 5, the joining of all creation to sing the glory of God follows the celebration of the death of the Lamb whose blood has ransomed men for God. The point that we can only participate in the worship of heaven because Christ has died for us, seems to be given its proper emphasis when the sanctus follows the anamnesis or making present/effective to us the sacrifice of Christ. The inclusion of a final sanctus in three out of six prayers suggests that the committee was persuaded of the weight of this argument but equally unwilling to break with tradition.[40]

The second reason was pragmatic. Dr J. K. Gregory, another member of the Committee, had also experimented with closing the eucharistic prayer with the sanctus. His reason was that in *Congregational Praise*, the sursum corda, preface (Prayer Book version) and sanctus were provided for minister and people. The people said together the words leading to the sanctus, 'therefore with angels'. A problem arose as to when the people should sit; furthermore, not having a set text to follow, a Congregational congregation would have no idea when the minister would conclude the eucharistic prayer. It seemed a good idea to Gregory for the eucharistic prayer to follow the preface, and to conclude the prayer with 'therefore with angels' in which the people would join, and from which they would know that the prayer was coming to its conclusion. Gregory, therefore, for very different reasons, was happy to support Gibbons.[41]

Prayers IV and V, as with I, II and III, included the Prayer Book angelology. Prayer VI, undergoing several revisions of a prayer drafted by Stuart Gibbons, included:

O God, in mercy receive our sacrifice of praise, at the hand of Christ our great High Priest; and unite us by thy Holy Spirit with all thy saints on earth and all the company of heaven to laud and magnify thy glorious name, evermore praising thee, and saying . . .

It is somewhat ironical that the liturgical theory of an Anglican scholar of the Catholic wing of that Church should have found its practical application in a tradition widely regarded as hostile to liturgy, and indifferent to liturgical history and theory. Possibly only the freedom and openness which Congregationalism possessed made such a bold experiment possible at this time.

With the formation of the United Reformed Church in 1972 – a union between Congregationalists and Presbyterians in England – it was decided that a new liturgy was needed for the new Church. A eucharistic rite was published in booklet form in 1974, containing a form in traditional language and one in modern English. The modern rite alone was updated for inclusion in *A New Church Praise*, 1975; the definitive text appeared in *A Book of Services*, 1980.

Three eucharistic prayers, all in modern English, were provided in the 1980 book. Prayers II and III were, respectively, the ecumenical prayer of the British Joint Liturgical Group, and a Table Prayer by the Dutch priest, Huub Oosterhuis.[42] All three prayers contained the sanctus. This is also true of the *Service Book* published in 1989, which has three new eucharistic prayers, all with the sanctus. However, a second order is provided, reflecting the practice of the Churches of Christ which entered the United Reformed Church in 1981. This tradition has separate thanksgivings over the bread and wine, and the forms provided do not utilise the sanctus.

In France, the eucharistic liturgy of the Taizé community has been an important liturgical catalyst. The community's 1959 rite had a 're-cycled' Roman canon as its eucharistic prayer, with the sanctus following a brief preface and proper preface. The rite was revised in 1972 with traditional eucharistic prayers. The thanksgiving preface of VII is a fixed preface for the creation of the whole universe, mankind, the covenant and promises revealed through the prophets. However, this Reformed community is not necessarily typical of Continental Reformed liturgy, where the older tradition still makes its presence felt. The French Reformed Church's *Liturgie*, 1963, represents a blending of older Reformed tradition with the insights of modern scholarship.[43] It provides a sursum corda, preface and sanctus, the recitation of the institution narrative, and then a resumption of the prayer with anamnesis and epiklesis. The resulting sequence *appears* like the classical

Syro-Byzantine anaphora, but in fact there are two separate prayers surrounding the narrative which is read as a warrant – rather like the Mercersburg rite. In the 1982 revision of *Liturgie* further prayers were added, and in these the narrative was included as part of a single eucharistic prayer. In prayer II, the sanctus (and benedictus) is sung, 'with all the angels and archangels', after thanksgiving is made for God's creating activity and care; in IV it comes as a proclamation of God's glory for Christ. The sanctus comes after a preface in the Vaud rite 1963, the Swiss Romande rite 1979[44] and, for example, the Swiss German Reformed rites of Zurich 1969 and Berne 1983.[45]

Other Reformed rites, such as the Church of Scotland's *Book of Common Order*, 1979; the *Worshipbook*, 1970, of the Presbyterian Church in the United States of America and the Cumberland Presbyterian Church; and their 1984 Supplemental Liturgical Resource 1, all use the sanctus in a traditional manner in the eucharistic prayer.[46]

LUTHERANISM

A eucharistic prayer was prepared by the German Evangelical Brotherhood of Michael in 1961, giving a prayer with sursum corda, proper preface, sanctus and benedictus, followed by the institution narrative, anamnesis and epiklesis with fraction, terminating with 'maranatha'.[47] This liturgy, together with the impetus from new Roman Catholic forms, resulted in revisions in 1976 and 1977 of the German Lutheran Agenda of 1955.[48] After sursum corda, proper preface, sanctus and benedictus, provision was made for either the Lord's Prayer and institution narrative, or a eucharistic prayer (five alternatives, and the third without preface and sanctus), or an experimental type of eucharistic prayer. The general preface stands out from most major modern revisions on account of its profuse angelology, being an adaptation of the old Roman *Per quem maiestatem*:

Through him the angels praise your majesty, the heavenly hosts adore you, and the powers tremble; together with the blessed Seraphim all the citizens of heaven praise you in brilliant jubilation. Unite our voices with theirs and let us sing praise in endless adoration.

In the United States, The Lutheran Churches produced two new books for worship: The *Lutheran Book of Worship*, 1978 (LBW), and *Lutheran Worship* 1982 (LW). LBW was the result of the work of the Inter-Lutheran Commission on Worship. After the offertory comes the 'Great Thanksgiving' with sursum corda, appropriate preface, sanctus and benedictus. After this the book makes provision for three usages:

1 A full eucharistic prayer after the classical structure
2 The institution narrative as proclamation
3 The 1942 Swedish pattern – a short prayer, then the narrative as proclamation

Instead of the sanctus, Hymn 528 'Isaiah in a vision' – an English version of Luther's paraphrase – may be sung. The *Manual* which accompanies LBW explains:

Luther's 'Isaiah in a vision did of old' (hymn 528) may replace the sanctus on occasion. When it is used, the final phrase of the appointed preface should be modified to introduce the hymn which is not simply the cry of the seraphim but a paraphrase of the account in Isaiah. The Preface should include: 'And so with the church on earth and the hosts of heaven, we praise your name and join in adoring song.'[49]

Because of dissension from certain members of the Lutheran Church – Missouri Synod, this latter Church revised the material prepared for LBW to produce LW. There were strong objections to a eucharistic prayer,[50] on the grounds that this was a departure from the Lutheran formulae and therefore 'unlutheran'. Divine Service I reproduced the Common Service; Divine Service II provided sursum corda, preface, sanctus and benedictus, a short prayer similar to 3 in LBW, then the Lord's Prayer and institution narrative. Divine Service III claims to follow the DM of 1526, and uses chorales. It provides for an admonition, Lord's Prayer, narrative of institution and Hymn 214, 'Isaiah, Mighty Seer, in Spirit soared.' In LB, therefore, we find a reluctance to depart from the traditional interpretation of Luther's patterns, and the sanctus either terminates a preface or, as a hymn, may follow the narrative (as in FM rather than DM!).

In the Swedish alternative rite 1975–6,[51] a complete prayer is provided, with three alternative continuations after the sanctus. Sursum corda, preface and proper preface (ten provided) lead into the sanctus and benedictus with:

Therefore with all your faithful through all times, and with all the company of heaven, we praise your name and devoutly sing . . .

Thus this Swedish revision unites the sanctus with a full eucharistic prayer. Norway, however, 1979–84, has a similar pattern to LW Divine Service II, where a short prayer after the sanctus is followed by the

Lord's Prayer and institution.[52] In the Danish revision a similar pattern is given, and in the 1968 Finnish Evangelical Lutheran rite the same pattern is found, except that the Lord's Prayer follows the narrative of institution.[53] Thus, within this tradition, there is a trend towards using the sanctus in a unified eucharistic prayer, but the older Lutheran pattern – and the use of a sanctus paraphrase – is still prevalent.

Amongst eucharistic prayers which have been prepared on an ecumenical basis, mention should be made of the British Joint Liturgical Group's prayer of 1978 – included in the 1980 *Book of Services* of the United Reformed Church. This prayer was modelled partly upon the *Te Deum* which, as we have seen, was itself derived from an *inlatio* and its sanctus.

It becomes clear from this selected survey (but the same applies to rites such as *The Methodist Service Book*, 1975, of the British Methodist Church, and *At the Lord's Table*, 1981, of the United Methodist Church in America) that, in most of the official eucharistic rites of the major denominations, the sanctus occurs as a *sine qua non*, generally placed within a unified eucharistic prayer. Its usual place is as the conclusion to a thanksgiving preface which is mainly christological, and in introducing the sanctus, there is a marked tendency to play down, and even avoid, reference to celestial beings. Perhaps the most interesting experimentation with the sanctus has been in the English Congregationalist Church, where it was used as a climax to some eucharistic prayers.

11

⚘

The sanctus in perspective

THIS study of the anaphoral sanctus began with its pre-history in Judaism. The cultic chant is cited first in the Book of Isaiah, overheard being sung in honour of Yahweh by the seraphim who attended the throne. We may conjecture that this chant was probably part of the Temple liturgy at that time, and may reflect a combination of a Yahweh–Sabaoth–Zion cultic theology with the kabod theology which was later to replace it. It may be at least, therefore, as old as Isaiah's vision, 742 or 736–5 BCE. The prophetic concept of being admitted to God's throne-room or divine council recurs in later Jewish thought in the apocalyptic literature, such as Daniel, and in the eschatological community of Qumran. Righteous men and the elect may be admitted to God's presence with the angelic host. The sanctus, or *qeduššah*, was one of the chants that seers and the elect might hear, as witnessed in the Pseudepigrapha (even allowing for Christian interpolations). The 'mystical tendency' of the joining of earth and heaven in praise to God was kept alive and developed in various Jewish groups, making its mark on some of the Pseudepigrapha and *hekhalot* literature, and by the inclusion of *qeduššah* in the Synagogue *berakot*. This same tendency also influenced certain Christian groups, as is witnessed by John 12:41, Revelation 4 and the *Passio* of Perpetua and Felicity, as well as by the preservation of Pseudepigraphal works. Possibly the usage of the Synagogue, or the strong mystical Judaism of Babylonia, influenced Syrian and Palestinian Christians to adopt the sanctus as part of their anaphoras or, as has been suggested, biblically-minded celebrants drew on Nehemiah 9 in their initial praise of God and imaginatively inserted an adaptation of Isaiah 6:3, though no doubt aware of its liturgical use in Judaism. By the third century, and indisputably by the early fourth, it was part of the eucharistic prayer in some Syrian and Palestinian communities. From there – perhaps like the institution narrative – it became a near universal feature, eventually joined with benedictus in all traditions other than the Egyptian, and remained so until the Reformation.

In the sixteenth-century Lutheran and Anglican traditions the sanctus was retained, though its context and function was changed; the Reformed tradition, however, jettisoned it. From the nineteenth century onwards it has been recovered in this tradition, and has been given a more traditional setting in the Lutheran and Anglican traditions. It is an almost universal feature in modern eucharistic prayers.

Yet there is a small, but significant, number of recent eucharistic prayers which omit the sanctus. Some of these are from small Protestant denominations of a conservative nature who have felt no need to introduce 'traditional' elements into their prayers – such as The Disciples of Christ *Handbook for Christian Worship*, St Louis, 1970. There has also been the deliberate use of Hippolytus *without* alteration, as in the Altar edition of *LBW*. However, there have also been a number of unofficial eucharistic prayers[1] and certain official new compilations, such as the Roman Catholic eucharistic prayer for Australian Aborigines, and the ASB eucharistic prayer for Communion of the Sick, which have not utilised the sanctus. Taken together, these prayers confirm – if there was ever any doubt – that it is quite possible to compose eucharistic prayers without recourse to the sanctus.

Some of the unofficial prayers were discussed by John Barry Ryan. He made the following observation:

The frequent omission of the Sanctus and references to the saints, thereby leaving unexpressed the idea of an earthly liturgy joining in a heavenly liturgy, accents the community desire to assume responsibility for their worship and their work to bring all men into the Kingdom.[2]

These unofficial compositions, although being a very subjective expression of a particular community's thoughts, tend to concentrate on an *oratio christologica* where, as in Hippolytus, some sudden transition to something which apparently praises God's transcendant Being is out of context.

Such an observation, however, is applicable to many modern official eucharistic prayers. Very few are concerned with an *oratio theologica*, and very few, if any, have the approach of Cyril/St James where the creation *itself* praises God, leading into the sanctus in a logical manner. A large number have a Christological proper preface which does not actually need the sanctus at all. Their context is such that in many cases the sanctus and its introduction could be removed, and the flow of the prayer (cf. The Roman Canon missae) would be distinctly improved. Furthermore, it has been shown in the previous chapter that there is a distinct tendency to play down angelology, which in many eucharistic prayers is the only item which gives the sanctus any sort of context.

These observations raise a number of fundamental questions about the anaphoral sanctus today. If the sanctus is to be included in eucharistic prayers, how should it be used? Is it possible to separate the sanctus from its traditional angelological introduction? Is there a case for experimenting with its position and form? It is with these questions that the conclusion of this study is concerned.

A LOGICAL DOXOLOGICAL FUNCTION

In certain anaphoras, where the sanctus seems to have been an original element, its function was either as an expression of the praise of the whole cosmos (Cyril/St James) or a statement of the fact that God is hymned in heaven by the angelic host (Addai and Mari). However, what is true of these anaphoras has, it would seem, been extended to a generalisation to explain the function of the sanctus *wherever it occurs*. For example, J. J. Von Allmen, under the title 'The Participants in the Cult', wrote:

> In the preface to the Eucharist, the congregation, after declaring what God has done for the world and its salvation, chants the *sanctus* 'with angels and all the powers of heaven'. In so doing it avows that it is participating in the doxology of the heavenly beings described by the Book of Revelation (cf. 4:8); it draws near to the heavenly Jerusalem where are innumerable angels.   (Heb 12:22)[3]

After noting the secondary dogmatic nature of angels, and arguing that they include 'animal' categories as well as 'anthropological' categories, Von Allmen emphasised that the worship of the Church is joined to the worship of the angels in the heavenly sanctuary, and that they are also present in the Church's worship.[4]

As valid a general theology of worship as such statements undoubtedly are, they ignore totally the diversity of usage of the sanctus in the various eucharistic prayers. There is nothing to relate such a theology to in Hippolytus and its derivatives; in the Roman Canon Missae there is an abrupt transition to the angelic hierarchy, which seems to be an interpolation; in Egypt it interrupts the intercessions and has little logical context; many West Syrian anaphoras have used it as an excuse to build an *oratio angelologica*, going beyond the speculations of pseudo-Dionysius; and in many modern compositions, its inclusion

seems to have been based upon weight of tradition or musical considerations rather than on the logic of the prayer. However, history shows
that it is not essential and is least successful where it appears as an
abrupt interruption. There seems, therefore, very little justification for
including the sanctus unless it is given a logical setting. The brief Book
of Common Prayer (1928, Wales) introduction when united with a
'Prayer of Consecration' representing as it does a truncation of Roman
usage (itself almost certainly an intrusion), is an example of where the
sanctus has no logical context. Some general theology about heavenly
worship, or the weight of tradition, or musical considerations should
not be an excuse for simply inserting the sanctus; it ought to have a
logical doxological context.

THE PROBLEM OF THE ANGELS

The sanctus in both its biblical settings is a chant of heaven, sung by
celestial beings. With few exceptions in either ancient (some West
Syrian) or modern (Canadian) anaphoras, it is introduced as the song of
angelic beings. The 'toning down', common in most modern revisions,
seems to reflect the modern Western unease with angelological speculation.

It is of course true that many Christians in the modern West are quite
happy to believe in the existence of angels, either because the Church
teaches so, or because they are mentioned in the Bible. In a book aimed
at popular readership the American evangelist, Dr Billy Graham,
asserts:

I believe in angels because the Bible says there are angels; and I believe the
Bible to be the true Word of God.[5]

He further adds:

I also believe in angels because I have sensed their presence in my life on special
occasions.[6]

On the other hand, without accepting the full implications of Bultmann's call for demythologising, many would agree that on the question
of angels, the Christian is faced with an outdated *Weltanschauung*,[7]
entering Christianity from the religious milieu of late Judaism and in
conflict with a Copernican view of the world and scientific thought.[8]
Apart from the studies of Edward Langton and W. G. Heidt, the
absence of recent *extended* treatments[9] of the subjects tends to emphasise the uneasiness of devoting too much attention and thought to these

'essentially marginal figures'.[10] Amongst modern dogmatics, the treatment of the subject by Macquarrie, Rahner and Barth stands out against an otherwise deafening silence.[11]

It may be wise to make a distinction between, on the one hand, the possibility of supra-human beings who are included in the whole creation, described as visible and invisible (invisible from a human point of view) who – or which – may in fact be God's 'Laws of the Universe' or expressions of God's care ('guardians of the nations') or his ambassadors, and who by their very existence are, like all creation, a witness and a living doxology to God and which may be called by the general biblical name 'angels' or 'The host of heaven' and, on the other hand, acceptance of the definite existence of certain zoological species (zoa) classified as 'thrones', 'powers', 'cherubim' and 'seraphim', and so on.

The possible ancient Near Eastern background relating to cherubim and seraphim has been discussed earlier. As far as the New Testament use of 'thrones', 'powers', 'dominions' and so on is concerned, although scholarship in general is agreed that these represent classes of spiritual beings, exegetes are divided as to whether they represent good or evil forces.[12] Whatever the truth of the exegetical question, it has to be admitted that these beings are simply presumed to exist by the New Testament writers. Possibly, therefore, in order to avoid unnecessary speculation, it might be legitimate to see these angelic beings in terms of God's Laws of the Universe, and possibly (following one interpretation of certain Old Testament references) the wonder and awe of God's Universe represented by stars and planets. They actually serve as witnesses to God's mysterious and transcendant Being. Beyond this, it is perhaps wise to adopt a reverent agnosticism concerning the existence of celestial zoological species with the names given in the Bible.

It must be admitted that the language of worship is not the same as that of precise dogmatic formulations or a philosophy of religion; furthermore, it is well known that many liberal and radical theologians who question traditional ways of speaking of God and Christ are happy to use the 'poetic' language of worship.[13] Yet it has to be asked whether the eucharistic prayer is the right place to introduce, or preserve, speculative language or, as many would urge, mythological language in the form of biblical classes of celestial beings. It may be wise to extend the Reformation and modern tendency to keep the angelological introduction to the sanctus to a minimum. As a doxological hymn of praise to God the Creator and Redeemer it has been revealed to mankind for us to use, either with or without angelic participation! A legitimate introduction might be as follows:

Joining with the angels [or, 'celestial beings', or 'all creation, seen and unseen'] together with the heavenly chorus, with prophets, apostles, martyrs, and Christians in every generation who look to you in hope, we worship you, singing . . .

An emphasis on the unity of the earthly and heavenly Church rather than on celestial zoological species has much to commend it, and preserves the transcendent and immanent dimensions of the original biblical setting (and temple cultic setting?) of the sanctus. If the anaphora is to be concerned with the creation itself praising God, then perhaps:

The entire Universe, with all its Laws, all creation, seen and unseen, hymn you with the song of heaven.

CREATION

In most of the classical Eastern anaphoras, the sanctus occurs as a doxological climax to a praise of God, which includes his work as creator (Basil, Addai and Mari, AC 8) or as the praise of the whole creation itself (Cyril/St James). In modern eucharistic prayers this theme is rarely given extended treatment. The Roman prayer IV echoes Basil; however, the proper prefaces for use with the other anaphoras are either Christological or hagiological, related to the proper of the feast. In the Anglican Communion, extended praise of God as Creator is the exception rather than the rule. Only a short reference occurs in the Church of Scotland's *Book of Common Order*, 1979, third order; the French Reformed prayer II, 1982, manages a little better. Why then the apparent silence?

It is partly, no doubt, that being Western Churches, the inherited tradition has always been more concerned with redemption and a Christological preface. However, it is strange that although the Eastern anaphoras have been used as inspiration in many new compositions, their theme of creation should have been ignored. It may be that this represents an unconscious retreat in the West in the face of the disastrous Darwinian controversies, and a wish not to disturb the 'uneasy truce' between science and religion.[14] To say too much using biblical language might be mistaken for Creationism; to venture too much into scientific terminology runs the risk of sounding like a bad textbook, and with swift changes in scientific theory, might run the risk of being tomorrow's discredited theory. There is, perhaps, some wisdom in the Barthian position that the doctrine of creation is a matter of faith quite unaffected by the changes, chances and controversies of science. However, belief in God as Creator *is* a fundamental belief:

One God, the Father Almighty, is the Creator of heaven and earth and of all things visible and invisible, while the incarnate Son or Logos, through whom all things were made and in whom they hold together, is the central and creative source of all order and rationality within the created universe.[15]

There is reason to believe that the truce between religion and science is less 'uneasy' now than it was some twenty years ago. The present position regarding 'chance' and 'law' has been summarised by Arthur Peacocke as follows:

The character of this interplay of chance and law appears now to be of a kind which makes it 'inevitable' both that living structures should emerge and that they should evolve – given the physical and chemical properties of the atomic units (and presumably, therefore, of sub-atomic particles) in the Universe we actually have.[16]

This 'inevitability', together with admiration for the beauty, simplicity and complexity of the Universe,[17] has provoked some scientists to a sense of *mysterium tremendum et fascinosum*. The chemist James Lovelock went as far as to posit a common medium in our atmosphere which preserved life on earth, naming it Gaia after the Greek earth goddess.[18] Rather more restrained are the astronomers Henbest and Couper:

The long line of development that's led to our appearance on Earth has required a whole string of 'coincidences', working hand-in-glove. Some are fairly obvious, others fairly abstruse; and they range from the borderlines of philosophy to intricacies of nuclear physics.[19]

In the long line of development, these writers include the barely perceptible imbalance of matter over anti-matter which led to the Universe of stars, planets and galaxies; the laws of Nature favourable to the development of intelligent life; the razor-thin balance of the nuclear force needed to join sub-atomic particles to form the nuclei of atoms; and the masses of the subatomic particles leading to DNA.

There are far too many 'coincidences' to be mere chance. We must conclude that we are only here because the Universe has certain very specific rules built into it.[20]

Henbest and Couper point out that scientists (if they are true to their discipline) cannot invoke God at this point, but prefer what is called the 'anthropic principle'. But they state:

The anthropic principle underlies our interrelation with the Universe – and the only possible alternative, a Universe designed by God for man, makes the same point even more strongly. The Universe is part of every one of us, at many levels.[21]

T. F. Torrance has argued that the Christian doctrine of creation allows us to accept the Universe as divine and contingent. The combination of unpredictability and lawfulness in nature found in its capacity spontaneously to generate richer and more open-structured forms of order in the constantly expanding Universe, may be regarded as something like the signature of the Creator in the depths of contingent being.[22] Interestingly, Torrance anchors this in doxology:

Because the Universe is God's creation, theological science cannot but be deeply interested in uncovering through natural scientific inquiry of the rational patterns which God has conferred upon it, if only in Christian concern for praise and worship of the Creator by the creation.[23]

It is not our purpose to develop a discussion of science and creation, but merely to indicate that there are grounds for more confidence and boldness in this area than many new eucharistic prayers seem to acknowledge. In Basil, Addai and Mari and James, the sanctus occurs (so we have urged) logically and naturally as praise of the transcendent God who is also immanent in his world: Heaven and earth – the whole Universe – is full of his glory. The sanctus can, and should, be utilised with the same context in contemporary eucharistic prayers, as thanksgiving *for* and *with* creation. The American 'Star-trek' prayer is a good example of an attempt to use common English scientific terms without surrendering a prayerful style and without following a particular scientific school or thought. Such a thanksgiving quite logically flows into the sanctus; indeed, according to one interpretation, stars and planets can be seen as a twentieth-century update of Old Testament angelology. In giving thanks for the Universe, galaxies, planets and life, man, the stuff of the Universe made conscious, is rendering thanks to God for his own creation in the *imago dei*, and for all creation. Moltmann underscores this point admirably:

As God's gifts, all his creatures are fundamentally eucharistic beings also; but the human being is able – and designated – to express the praise of all created things before God. In his own praise he acts as representative for the whole of creation. His thanksgiving, as it were, looses the dumb tongue of nature. It is here that the priestly dimension of his designations is to be found. So when in the 'creation' psalms thanks are offered *for* the sun and the light, *for* the heavens and the fertility of the earth, the human being is thanking God, not merely on his own behalf, but also in the name of heaven and earth and all created beings in them. Through human beings the sun and moon also glorify the Creator. Through human beings plants and animals adore the Creator too. That is why in the praise of creation the human being sings the cosmic liturgy, and through him the cosmos sings before its Creator the eternal song of creation.[24]

In this context the New Zealand rite, while having very little on creation itself, has an excellent variant form of the sanctus:

Holy, holy, holy, God of mercy, given of life; earth and sea and sky and all that lives, declare your presence and your glory

TRINITARIAN THANKSGIVING AND THE SANCTUS

Certain of the classical anaphoras mention the Trinity, either indirectly (by addition perhaps in Addai and Mari) or directly. A few Syro-Byzantine anaphoras give a doctrinal qualification: Eustathius has 'You are equal in ousia and worshipped in three persons of Father and Son and Holy Spirit'. Clement has 'Father, Son and Holy Spirit, true God, one nature on high, one substance, who in three persons is adored and praised by all things.' Syriac John Chrysostom has 'the one majesty of the Trinity, of equal substance, adored in three persons, Father, Son and Holy Spirit'. In this context, the sanctus came later in the anaphora, reinforcing the doctrine, since Isaiah 6:3 was a useful proof text.

In much contemporary theology the doctrine of the Trinity has fallen into oblivion, and there is also a tendency to move towards a unitarianism or, more commonly perhaps, a binitarianism.[25] However, some recent studies have been concerned with defending the centrality of a critical, rational and strong doctrine of the Trinity.[26] David Brown, for example, affirms that there are sufficient grounds for believing the doctrine if it is set in the wider framework of a justified belief in an interventionist God who engages in a particular form of revelatory dialogue with man.[27] Modern anaphoras do not necessarily reflect the neglect of this doctrine, though apart from a proper preface for the feast, there is a reluctance to mention the Trinity itself. This is probably due to the fact that modern revisers are concerned with the anaphora as a prayer, and not as an extension of Council decrees. However, although no attempt is made to expound the Substantial Trinity, in the Anglican, Methodist and some Reformed traditions there is a tendency to use a long preface leading up to the sanctus, which is a thanksgiving for the Trinitarian history of God in terms of Theology, Christology and Pneumatology. God is thanked as Father and Creator (briefly!), giving a soteriological understanding of the work of creation. Then follows extended treatment of the work of Christ and the Holy Spirit. The latter is sometimes just mentioned, but in some prayers the work of the Spirit in renewing men and women and bringing about their new solidarity and fellowship – the Holy Spirit glorifying the risen Lord and through him the Father – is recounted. Yet, as Moltmann has pointed out, there is only one, single, divine Trinity and one, single, divine history of salvation. The triune God can only appear in history as he is in himself, and in no other way.[28] Thus, although the new prefaces covering the work of creation, Christology and the work of the Spirit represent a new departure, the Trinitarian history with which they are concerned is simply the 'Economic' side of the immanent Trinity. To conclude such a preface with the sanctus is therefore highly appropriate, even if today Isaiah 6:3 cannot be used as a proof text. It may be, however, that Revelation 4:8 would be a more logical doxology to the Trinitarian history of God – who was, who is and who is to come. Precedents for its use in the anaphora are few – a Coptic fragment, the liturgy of Stephens, the Danish liturgy of 1912 – but this should not prevent or discourage its use in the anaphora.

JUSTIFICATION/SANCTIFICATION AND THE SANCTUS

Ultimately the eucharistic prayer, at least in its classical forms – and as it is conceived by most scholars and Churches at present – is a doxology glorifying God for the fact of justification and sanctification. At the heart of the prayer is God's saving work pinpointed in the sacrifice on the cross for our redemption, of which the eucharist itself is the anamnesis. By the sacrificial death of Jesus we have been placed on God's side and consecrated to him for ever.

The Church is a holy temple (1 Cor 3:16–17; Eph 2:21); believers are to present their bodies to God in the form of living, holy sacrifices (Rom.12:1). In fact, Christ sanctified the whole Church and made it his own by his sacrifice at Calvary, so he could present it as a pure, spotless sacrifice at the end of the age (Eph.5:27).[29]

Indeed, in the eucharistic memorial, the Church pleads Christ's sacrifice on the cross, and offers itself in, with and through Christ.[30] We are united with Jesus Christ in his vicarious humanity, and participate in his vicarious self-offering to the Father.

It may be argued that justification and sanctification, concepts from the realms of the Jewish lawcourts and the sanctuary, are complimentary models whose truth should not be pressed into a logical or a chronological relationship.[31] Nevertheless, the anaphoras tend to move from justification to the idea of sanctification. Salvation from God includes the call to a new life within the community of the discipleship of Jesus, with goals set by him and achieved through the power of his Spirit. The Syro-Byzantine anaphoras, and many modern anaphoras, include a petition for the communicants within the epiklesis. The Holy Spirit as the paraclete sets people apart for God because of the sacrificial blood of Jesus, shed for the remission of sins. The Church is also prayed for in the anaphoral intercessions which, apart from Egypt and part of the Roman canon, come after the anamnesis (or in East Syria, after the institution narrative) and epiklesis. The thought is to associate the whole Church with the eucharistic feast. Since the eucharist is a foretaste of the heavenly banquet (Lk 13:29), where we eat in the presence of God, it is not surprising that some anaphoras conclude on this eschatological note. Addai and Mari in particular expresses this:

And because of all your wonderful dispensation towards us, with open mouths and uncovered faces let us give you thanks and glorify you without ceasing in your Church, which has been redeemed by the precious blood of your Christ, offering up praise, honour, thanks and adoration to your holy and life-giving name, now and at all times for ever and ever.

A similar type of eschatological thought is expressed in the Roman Catholic Eucharistic Prayer for Reconciliation II:

You have gathered us here around the table of your Son, in fellowship with the Virgin Mary, Mother of God, and all the saints.
In that new world where the fullness of your peace will be revealed, gather people of every race, language, and way of life to share in the one eternal banquet with Jesus Christ the Lord.

And in the second prayer of the ASB rite A:

Accept through him this offering of our duty and service and as we eat and drink these holy gifts in the presence of your divine majesty, fill us with your grace and heavenly blessing; nourish us with the body and blood of your Son, that we may grow into his likeness and, made one by your Spirit, become a living temple to your glory.

Through Jesus Christ our Lord, by whom, and with whom, and in whom, in the unity of the Holy Spirit, all honour and glory be yours, almighty Father, from all who stand before you in earth and heaven, now and for ever. Amen.

Here we find the model of justification/sanctification resulting in the Church being admitted into the presence of God, just as the cleansing of Joshua the High Priest in the vision of Zechariah resulted in him being given access 'among those [the celestial host] who are standing here [before God's throne]'. As Moltmann says,

According to Christian understanding, the beginning of heavenly bliss is already present – and is also already experienced – in the grace of Christ and in the Church of Christ; and this means that heaven has already been thrown open here.[32]

Within this theological context the sanctus provides a fitting *conclusion to the whole eucharistic prayer*. This suggestion may seem to be letting Ratcliff's theory of the sanctus in again at the back door. It must be stressed, therefore, that there seems not the slightest historical evidence to support Ratcliff's view. As a termination of the eucharistic prayer, it appears first with Luther (though of course there is little in the way of eucharistic prayer), and more obviously in certain Presbyterian rites. In the context suggested here, it appears in some of the eucharistic prayers of the 1970 English Congregationalist liturgy; the anaphora used in the community at West Malling Abbey; and it concludes two of four eucharistic prayers in the Church of England Liturgical Commission's publication, *Patterns for Worship*, 1989, for proposed use in Family Services and Urban Priority congregations.[33] Its use as a conclusion is suggested not on historical grounds at all, but purely on logical theological and doxological grounds. As Stuart Gibbons, one of the authors of the Congregationalist prayers, argued:

The point that we can only participate in the worship of heaven because Christ died for us, seems to be given its proper emphasis when the sanctus follows the anamnesis or making present/effective to us the sacrifice of Christ.[34]

Used as the terminating doxology, the sanctus then forms the crescendo of praise and expresses the eschatological status of the people of God. The form could be the usual liturgical adaptation of Isaiah 6:3, or Revelation 4:8, or could even be a sanctus 'proper', reminiscent of the tropes. What is important, however, is that the sense of the prayer should dictate the use or non-use of the sanctus, and its position and musical considerations must come second.

As far as the benedictus is concerned, whether its Hosanna is to remain attached to the sanctus, or whether the benedictus itself is added to the sanctus or omitted, should depend on whether it is appropriate to the context.

Although it is quite possible, and in some cases perhaps desirable, to compile eucharistic prayers *without* the sanctus, there is every reason to expect that this ancient chant will continue to be utilised in some form in the eucharistic prayer – not because of tradition, but because it is appropriate. For, in Christian theology, the glory of God was revealed in Christ whose love and grace is revealed in the eucharistic feast. In Christ the space of heaven and the region of the earth are united. In the eucharist the worshipper enters heaven through Christ, and is represented by our true High Priest. Here time and eternity intersect and become one, and this world and the world to come elide. The words of the sanctus, whether said quietly, sung to a solemn but simple Gregorian chant, or to an elaborate polyphonic setting, can give the worshipper that glimpse of eternity which Isaiah experienced. Perhaps the last word belongs to Rudolph Otto who reminded the Church of the *mysterium tremendum et fascinosum* – something which is sometimes forgotten in contemporary liturgical formulation:

I have heard the *Sanctus Sanctus Sanctus* of the cardinals in St Peter's, the *Swiat Swiat Swiat* in the Kreml Cathedral, and the *Hagios Hagios Hagios* of the patriarch in Jerusalem. In whatever language they resound, these most sublime words that have come from human lips always grip one in the depths of the soul, with a mighty shudder, exciting and calling into play the mystery of the otherworldly latent therein.[35]

—— ✠ ——

Notes

Introduction: The enigma of the sanctus

1 In this study, *trisagion* is used in reference to the biblical text of Isaiah 6:3, together with 'thrice-holy'. It does not refer to the Christian liturgical Trisagion, 'Holy God, Holy Mighty, Holy Immortal' and its variants found in the Eastern eucharistic and other rites. The Jewish liturgical use of the *trisagion* is referred to as *qeduššah*; sanctus, unless the context shows otherwise, is used to refer to the anaphoral sanctus.

2 M. A. Smith, 'The Anaphora of Apostolic Tradition re-considered', *SP* 10 (1970), pp. 426–30.

3 L. Bouyer, *Eucharist*, trans. C. U. Quinn (Indiana 1968), pp. 115–19; W. Rordorf, 'Les Prières Eucharistiques de la Didaché', in *Eucharisties d'Orient et d'Occident*, I (Paris 1970), pp. 65–82. L. Finkelstein had drawn attention to this some years before: 'The Birkat Ha-mazon', *JQR* ns 19 (1928), pp. 211–62.

4 E. C. Ratcliff, 'The Original Form of the Anaphora of Addai and Mari: A Suggestion', *JTS* 30 (1928–9), pp. 23–32; G. Dix, *The Shape of the Liturgy* (London 1945), p. 181; B. Botte, 'L'Anaphore Chaldéene des Apôtres', *OCP* 15 (1949), pp. 259–76; 'Problèmes de l'Anaphore syrienne des Apôtres Addaï et Mari', *Or. Syr.* 10 (1965), pp. 86–106; Bouyer, *Eucharist*, pp. 146–8; L. Ligier, 'From the Last Supper to the Eucharist', in L. Sheppard (ed.), *The New Liturgy* (London 1970), pp. 113–50, 132.

5 See especially W. C. van Unnik, '1 Clement 34 and the Sanctus', *VC* 5 (1951), pp. 204–48.

6 G. J. Cuming, 'The Anaphora of St Mark: A Study in Development', *Mu* 95 (1982), pp. 115–29, 123.

7 G. Kretschmar, *Studien zur frühchristlichen Trinitätstheologie* (Tübingen 1956).

8 G. Dix, *The Shape*, p. 165.

9 'Primitive Consecration Prayers', *Theology* 37 (1938), pp. 261–83.

10 PG xiii. 221.

11 Kretschmar, *Studien*, pp. 180, 182.

12 B. Botte, 'L'Eucologe de Sérapion est-il authentique?', *OC* 48 (1964), pp. 50–7.

13 See chapter 5.

14 Dix, 'Primitive Consecration Prayers', p. 274.

15 *Ibid.*, p. 277.

16 A. A. Milne, *Winnie-The-Pooh* (London 1926), pp. 32ff. Pooh and Piglet followed tracks of their own making.

17 *The Shape*, pp. 165, 221, 225–7.

18 *JEH* 1 (1950), pp. 29–36 and 125–34. Reprinted in *Liturgical Studies* (London 1976), pp. 18–40.

19 *JEH* 1, p. 126.

20 Bryan D. Spinks, 'The Cleansed Leper's Thankoffering Before the Lord: Edward Craddock Ratcliff and the Pattern of the Early Anaphora', in Bryan D. Spinks (ed.), *The Sacrifice of Praise*, Bibliotheca Ephemerides Liturgicae Subsidia 19 (Rome 1981), pp. 161–78.

21 Ratcliff, *The Sanctus and the Pattern of the Early Anaphora*, p. 134.

22 In J. N. Birdsall and R. W. Thompson (eds.), *Biblical and Patristic Studies in Memory of Robert Pierce Casey* (Freiburg and New York 1963), pp. 235–49; *Liturgical Studies*, pp. 66–79.

23 *The Sacrifice of Praise*, p. 167.

24 A. H. Couratin, 'The Sanctus and the Pattern of the Early Anaphora: A note on the Roman Sanctus', *JEH* 2 (1951), pp. 19–23; G. A. Michell, 'Firmilian and Eucharistic Consecration', *JTS* ns 5 (1954), pp. 215–20; W. E. Pitt, 'The Origin of the Anaphora of St Basil', *JEH* 12 (1961), pp. 1–13.

25 Couratin, 'The Sanctus', p. 21. 'Endlessly saying, Holy, holy, holy Lord God of Sabaoth. Full are heaven and earth of your glory, throughout all the ages of ages. Amen.'

26 Michell, 'Firmilian', pp. 217–18.

27 R. J. Ledogar, *Acknowledgement: Praise Verbs in the Early Greek Anaphora* (Rome 1968). Generally it seems that the compilers of liturgies used a large amount of freedom in rendering words from one language to another.

28 Bryan D. Spinks, 'A Note on the Anaphora outlined in Narsai's Homily XXXII', *JTS* ns 31 (1980), pp. 82–93.

29 E. Dekkers, 'Van profetie tot canon', *TL* 25 (1946), pp. 8–25.

30 B. Capelle, 'Les liturgies "basiliennes" et S. Basile', in J. Doresse and E. Lanne, *Un témoin archaïque de la liturgie copte de S. Basile* (Louvain 1960); B. Bobrinskoy, 'Liturgie et ecclésiologie trinitaire de Saint Basile', *Verbum Caro* 23 (1969), pp. 1–32; J. R. K. Fenwick, 'An Investigation into the Common Origin of the Anaphoras of the Liturgies of St Basil and St James', Ph.D. Thesis, London University, 1985.

1 The Old Testament background and setting

1 H. Wheeler Robinson, 'The Council of Yahweh', *JTS* 45 (1944), pp. 151–7; *Inspiration and Revelation in the Old Testament* (Oxford 1946), pp. 166–70.

2 G. E. Wright, *The Old Testament Against its Environment* (London 1950), pp. 32–3.

3 *Ibid.*, pp. 31–2.

4 E. T. Mullen, *The Assembly of the Gods* (Chico 1980).

5 For the Ugaritic terms see Mullen, *The Assembly*, pp. 117ff.

6 F. M. Cross, 'The Council of Yahweh in Second Isaiah', *JNES* 12 (1953), pp. 274–7; 'Yahweh and the God of the Patriarchs', *HTR* 55 (1962), pp. 225–59; R. E. Brown, 'Pre-Christian Semitic Concept of Mystery', *CBQ* 20 (1958), pp. 417–43; J. A. Wilson, 'The Assembly of a Phoenician City', *JNES* 4 (1945), p. 245. Cf. also Patrick D. Miller, *The Divine Warrior in Early Israel* (Cambridge Mass. 1973).

7 F. J. Neuberg, 'An Unrecognised Meaning of Hebrew DÔR', *JNES* (1950),

pp. 215–17; P. Ackroyd, 'The Meaning of Hebrew *Dôr* Considered', *JSS* 13 (1968), pp. 5–8.

8 T. H. Gaster, *IDB* 1, p. 131.

9 W. G. Heidt, *Angelology of the Old Testament* (Minnesota 1949), pp. 7–14; Wright, *The Old Testament*, p. 33.

10 For the vocabulary regarding 'standing' in this context, see Mullen, p. 231.

11 T. H. Gaster, *IDB* 1, p. 129.

12 Ivan Engnell, *The Call of Isaiah* (Uppsala 1949); R. E. Clements, *Isaiah 1–39* (London 1980); Otto Kaiser, *Isaiah 1–12* (London 1983, 2nd edn).

13 G. B. Gray, *Isaiah 1–25* (Edinburgh 1912), pp. 102–3; Kaiser, *Isaiah 1–12*, following the observations of G. R. Driver, 'Isaiah 6:1 His train filled the temple', in H. Goedicke (ed.), *Near Eastern Studies in Honor of W. F. Albright* (Baltimore and London 1971) that the garments of gods and rulers did not have flowing trains, translates as 'the hem of his garment'.

14 Engnell, *The Call of Isaiah*.

15 J. Bright, *A History of Israel* (London 1960, 1st edn); Bernhard W. Anderson, *The Living World of the Old Testament* (London 1978, 3rd edn).

16 Kaiser, *Isaiah 1–12* (London 1972, 1st edn), p. 3, footnote b.

17 G. Fohrer suggested that it was simply a vision of the temple. Clements, *Isaiah 1–39*, p. 73.

18 Edwin C. Kingsbury, 'The Prophets and the Council of Yahweh', *JBL* 83 (1964), pp. 279–86.

19 Julian Morgenstern, 'The Gates of Righteousness', *HUCA* 6 (1929), pp. 1–37; S. Mowinckel, *The Psalms in Israel's Worship* (Oxford 1982), pp. 118–30.

20 Kaiser, *Isaiah 1–12*, 1st edn, pp. 74, 76; Bright, Isaiah 1, *Peake's Commentary on the Bible* (London 1962); Engnell, *The Call of Isaiah*.

21 Mowinckel, *The Psalms*; S. H. Hooke, *Myth, Ritual and Kingship* (New York and Oxford 1958); A. R. Johnson, *Sacral Kingship in Ancient Israel* (Cardiff 1967); J. H. Eaton, *Kingship and Psalms* (London 1976), *Festal Drama in Deutero-Isaiah* (London 1979); *Vision in Worship* (London 1981); Clements, *God and Temple* (Oxford 1965), pp. 69–70.

22 D. J. A. Clines, *IDB*, Supplementary Volume (Nashville 1976), pp. 625ff. See also H. J. Kraus, *Worship in Israel* (Oxford 1966); M. Noth, 'God, King, and Nation in the Old Testament', in *The Laws in the Pentateuch and Other Studies* (Edinburgh 1966).

23 Kaiser, *Isaiah 1–12*, 2nd edn, pp. 124–5.

24 Gray, *Isaiah 1–25*, pp. 105, 107–8.

25 Kaiser, *Isaiah 1–12*, 1st edn, p. 76.

26 F. H. W. Gesenius, *Lexicon Manuale Hebraicum et Chaldaicum* (Lipsiae 1885), p. 970.

27 So Kaiser, *Isaiah 1–12*, 1st edn, p. 76, note c; E. Jacob, *Theology of the Old Testament* (London 1958), p. 69; Engnell, *The Call of Isaiah*, p. 33.

28 Jacob, *Theology of the Old Testament*.

29 Kaiser, *Isaiah 1–12*, 1st edn, p. 76.

30 Karen R. Joines, 'Winged Serpents in Isaiah's Inaugural Vision', *JBL* 86 (1966), pp. 410–15.

31 *Ibid.*, p. 413.

32 *Ibid.*, pp. 413–14.

33 J. de Savignac, 'Les "Seraphim"', *VT* 22 (1972), pp. 320–5.

34 Kaiser, *Isaiah 1–12*, 2nd edn, p. 125.
35 1 Kings 6:24; Exodus 25:20.
36 Walter Zimmerli, *Ezekiel 1* (chapters 1–24) (Philadelphia 1979), p. 99 suggests in a similar manner to that which may have been used by the priests at the temple against worshippers who made their confession of sin.
37 De Savignac, 'Les "Seraphims"', p. 322. He also suggests a connection between the *Uraeus* and Anat (Antit, Beth Shan) and Anath, the consort of Yaho at Elephantine.
38 Kaiser, *Isaiah 1–12*, 1st edn, p. 76; Bright, Isaiah 1, p. 494; Clements, *God and Temple*, p. 74.
39 Engnell, *The Call of Isaiah*, p. 35.
40 *Ibid.*, p. 36.
41 Kaiser, *Isaiah 1–12*, 2nd edn, p. 126.
42 Engnell, *The Call of Isaiah*, p. 36.
43 N. Walker, 'The Origin of the "Thrice Holy"', *NTS* 5 (1958–9), pp. 132–3.
44 *Ibid.*, p. 133.
45 Gesenius and Kautzch, *Hebrew Grammer* (Oxford 1898), pp. 59–60, note 2.
46 B. M. Leiser, 'The Trisagion of Isaiah's Vision', *NTS* 6 (1959–60), pp. 261–3.
47 *Ibid.*, p. 263.
48 So apparently O. Keel; Kaiser, *Isaiah 1–12*, 2nd edn, p. 126, note 45.
49 G. Von Rad, *Old Testament Theology*, I (Edinburgh 1962), p. 19. Jacob, *Theology of the Old Testament*, p. 54, counts 279.
50 *Ibid.*, Patrick D. Miller, *The Divine Warrior in Early Israel*, (Cambridge Mass. 1973), pp. 152–3.
51 J. A. Emerton, 'New Light on Israelite Religion: The Implications of the Inscriptions from Kuntillet "Ajrud"', *ZAW* 94 (1982), pp. 2–20, 4.
52 *Ibid.*, pp. 3–9.
53 Miller, *The Divine Warrior*, p. 154; Jacob, *Theology of the Old Testament*, pp. 54–5; J. Gray, *1 and 2 Kings* (London 1964, 1st edn), p. 402.
54 Von Rad, *Old Testament Theology*, p. 18; Jacob, *Theology of the Old Testament*; Miller, *The Divine Warrior*, p. 155; F. M. Cross, 'Yahweh and the God of the Patriarchs', *HTR* 55 (1962), pp. 225–59, 256.
55 Miller, *The Divine Warrior*, p. 10.
56 *Ibid.*, p. 154. According to Miller, *yhwh* is a causative imperfect of 'to be'. He follows W. F. Albright, 'Review of L'épithète divine Jahve Ṣ°bā'ôt: Etude philologique, historique, et exégétique', *JBL* 67 (1948), pp. 377–81, Cross, 'Yahweh' and *Canaanite Myth and Hebrew Epic* (Cambridge Mass. 1973), and links *yhwh* with a longer name, *el du yahwe*, 'El who creates'. He suggests that *yahweh ṣ°bā'ôt* meant 'He who creates the divine armies'.
57 Von Rad, *Old Testament Theology*, I, p. 19.
58 Clements, *Isaiah 1–39*, p. 32.
59 Tryggve N. D. Mettinger, *The Dethronement of Sabaoth*, Studies in the Shem and Kabod Theologies (Lund 1982), pp. 13–15.
60 *Ibid.*, p. 15.
61 *Ibid.*, *passim*.
62 Cf. E. Tov, *The Septuagint Translation of Jeremiah and Baruch* (Missoula 1976), p. 31, note 20. Theodotion used *kurios tōn dunameōn*, and Aquila used . . . *stratiōn*. Symmachus used both terms.
63 Jacob, *Theology of the Old Testament*, pp. 79ff; Kittel, *TDNT* 2, pp. 238ff.
64 Zimmerli, *Ezekiel 1*, pp. 3, 75ff; E. Eichrodt, *Ezekiel* (London 1970), see the discussion of the translation, *passim*.

65 For example, Zimmerli, pp. 231ff; Eichrodt, pp. 115ff; John W. Wevers, *Ezekiel* (London 1969), pp. 73ff; J. Muilenburg, Ezekiel in *Peake's Commentary*, p. 574; D. M. G. Stalker, *Ezekiel* (London 1968), pp. 94–5.

66 Zimmerli, p. 120.

67 Eichrodt, p. 55.

68 *Ibid.*

69 Zimmerli, p. 128, but see also Bertholet's suggestion below.

70 Zimmerli, p. 129.

71 Zimmerli, p. 251.

72 Eichrodt, p. 116.

73 Menahem Haran, 'The Ark and the Cherubim: Their Symbolic Significance in Biblical Ritual', *Israel Exploration Journal* 9 (1959), pp. 30–8; 89–94; *Temples and Temple-Service in Ancient Israel* (London 1978), pp. 246–59.

74 Clements, *God and Temple*, p. 30.

75 Haran, *The Ark*, p. 34; Zimmerli, p. 128.

76 M. Metzger, *Königsthron und Gottesthron. Thronformer und Throndarstellungen in Ägypten und im Vorderen Orient im 3. und 2. Jahrtausend vor Christus und deren Bedeutung für das Verständnis über den Thron im Alten Testament* (Kevelaer 1985). I am grateful for a copy of the review of this book by Dr G. I. Davies, who drew my attention to it.

77 E. Dhorme, 'Le nom des chérubins', *Recueil Edouard Dhorme* (Paris 1951), pp. 671–83.

78 A. S. Kapelrud, 'The Gates of Hell and the Guardian Angels of Paradise', *Journal of the American Oriental Society* 70 (1950), pp. 151–6.

79 W. F. Albright, 'What were the Cherubim?' *The Biblical Archaeologist* 1 (1938), pp. 1–3; Metzger, *Königsthron*.

80 R. de Vaux, 'Les chérubins et l'arche d'alliance. Les sphinx gardiens et les trônes divins dans l'ancien Orient', *Mélanges de l'Université Saint Joseph* (Beirut 1961), pp. 93–124.

81 R. H. Pfeiffer, 'Cherubim', *JBL* 41 (1922), pp. 249–50. See also O. Keel, *The Symbolism of the Biblical World* (London 1978), pp. 167ff.

82 Mettinger, *The Dethronement*, p. 34. According to Metzger, *Königsthron*, *yōšēb hakkᵉrûbîm* was originally a title of Baal, with no connection with the ark.

83 Haran, *The Ark*, p. 38.

84 A. Bertholet and K. Galling, *Hesekiel* HAT 13 (Tübingen 1936).

85 Mettinger, *The Dethronement*, p. 104.

86 *Ibid.*, p. 105.

87 *Ibid.*, p. 115.

88 E. W. Heaton, *Daniel* (London 1956), pp. 178–80; J. A. Emerton, 'The Origin of the Son of Man Imagery', *JTS* NS 11 (1958), pp. 225–42. N. Porteous, *Daniel* (London 1965), pp. 95ff; Mullen, *The Assembly of the Gods*, pp. 159–61.

89 For a discussion on the cultic significance of 'standing before', see Mullen, p. 231, and *THAT* 2, cols. 330–1.

2 The worship of heaven and the qeduššah in Judaism

1 Millar Burrows, *More Light on the Dead Sea Scrolls* (New York 1958) pp. 278ff.

2 B. Gartner, *The Temple and the Community in Qumran and the New Testament* (Cambridge 1965), pp. 10–11.

3 Texts: G. Vermes, *The Dead Sea Scrolls in English* (London 1975, 2nd edn).

4 Cf. Malachi 2:7 'For the lips of a priest should guard knowledge, and man should seek instruction from his mouth, for he is the messenger [angel] of the Lord of hosts' (RSV).

5 J. Strugnell, 'The Angelic Liturgy at Qumran – 4Q Šîrôt Ôlat Haššabbat', in *Congress Volume, Oxford 1959 VT* Supplement 7 (Leiden 1960), pp. 318–45.

6 Moshe Weinfeld, 'Traces of Kedushat Yozer and Pesukey De-Zimra in the Qumran Literature and in Ben-Sira', *Tarbiz* 45(1975–6), pp. 13–26.

7 ET in J. A. Sanders, *The Dead Sea Psalms Scroll* (New York 1967), p. 131.

8 Even these categories are not necessarily particularly helpful. See, Samuel Sandmel, *The First Christian Century in Judaism and Christianity: Certainties and Uncertainties* (London 1969), chapter 2. Martin Hengel, *Judaism and Hellenism: Studies in Their Encounter in Palestine During the Early Hellenistic Period*, 2 vols., (Philadelphia 1974); J. Daniélou, *The Theology of Jewish Christianity* (London 1964); *Gospel Message and Hellenistic Culture* (London 1973); *The Origins of Latin Christianity* (London 1977).

9 James H. Charlesworth, *The Pseudepigrapha and Modern Research. With a Supplement*, (Chico 1981), p. 21.

10 *Ibid.*, p. 125; Daniélou, *The Theology of Jewish Christianity*, pp. 12–14.

11 *Ibid.*, p. 21.

12 C. C. Rowland, 'The Visions of God in Apocalyptic Literature', *JSJ* 10(1979), pp. 137–54, 138.

13 Mary Dean-Otting, *Heavenly Journeys. A Study of the Motif in Hellenistic Jewish Literature* (Frankfurt am Main, Bern, New York 1984), pp. 5–6.

14 Ithamar Gruenwald, *Apocalyptic and Merkavah Mysticism* (Leiden 1980), p. 31.

15 R. A. Kraft, *The Testament of Job* (Missoula, Montana 1974), pp. 82–3.

16 Unless otherwise noted, quotations are from Charlesworth (ed.), *The Old Testament Pseudepigrapha*, 2 vols. (London 1983 and 1986). *OTP* 1, pp. 682–3.

17 *OTP* 1, pp. 989ff.

18 Charlesworth, *The Pseudepigrapha*, p. 70.

19 Michael E. Stone, *The Testament of Abraham. The Greek Recensions* (Montana 1972).

20 *Ibid.*, p. 7.

21 G. H. Box, *The Testament of Abraham* (London 1927), pp. 57–75; *OTP* 1, p. 904.

22 So the translation in Box.

23 See below on the forms of the Christian sanctus in the eucharistic prayer.

24 R. H. Charles, *APOT* 2, p. 154.

25 *Ibid.*

26 *OTP* 2, p. 295, note 43c.

27 Charlesworth, *The Pseudepigrapha*, pp. 130–1.

28 *OTP*, p. 404.

29 M. R. James, *The Lost Apocrypha of the Old Testament* (London 1920) pp. 97–8.

30 J. T. Milik, 'Problèmes de la littérature hénochique à la lumière des fragments araméens de Qumrân', *HTR* 64 (1971), pp. 333–78; *The Books of Enoch: Aramaic Fragments of Qumran Cave 4* (Oxford 1976).

31 Joseph A. Fitzmyer, 'Implications of the New Enoch Literature from Qumran', *TS* 38(1977), pp. 332–45; M. A. Knibb, 'The Date of Parables of Enoch: A Critical Review', *NTS* 25(1978–9), pp. 345–59; Christopher L. Mearns, 'The Parables of Enoch – Origin and Date', *ET* 89(1978), pp. 118–19; 'Dating the Similitudes of Enoch', *NTS* 25 (1978–9), pp. 360–9. See also H. Odeberg, *3 Enoch*, revised by J. Greenfield (New York 1973), p. xvii.

32 Charlesworth, 'The SNTS Pseudepigrapha Seminars at Tübingen and Paris on the Books of Enoch', *NTS* 25(1979), pp. 315–23.

33 David W. Suter, *Tradition and Composition in the Parables of Enoch*, SBL Dissertation Series 47 (Missoula 1979), p. 23.

34 Rowland, 'The Visions of God'; Gruenwald, *Apocalyptic and Merkavah Mysticism*.

35 Suter, *Tradition and Composition*, p. 32.

36 Daniélou, *The Theology of Jewish Christianity*, p. 16; J. Greenfield in Odeberg, *3 Enoch*; Charlesworth, p. 104.

37 G. Scholem, *Jewish Gnosticism, Merkabah Mysticism, and Talmudic Tradition* (New York 1965, 2nd edn); Gruenwald, *Apocalyptic and Merkavah Mysticism*; P. Schafer, *Synopse zur Hekhalot Literatur* (Tübingen 1982). Cf. also Rowland, *The Open Heaven* (London 1982).

38 Gruenwald, p. vii.

39 Lawrence A. Hoffman, *The Canonization of the Synagogue Service* (Indiana 1979), p. 60.

40 *Ibid.*, p. 61.

41 Dean-Otting, *Heavenly Journeys*, p. 25, points out an important difference between the ascents in the Pseudepigrapha and those in later developed Hekhalot literature; the ascents of the Pseudepigrapha take the one ascending by surprise, while the *Merkāvāh* ascent in the latter literature comes about as a result of theurgic practices.

42 Samson H. Levey, 'The Targum of Ezekiel', *HUCA* 46(1975), pp. 139–58. Levey, p. 143, suggests it reflects the situation in Palestine immediately following the catastrophe of 70 CE. See, also, Levey, *The Targum of Ezekiel* (Edinburgh 1987).

43 J. Neusner, *A History of the Jews in Babylonia*, I, *The Parthian Period* (Leiden 1969); *A Life of Rabban Yohanan Ben Zakkai ca.1–80 CE* (Leiden 1962), pp. 97–8; E. E. Urbach, 'The Traditions about the Merkabah Mysticism in the Tannaitic Period', in *Studies in Mysticism and Religion presented to Gershom G. Scholem on his Seventieth Birthday* (Jerusalem 1967), pp. 7ff; Rowland, *The Open Heaven*, pp. 228ff.

44 Leon Cornet, 'Sanctus et Merkaba', *QL* 59(1978) pp. 23–37; Bryan D. Spinks, 'The Jewish Liturgical Sources for the Sanctus', *HJ* 21(1980), pp. 168–79.

45 Scholem, *Jewish Gnosticism*, pp. 20–1.

46 I am indebted to Professor Morton Smith for kindly allowing me to use his translation of *Hekhalot Rabbati*.

47 Scholem, *Jewish Gnosticism*, p. 106.

48 For a discussion on *berakot*, see J. Heinemann, *Prayer in the Talmud* (Berlin and New York 1977), pp. 77ff.

49 Scholem, *Jewish Gnosticism*, p. 110; cf. pp. 116–17.

50 For a full discussion, see I. Elbogen, *Der jüdische Gottesdienst in seiner geschichtlichen Entwicklung* (Frankfurt 1931); A. Z. Idelsohn, *Jewish Liturgy and its Development* (New York 1960).

51 Conveniently summarised by Eric Werner, 'The Doxology in Synagogue and Church', *HUCA* 19(1945–6), reprinted in Jakob J. Petuchowski (ed.), *Contributions to the Scientific Study of Jewish Liturgy* (New York 1970), pp. 318–70.

52 Shabbath 115b.

53 Hoffman, *The Canonization*, pp. 1–9; David Hedegard, *Seder R. Amran Gaon*, Part I (Lund 1951); Tryggive Kronholm, *Seder R. Amran Gaon*, Part II, 'The Order of Sabbath Prayer' (Lund 1974).

54 Heinemann, *Prayer in the Talmud*, p. 30.

55 *Ibid.*, pp. 7–8.

56 Richard S. Sarason, 'On the Use of Method in the Modern Study of Jewish Liturgy', in W. S. Green (ed.), *Approaches to Ancient Judaism: Theory and Practice* (Missoula 1978), pp. 97–172.

57 Heinemann, *Prayer in the Talmud*. For Spanier, see Petuchowski, *Contributions*, p. xi.

58 P. Bloch, 'Die *Yordei Merkavah*, die Mystiker der Gaonzeit, und ihr Einfluss auf die Liturgie', *MGWJ* 37 (1893), pp. 22ff.

59 Heinemann, *Prayer in the Talmud*, p. 24.

60 Hedegard, *Seder*, pp. 46–9 for the full text.

61 Kronholm, *Seder*, pp. 74–80.

62 Heinemann, *Prayer in the Talmud*, pp. 126, 129, 230.

63 C. W. Dugmore, *The Influence of the Synagogue upon the Divine Office* (Oxford 1944; London 1964).

64 L. Finkelstein, 'La Kedouscha et les Bénédictions du Schema', *REJ* 93(1932), pp. 1–26.

65 L. Zunz, *Die gottesdienstlichen Vorträge der Juden* (Frankfurt 1892), p. 382.

66 J. Mann, 'Geniza Fragments of the Palestinian Order of Service', *HUCA* 2 (1925), pp. 269–338, reprinted in Petuchowski, *Contributions*, p. 400.

67 Hedegard, *Seder*, p. 49, notes.

68 E. Fleischer, 'The Diffusion of the Qedushot of the Amidah and the Yozer in the Palestinian Ritual', *Tarbiz* 38(1968–9), pp. 255–84.

69 Kronholm, *Seder*, for the texts.

70 *Ibid.*, p. 76, note 8.

71 S. Schechter, in the *David Kaufman Memorial Volume*, ed. M. Brann and F. Rosenthal (Breslau 1900), Hebrew Section, p. 52.

72 Finkelstein, 'The Development of the Amidah', *JQR*, ns 16 (1925–6), pp. 1–43, 127–70; reprinted in Petuchowski, *Contributions*, pp. 109, 119ff.

73 K. Kohler, 'The Origins and Composition of the Eighteen Benedictions with a Translation of the Corresponding Essene Prayers in the Apostolic Constitutions', *HUCA* 1 (1924), pp. 387–425, reprinted in Petuchowski, *Contributions*, pp. 62–3.

74 Hedegard, *Seder*, p. 49.

75 Fleischer, 'The Diffusion', pp. 261–6.

76 L. J. Liebreich, 'An Analysis of U-Ba Le Ziyyon', *HUCA* 21(1948) pp. 176–209.

77 Werner, 'The Doxology'.

3 Continuity and influence in early Christian documents

1 D. Flusser, 'Sanktus und Gloria' in O. Betz *et al.* (ed.), *Abraham unser Vater*, Festschrift Otto Michael (Leiden 1963), pp. 129–52.

2 B. Lindars, *The Gospel of John*, New Century Bible (London 1972), p. 439; R. E. Brown, *The Gospel According to John* (i–xii), Anchor Bible (New York 1966), p. 487.

3 R. H. Charles, *The Revelation of St John*, I (Edinburgh 1920), p. 109.

4 O. A. Piper, 'The Apocalypse of John and the Liturgy of the Ancient Church', *Church History* 20 (1950), pp. 10–22; Lucetta Mowry, 'Revelation 4–5 and Early Christian Liturgical Usage', *JBL* 71 (1952), pp. 75–84; Ralph P. Martin, *Worship in the Early Church* (Edinburgh 1965), p. 45; Ferdinand Hahn, *The Worship of the Early Church* (Philadelphia 1973), p. 101. It is evident that liturgical allusions are to

be found throughout Revelation. J. Comblin, 'La liturgie de la Nouvelle Jérusalem', *ETL* 29 (1953), pp. 5–40.

5 P. Prigent, *Apocalypse et liturgie* (Neuchâtel 1948), p. 68.

6 Mowry, 'Revelation 4–5', p. 84.

7 A. Cabaniss, 'A Note on the Liturgy of the Apocalypse', *Interpretation* 7 (1953), pp. 78–86.

8 Charles, *The Revelation of St John*, *passim*; Gruenwald, *Apocalyptic and Merkavah Mysticism*; Rowland, *The Open Heaven*.

9 Gruenwald, p. 62.

10 Rowland, 'The Visions of God in Apocalyptic Literature', p. 145.

11 Charles, pp. 129ff.; Gruenwald, pp. 64–6.

12 Charles lists other differences, pp. 119–20.

13 *Ibid.*, p. 127.

14 G. B. Caird, *The Revelation of St John the Divine* (London 1966), p. 16.

15 Martin McNamara, *The New Testament and the Palestinian Targum to the Pentateuch* (Rome 1966), p. 100.

16 *Ibid.*, pp. 102–5.

17 *Ibid.*, pp. 106–9.

18 *Ibid.*, pp. 110–12.

19 *Ibid.*, p. 112.

20 W. C. van Unnik, '1 Clement 34 and the Sanctus', *VC* 5 (1951), pp. 204–48.

21 Georges Blond, 'Clement of Rome', in *The Eucharist of the Early Christians*, ed. W. Rordorf (New York 1978), pp. 24–47; Allen Bouley, *From Freedom to Formula* (Washington 1981).

22 J. B. Lightfoot, *The Apostolic Fathers*, I (London 1907); van Unnik, '1 Clement 34', pp. 207–8.

23 Van Unnik, p. 245.

24 Donald A. Hagner, *The Use of the Old and New Testaments in Clement of Rome* (Leiden 1973).

25 *Ibid.*, pp. 62–3.

26 R. M. Grant and H. H. Graham, *First and Second Clement* (New York 1965).

27 R. Murray, 'Hellenistic–Jewish Rhetoric in Aphrahat', *Symposium Syriacum 1980*, *OCA* 221 (Rome 1983), pp. 79–85.

28 R. Murray, *Symbols of Church and Kingdom* (London 1975), pp. 4ff.

29 Text in Herbert Musurillo, *The Acts of the Christian Martyrs* (Oxford 1955), pp. 293ff.

30 J. Daniélou, *The Origins of Latin Christianity* (London 1977), pp. 59ff.; Rowland, *The Open Heaven*, pp. 396–402.

31 A. Gerhards, 'Le Phénomène du Sanctus addressé au Christ' in *Le Christ dans la Liturgie*, (Rome 1981), pp. 65–83, 70.

32 Charlesworth, *The Pseudepigrapha*, pp. 125–130; text, *OTP* 2, pp. 156–76.

33 Charlesworth, *The Pseudepigrapha*, p. 126.

34 Gruenwald, *Apocalyptic and Merkavah Mysticism*, p. 57.

35 Ratcliff, 'The Sanctus and the Pattern of the Early Anaphora', p. 131.

36 ET in E. Evans, *Tertullian's Tract on Prayer* (London 1953).

37 G. J. Cuming, 'The Early Eucharistic Liturgies in Recent Research' in Bryan D. Spinks (ed.), *The Sacrifice of Praise* (Rome 1981), pp. 65–9; D. Hagedorn, *Der Hiobkommentar des Arianers Julian* (Berlin 1973).

38 M. Metzger, 'The Didascalia and the Constitutiones Apostolorum', in W. Rordorf (ed.), *The Eucharist of the Early Christians* (New York 1978), pp. 194–219.

39 Kohler, 'The Origins and Composition'.
40 W. Bousset, 'Eine jüdische Gebetssammlung in siebenten Buch der apostolischen Konstitutionen', *Nachrichten von der Königlichen Gesellschaft der Wissenschaften zu Göttingen* (Berlin 1916).
41 E. R. Goodenough, *By Light, Light* (New Haven 1935).
42 L. Bouyer, *Eucharist* (Indiana 1968), pp. 119–35, 252.
43 D. A. Fiensy, 'A Redactional Examination of Prayers Alleged to be Jewish in the Constitutiones Apostolorum', Ph.D. Thesis, Duke University 1980, published as *Prayers Alleged to be Jewish* (Chico 1985).
44 *Ibid.*, pp. 215–28.
45 *Ibid.*, p. 177.
46 *Ibid.*, p. 178.
47 Eric Werner, 'The Doxology in Synagogue and Church', *HUCA* 19 (1945–6), pp. 276–328.

4 The sanctus in the East Syrian and Syro-Byzantine eucharistic prayers

1 The name *sharar* is derived from the first word of the first pro-anaphoral prayer, 'Confirming'.
2 Bryan D. Spinks, *Addai and Mari – The Anaphora of the Apostles: A Text for Students*, Grove Liturgical Study 24 (Bramcote 1981), p. 3; see p. 33 for full bibliography.
3 E. C. Ratcliff, 'The Original form of the Anaphora of Addai and Mari: a suggestion', *JTS* 30 (1928–9), p. 29.
4 Spinks, 'The Cleansed Leper's Thankoffering'; Pitt, 'The Origin of the Liturgy of St Basil'.
5 Dix, 'Primitive Consecration Prayers', p. 271; *The Shape of the Liturgy*, p. 180; B. Botte, 'L'Anaphore Chaldéene des Apôtres', p. 264; 'Problèmes de l'Anaphore', p. 93; Bouyer, *Eucharist*, p. 154.
6 W. F. Macomber, 'The Oldest known text of the Anaphora of the Apostles Addai and Mari', *OCP* 32 (1966), pp. 335–71.
7 *Ibid.*, pp. 347–8.
8 J. M. Sánchez Caro, 'La anafora de Addai y Mari y la anafora meronita Sarrar: intento de reconstruccion de la fuente primitiva comun', *OCP* 43 (1977), pp. 41–69; H. A. J. Wegman, 'Pleidoor voor een Tekst de Anaphora van de Apostelen Addai en Mari', *Bijdragen* 40 (1979), pp., 15–43; Jean Magne, 'L'anaphore nestorienne dite d'Addée et Mari et l'anaphore maronite dite de Pierre III' *OCP* 53 (1987), pp. 107–59.
9 Texts: Hippolytus in *PEER*; Ethiopic Apostles, *LEW*.
10 Tongue, Name – Philippians 2:11; Worthy of praise – Revelation 4:11, 5:12; Name – Psalms 7:17, 9:2, 29:2, Philippians 2:9–10, Romans 15:9; Glory – Psalm 19:1; Luke 2:14, Revelation 4:11; created the world – Genesis 1:1, Revelation 4:11.
11 See Spinks, 'Eucharistic Offering in the East Syrian Anaphoras', *OCP* 50 (1984), pp. 347–71.
12 J. Vellian, 'The Anaphoral Structure of Addai and Mari Compared to the Berakoth Preceding the Shema in the Synagogue Morning Service', *Mu* 85 (1972), pp. 201–23.
13 T. J. Talley, 'The Eucharistic Prayer: Tradition and Development', in Kenneth W. Stevenson (ed.), *Liturgy Reshaped* (London 1982), pp. 48–64.
14 Spinks, *Addai and Mari*, pp. 24–5.

15 Cf. Pliny, Epist. 10, 96, 7: 'Carmen Christo quasi deo dicere'.

16 It is important not to judge such texts by later trinitarian theology.

17 Macomber, 'The Ancient Form of the Anaphora of the Apostles', in *East of Byzantium. Syria and Armenia in the Formative Period*, (Washington 1982), pp. 109–23.

18 Massey H. Shepherd, 'Eusebius and the Liturgy of Saint James', in *Yearbook of Liturgical Studies* 4 (1963), pp. 109–23.

19 W. J. Swaans, 'A propos des "Catéchèses Mystagogiques" attribuées à S. Cyrille de Jérusalem', *Mu* 55 (1942), pp. 1–43; F. L. Cross, *St Cyril of Jerusalem's Lectures on the Christian Sacraments* (London 1966), pp. xxxvi–xxxix.

20 E. Yarnold, 'The Authorship of the Mystagogic Catecheses attributed to Cyril of Jerusalem', *HJ* 19 (1978), pp. 143–61.

21 G. J. Cuming, 'Egyptian Elements in the Jerusalem Liturgy', *JTS* ns 25 (1974), pp. 117–24.

22 'The Jerusalem Liturgy of the Catecheses Mystagogicae: Syrian or Egyptian?'

23 E. C. Cutrone, 'Cyril's Mystagogical Catecheses and the Evolution of the Jerusalem Anaphora', *OCP* 44 (1978), pp. 52–64; Spinks, 'The Consecratory Epiklesis in the Anaphora of St James', *SL* 11 (1976), pp. 19–38.

24 J. R. K. Fenwick, 'An Investigation into the Common Origin of the Anaphora of the Liturgies of St Basil and St James', Ph.D. Thesis, London University, 1985; also, *Fourth Century Anaphoral Construction Techniques*, Grove Liturgical Study 45 (Bramcote 1986).

25 G. Kretschmar, 'Die frühe Geschichte der Jerusalemer Liturgie', in *Jahrbuch für Liturgik und Hymnologie* 2 (1956), pp. 22–46.

26 Dix, *The Shape*, p. 197; Cuming, 'Egyptian Elements'.

27 The texts used here are Vat.gr.2282 in PE, and BM.293 Add. 14.499 in *AS*.

28 Cf. O. Heiming, *AS* II.2, p. 125; A. Tarby, *La Prière Eucharistique de L'Eglise de Jérusalem* (Paris, 1972), p. 33.

29 R. H. Connolly and H. W. Codrington, *Two Commentaries on the Jacobite Liturgy* (London 1913).

30 For example, Pitt, 'The Origin of the Liturgy of St Basil'; H. Lietzmann, *Mass and Lord's Supper: A Study in the History of the Liturgy* (Leiden 1979), p. 116; Dix, *The Shape*, p. 204; Michell, 'Firmillian and Eucharistic Consecration', p. 218.

31 Fenwick, 'An Investigation', and *Fourth Century Anaphoral Construction Techniques* (Grove Liturgical Study 45, Bramcote 1986).

32 'An Investigation', pp. 137–8.

33 PE, pp. 244–6.

34 Ledogar, *Acknowledgement: Praise-Verbs in the Early Greek Anaphoras*, pp. 22ff.

35 *Eucharist*, pp. 270–1.

36 'An Investigation', p. 132.

37 In Connolly and Codrington, *Two Commentaries*, pp. 48–50.

38 M. Richard, *Asterii Sophistae Commentariorum in Psalmos quae supersunt accedunt aliquot homiliae anonymae* (Oslo 1956).

39 H.-J. Auf der Maur, *Die Osterhomilien des Asterios Sophistes als Quelle für die Geschichte der Osterfeier* (Trier 1967).

40 *Ibid.*, pp. 79–80; PG 46.421c; 61.527.

41 Auf der Maur, p. 84; Richard, *Asterii*, p. 115.

42 Auf der Maur, p. 85; Richard 233.

43 Auf der Maur, 187ff.

44 H. Engberding, *Das eucharistische Hochgebet der Basileiosliturgie: Textgeschicht-lichte Untersuchungen und kritische Ausgabe* (Münster 1931).

45 J. Doresse and E. Lanne, *Un témoin archaïque de la liturgie copte de S. Basile* (Louvain 1960).

46 B. Bobrinskoy, 'Liturgie et Ecclésiologie Trinitaire de Saint Basile', in *Eucharisties d'Orient et d'Occident* II (Paris 1970), pp. 197–240.

47 Fenwick, 'An Investigation', and *Fourth Century Anaphoral Construction Techniques*.

48 A. Houssiau, 'The Alexandrine Anaphora of St Basil', in *The New Liturgy*, pp. 228–43, 230.

49 Fenwick, 'An Investigation', p. 115.

50 See below.

51 On this point, see Kenneth W. Stevenson, *Eucharist and Offering*, (New York 1986).

52 Fenwick, 'An Investigation', pp. 130, 138.

53 B. Capelle, in Doresse and Lanne, *Un témoin archaïque*, p. 56.

54 A. Baumstark, 'Die Chrysostomosliturgie und die syrische Liturgie des Nestorios', in *Chrysostomika* (Rome 1908), pp. 846–8; Bouyer, *Eucharist*, p. 341.

55 For a brief description see S. De Beaurecueil, 'La prière eucharistique dans la liturgie égyptienne de Saint Grégoire', *Les Cahiers Coptes* 7–8 (1954), pp. 6–10.

56 J. Jungmann, *The Place of Christ in Liturgical Prayer*, 2nd edn (London 1965), p. 227.

57 E. Hammerschmidt, *Die koptische Gregoriosanaphora* (Berlin 1957), p. 179.

58 J. M. Sánchez Caro, *Eucharistia E Historia de la Salvacion* (Madrid 1983), pp. 310ff.

59 A. Gerhards, *Die griechische Gregoriosanaphora* (Münster 1984).

60 *Ibid.*, p. 52.

61 *Ibid.*, pp. 114–21.

62 *Ibid.*, p. 171; cf Hammerschmidt, *Die koptische*, p. 177.

63 See chapter 7.

64 Gerhards, *Die griechische*, p. 60.

65 *Ibid.*, pp. 176–210.

66 Shepherd, 'The Formation and Influence of the Antiochene Liturgy', in *Dumbarton Oaks Papers* 15 (1961), pp. 25–44.

67 Robert M. Grant, 'The Early Antiochene Anaphora', *ATR* 30 (1946), pp. 91–4.

68 LEW, pp. 470–81.

69 F. Van de Paverd, *Zur Geschichte der Messliturgie in Antiocheia und Konstantinopel gegen Ende des vierten Jahrhunderts*, OCA 187, (Rome 1970).

70 *Ibid.*, pp. 266–87.

71 A. Mingana (ed.), Woodbrook Studies vol. VI (Cambridge 1933), p. 100.

72 *Ibid.*, p. 101.

73 Macomber, 'An Anaphoral Prayer composed by Theodore of Mopsuestia', *Parole de l'orient* 6–7 (1975–6) (Mélanges offerts au R. P. Francois Graffin sj), pp. 341–7.

74 *Ibid.*

75 E. Mazza, 'La Struttura dell'anafora nelle Catechesi di Teodoro di Mopsuestia', *EL* 102 (1988), pp. 147–83.

76 Georg Wagner, *Der Ursprung der Chrysostomusliturgie*. Liturgie wissenschaftlicher Quellen und Forschungen (Münster 1973), p. 59.

77 Cuming, 'Pseudonymity and Authenticity, with special reference to the Liturgy of St John Chrysostom', *SP* 15 (Berlin 1984), pp. 532–8, 535.

78 *Ibid.*, p. 536.
79 R. F. Taft, 'The Authenticity of the Chrysostom Anaphora Revisited. Determining the Authorship of Liturgical Texts by Computer', *OCP* 56 (1990) 5–51. See also Fenwick, *The Missing Oblation: The Contents of the Early Antiochene Anaphora* (Bramcote 1989).
80 H. Engberding, 'Die syrische Anaphora der zwölf Apostel und ihre Paralleltexte', *OC* 12 (1937), pp. 213–47.
81 A. Raes, 'L'Authenticité de la Liturgie Byzantine de S. Jean Chrysostome', *OCP* 24 (1958), pp. 5–16; G. Khouri-Sarkis, 'L'Origine syrienne de l'anaphore byzantine de saint Jean Chrysostome', *Or-Syr* 7 (1962), pp. 3–68.
82 In a private communication.
83 Wagner, *Der Ursprung*.
84 PE, p. 224.
85 Wagner, *Der Ursprung*, p. 76.
86 Macomber, 'A Theory on the Origins of the Syrian, Maronite and Chaldean Rites', *OCP* 39 (1973), pp. 235–42.
87 Cuming, Review article in *Eastern Churches Review* 7 (1975), pp. 95–7.
88 My opinion is supported by Professor Brock, private communication.
89 Chapter 3.
90 Bouley, *From Freedom to Formula*, p. 232.
91 Marcel Metzger, 'The Didascalia and the Constitutiones Apostolorum', in *The Eucharist of the Early Christians*, ed. W. Rordorf (New York 1978), p. 208.
92 W. H. Bates, 'The Composition of the Anaphora of Apostolic Constitutions VIII', *SP* 13 (Berlin 1975), pp. 343–55, 345.
93 Chapter 3.
94 E. Beck, *Des Heiligen Ephraem des Syrers Hymnen de Nativitaté (Epiphania)*, CSCO 187, Syri 83 (Louvain 1959).
95 *Première homélie sur la Pâque de Seigneur*, ed. G. Bickell, *ZDMG* 27 (1878), pp. 569–75.
96 *PG* 86.1386c.
97 Spinks, 'Eucharistic Offering in the East Syrian Anaphoras', *OCP* 50 (1984), pp. 347–71, 355–6.
98 R. H. Connolly, *The Liturgical Homilies of Narsai*, Texts and Studies 8 (Cambridge 1909), pp. 12–13.
99 Spinks, 'A Note on the Anaphora outlined in Narsai's Homily XXXII', *JTS* ns 31 (1980), pp. 82–93.
100 Spinks, 'Eucharistic Offering in the East Syrian Anaphoras', p. 356, and notes 30 and 31.
101 Wagner, *Der Ursprung*, pp. 51–63.
102 Spinks, 'The East Syrian Anaphora of Theodore: Reflections upon its sources and theology', *EL* 103 (1989), pp. 441–55.
103 Spinks, 'Eucharistic Offering in the East Syrian Anaphoras'.
104 Urmiah edition, 1890–3.
105 Spinks, 'Eucharistic Offering', p. 365.

5 The sanctus in the Egyptian and Western eucharistic prayers

1 Texts in *PE* and *PEER*. For the Barcelona text, see S. Jameras, 'L'Original grec del fragment copte de Lovaina Num. 27 en l'Anafora di Barcelona', in *Miscellania*

Liturgica Catalana III (1984), pp. 13–25. I am grateful to Geoffrey Cuming for drawing my attention to the text, and providing me with a transcript from the published article.

2 R.-G. Coquin, 'L'anaphore alexandrine de saint Marc', *Mu* 82(1969), pp. 307–56.

3 E. Kilmartin, 'Sacrificium Laudis: Content and Function of Early Eucharistic Prayers', *TS* 35(1974), pp. 268–87.

4 W. H. Bates, 'Thanksgiving and Intercession in the Liturgy of St Mark', in Bryan D. Spinks (ed.), *The Sacrifice of Praise*, pp. 107–19; H. A. J. Wegman, 'Un anaphore incomplète?', in R. Van Den Broek and M. J. Vermaseren (eds.), *Studies in Gnostic and Hellenistic Religions* (Leiden 1981), pp. 432–50; 'Généalogie hypothétique de la prière eucharistique', *QL* 61(1980), pp. 263–78; G. J. Cuming, 'The anaphora of St Mark: A Study in Development', *Mu* 95(1982), pp. 115–29 (read as a master theme at the Oxford Patristic Conference, 1979).

5 Spinks, 'A Complete Anaphora? A Note on Strasbourg Gr.254', *HJ* 25(1984), pp. 51–9. It is possible that the papyrus preserves the first of two or even more prayer units.

6 See T. J. Talley, 'The Eucharistic Prayer: Tradition and Development', in Kenneth W. Stevenson (ed.), *Liturgy Reshaped*; E. Mazza, 'Una Anafora Incompleta? Il Papiro Strasbourg Gr.254', *EL* 99 (1985) pp. 425–36.

7 Cuming, *The Liturgy of St Mark*, OCA 234 (Rome 1990).

8 My thanks to Professor Martin Plumley for kindly expressing his opinion on the matter in a private communication.

9 My thanks to Dr Anthony Gelston of Durham University for his guidance on this question.

10 W. Rudolph, *Micha-Nahum-Habakuk-Zephanja Kommentar zum Alten Testament* (Gütersloh 1975), pp. 242–3.

11 Dix, 'Primitive Consecration Prayer'. See Introduction.

12 Clement, *Stromateis* 7:12.

13 Athanasius, *In illus, omnia mihi tradita sunt*, PG 25.220.

14 Cyril of Alexandria, *Commentariis in Habacuc Prophetum*, PG 71.900.

15 I am grateful to Professor Plumley for drawing my attention to this fragment, which he dates ninth century CE. The work itself is more difficult to date.

16 Cuming, 'The Anaphora of St Mark', p. 119; Bates, 'Thanksgiving and Intercession', pp. 115–16.

17 A. Baumstark, 'Zwei nicht erkannte Bruchstücke frühchristlich-griechischer Liturgie Ägyptens', *JLW* 1(1921), pp. 132–4.

18 B. Botte, 'L'Eucologe de Sérapion est-il Authentique?', *OC* 48(1964), pp. 50–7; Cuming, 'Thmuis Revisited: another look at the prayers of Bishop Sarapion', *TS* 41(1980), pp. 568–75.

19 *PE*, 124.

20 *PE*, 120.

21 *PEER* 81; S. Janeras, 'L'Original grec'.

22 For the latter, see *The Egyptian Church Order*.

23 L. Bouyer, *Eucharist* (Indiana, 1968), p. 218.

24 E. E. Urbach, *The Sages – Their Concepts and Beliefs* (Jerusalem 1975), p. 98. Cf. p. 124.

25 Irenaeus. *Contra Haer.* ii.35.3; Origen, *Philocalia* 17; *Contra Celsus* Bk 1, chapters 24 and 25.

26 Scholem, *Jewish Gnosticism*, pp. 67–8.

27 Ed. J. M. Robinson (Leiden 1977), p. 165.

28 *Ibid.*, p. 294.
29 Hans Dieter Betz (ed.), *The Greek Magical Papyri in Translation*, I (Chicago 1985), p. 62.
30 Cited in E. R. Goodenough, *Jewish Symbols in the Greco-Roman Period*, II (New York 1953), p. 172; A. Kropp, *Demotische und Koptische Texte*, 3 vols. (Brussels 1930–1), II, p. 50.
31 *OTP* 2, pp. 715ff.
32 J. A. Jungmann, *The Mass of the Roman Rite*, 2 vols. (New York 1955); T. Klauser, *A Short History of the Western Liturgy* (Oxford 1979, 2nd edn); Botte, *Le Canon de la messe romaine* (Louvain 1935); Ralph A. Keifer, 'The Unity of the Roman Canon: An Examination of its unique structure', *SL* 11(1976), pp. 39–58.
33 *De Sacramentis*, Book 4.
34 E. C. Ratcliff and A. H. Couratin, 'The Early Roman Canon Missae', *JEH* 20(1969), pp. 211–24; E. C. Ratcliff, 'The Institution Narrative of the Roman Canon Missae: Its Beginnings and Early Background', *Studia Patristica* 2 (1957), pp. 64–82; C. Mohrmann, *Liturgical Latin. Its Origin and Character* (Washington 1957); 'Les origines de la latinité chrétienne à Rome', *VC* 3(1949), pp. 47–106, 163–83.
35 See below on the problem of the translation of 'the heaven of heavens and virtues', p. 97.
36 These are tabulated in P. Cagin, *Te Deum ou Illatio* (Oxford and Rome 1906).
37 L. Chavoutier, 'Un Libellus Pseudo-Ambrosien sur le Saint-Esprit'.
38 B. Botte and C. Mohrmann, *L'Ordinaire de la messe* (Paris and Louvain 1953), p. 75.
39 E. C. Ratcliff, 'Christian Worship and Liturgy' in K. E. Kirk (ed.), *The Study of Theology* (London 1939), p. 443; G. G. Willis, *Essays in Early Roman Liturgy* (London 1964), p. 124.
40 *PE*, p. 422; *PEER*, p. 116.
41 L. Duchesne (ed.), *Liber Pontificalis*, 3 vols. (Paris 1955–7), I, p. 128.
42 K. Gamber, *Missa Romensis* (Regensburg 1970), p. 65.
43 Chavoutier, 'Un Libellus', p. 149.
44 *Ibid.*, pp. 180–91.
45 Unpublished paper, 'Sanctus', p. 47.
46 P.-M. Gy, 'Le Sanctus Romain et les Anaphores Orientales', in *Mélanges Liturgiques offerts au R. P. Dom Bernard Botte* (Louvain 1972), pp. 167–74.
47 A. P. Lang, *Leo der Grosse und die Texte des Altgelasianums* (Steyle 1957); 'Leo der Grosse und die Dreifaltigkeitspräfation', *SE* 9 (1957), pp. 116–62.
48 Gy, 'Le Sanctus Romain', pp. 169–70.
49 *Ibid.*, p. 171.
50 B. Capelle, 'Problèmes textuels de la préface romaine. II.Caeli caelorumque virtutes', *RSR* 40(1951–2), pp. 145–50.
51 M.-F. Lacan, 'Caeli caelorumque virtutes', *RSR* 51(1963), pp. 240–6.
52 Gy, 'Le Sanctus Romain', p. 172.
53 Jean Magne, 'Carmina Christo I. Le "Sanctus" de la Messe Latine', *EL* 100 (1986), pp. 3–27, 12–15.
54 Gy, 'Le Sanctus Romain', pp. 173–4.
55 See above in relation to the Syro-Byzantine and later East Syrian rites.
56 *De Sacramentis*.
57 Cagin, *Te Deum*, pp. 481ff.

58 A. A. King, *Liturgies of the Primatial Sees* (London 1957), pp. 428–9.

59 A. Paredi, *I Prefazi ambrosiani* (Milan 1937).

60 Dix, *The Shape*, p. 541.

61 See the article by Gy, and Chavoutier's arguments.

62 E. Bishop, 'Spanish Symptoms', in *Liturgica Historica* (Oxford 1918), pp. 165–202; G. Mercati, 'More Spanish Symptoms', in *ibid.*, pp. 203–10; Bouley, *From Freedom to Formula*, pp. 169–80. Cf. W. C. Bishop, *The Mozarabic and Ambrosian Rites* (London 1924).

63 C. Coebergh, 'Sacramentaire léonien et liturgie mozarabe', in *Miscellanea Liturgica in honorem Cuniberti Mohlberg*, II (Rome 1949), pp. 295–304.

64 A. Allgeier, 'Das afrikanische Element im altspanischen Psalter', *Spanische Forschungen* 2 (1930), pp. 196–228; J. Pinell, 'De liturgiis occidentalibus' (manuscript 2 vols., Rome 1967), I, p. 69.

65 See the discussion in Bouley, *From Freedom to Formula*.

66 M. Ferotin, *Le Liber Mozarabicus Sacramentorum* (Paris 1912), p. xiv.

67 King, *Liturgies*, p. 480.

68 Ferotin, *Le Liber Mozarabicus*, p. xv.

69 Ferotin, *Le Liber Ordinum* (Paris 1904).

70 M. Simonetti (ed.), *Pseudo-Athanasii de Trinitate libri X-XII* (Bologna 1956).

71 Ferotin, *Le Liber Mozarabicus*, col.341; Bishop, 'The Genius of the Roman Rite', in *Liturgica Historica*, p. 5.

72 Bishop, 'Spanish Symptoms', pp. 15, 19.

73 Magne, 'Carmina Christo I', pp. 11–12.

74 See King, *Liturgies*, p. 603.

75 See chapter 6.

76 Cagin, *Te Deum ou Illatio*.

77 E. Kahler, *Studien zum Te Deum* (Göttingen 1956).

78 P. Le Brun, *Explication littérale, historique et dogmatique des prières et des cérémonies de la messe*, 4 vols. (Paris 1716–26), II, p. 233; J. M. Neale and G. H. Forbes, *Ancient Liturgies of the Gallican Church* (Burntisland 1855), p. v; Duchesne, *Christian Worship* (London 1904), pp. 90–5; Bouyer, *Eucharist*, pp. 305–18.

79 E. Griffe, 'Aux origines de la liturgie gallicane' in *Bulletin de Littérature Ecclésiastique* 1 (1955), pp. 17–43; John A. Frendo, *The 'Post Secreta' of the 'Missale Gothicum' and the Eucharistic Theology of the Gallican Anaphora* (Malta 1977).

80 Bouley, *From Freedom to Formula*, pp. 181ff.

81 Both cited by Chavoutier, 'Un Libellus', pp. 165–6.

82 Bouley *From Freedom to Formula*, p. 187. For the text, see L. C. Mohlberg, *Missale Gallicanum vetus* (Rome 1958), pp. 74–91.

6 The possible origins of the sanctus in the eucharistic prayer

1 W. O. E. Oesterley, *The Jewish Background of the Christian Liturgy* (Oxford 1925); F. Gavin, *The Jewish Antecedents of the Christian Sacraments* (London 1928); Dix, *The Shape of the Liturgy*; J.-P. Audet, 'Literary Forms and Contents of a Normal Eucharistia in the First Century', *TU* 18 (1959), pp. 643–62.

2 Dix, *The Shape*, pp. 52ff., 215ff.

3 T. J. Talley, 'From Berakah to Eucharistia: A Reopening Question', *Worship* 50 (1976), pp. 115–37, 120–1.

4 *PEER*, p. 10.

5 Dr Ithamar Gruenwald informs me that several of the Jewish Hekhalot texts refer to special meals which the mystic preparing for his special experience had to prepare himself, but unfortunately they did not preserve the *berakot* which would have accompanied them. In view of the general importance of *qeduššah* in this tendency, it is tempting to speculate that it found a place in these meal prayers.

6 *Eucharist*, p. 102.

7 Louis Ligier, 'From the Last Supper to the Eucharist'; 'The Origins of the Eucharistic Prayer: from the Last Supper to the Eucharist', *SL* 9 (1973), pp. 176–85; 'Anaphores orientales et prières juives', *Proche-Orient Chrétien* 13 (1963), pp. 3–20.

8 'From the Last Supper', p. 129.

9 'The Origins', p. 168.

10 *Ibid.*, p. 182.

11 Talley, *Worship*, p. 119.

12 'The Eucharistic Prayer of the Ancient Church According to Recent Research: Results and Reflections', *SL* 9, pp. 140–2.

13 *Ibid.*, pp. 148–9.

14 *Worship* 50, p. 124.

15 *Ibid.*, pp. 129–30.

16 *Ibid.*, p. 131.

17 *Ibid.*, p. 135.

18 'The Eucharistic Prayer: Directions for Development', *Worship* 51 (1977), pp. 316–25, 317–18; 'The Eucharistic Prayer: Tradition and Development', pp. 53, 58.

19 'The Eucharistic Prayer: Tradition and Development', p. 55; 'The Literary Structure of the Eucharistic Prayer', *Worship* 58 (1984), pp. 404–20, 415.

20 *Worship* 58, p. 415.

21 'Généalogie hypothétique de la prière eucharistique', p. 263, note 2.

22 *Ibid.*, p. 275.

23 *Ibid.*, p. 272.

24 For Giraudo, see Talley, *Worship* 58.

25 Sánchez Caro, *Eucharistia*, pp. 51, 126, 129.

26 Paul F. Bradshaw, 'The Search for the Origins of Christian Liturgy: some Methodological Reflections', *Gratias Agamus*, *SL* 17 (Jubilee Volume, 1987), pp. 26–34, 31.

27 Ligier, 'The Origins', p. 178. My italics.

28 *Ibid.*, p. 179.

29 *Ibid.*

30 'Four Very Early Anaphoras', *Worship* 58 (1984), pp. 168–72.

31 See above, chapter 4.

32 'Four Very Early Anaphoras'.

33 Cuming, 'The Anaphora of St Mark: A Study in Development'.

34 Fenwick, 'An Investigation', and *Fourth-Century Anaphoral*.

35 J. Neusner, *A History of the Jews in Babylonia, I. The Parthian Period* (Leiden 1969, 2nd edn), p. 161.

36 Bouley, *From Freedom to Formula*, pp. 79–80.

37 Heinemann, *Prayer in the Talmud, passim.*

38 *Ibid.*, p. 191.

39 *Ibid.*, p. 189.

40 Charlesworth, 'Jewish Hymns, Odes, and Prayers', in R. A. Kraft and G. W. E. Nickelsburg (eds.), *Early Judaism and its Modern Interpreters* (Atlanta, Georgia 1986); 'A Prolegomenon to a New Study of the Jewish Background of the Hymns and Prayers in the New Testament', *JJS* 33 (1982), pp. 265–85.

41 J. D. G. Dunn, *Unity and Diversity in the New Testament* (London 1981, 2nd edn); G. Theissen, *Sociology of Early Palestinian Christianity* (Philadelphia 1978); *The Social Setting of Pauline Christianity* (Edinburgh 1982).

42 R. P. C. Hanson, 'The Liberty of the Bishop to Improvise Prayer in the Eucharist', *VC* 15 (1961), pp. 173–6.

43 Fenwick, 'An Investigation', and *Fourth-Century Anaphoral*. See also, Spinks, 'Beware the Liturgical Horse! An English Interjection on Anaphoral Evolution', *Worship* 59 (1985), pp. 211–19. At the 1987 Oxford Patristic Conference, G. J. Cuming read a paper entitled 'The Shape of the Anaphora' and concluded that some early anaphoras owe nothing to the BHM, and that the Bible and the Psalms have exerted an influence on the shape of some eucharistic prayers.

44 C. P. Price, 'Jewish Morning Prayers and Early Christian Anaphoras', *ATR* 43 (1961), pp. 153–68.

45 *Ibid.*, p. 155.

46 *Ibid.*, p. 162.

47 *Ibid.*, p. 168.

48 Vellian, 'The Anaphoral Structure'.

49 Spinks, 'The Original Form of the Anaphora of the Apostles: A Suggestion in the Light of Maronite Sharar'.

50 See chapters 3 and 4.

51 R. Murray, *Symbols of Church and Kingdom. A Study in Early Syriac Tradition* (Cambridge 1975).

52 Neusner, *A History of the Jews in Babylonia*, I, p. 170.

53 Though Rev 4:8 seems to have been ignored in favour of Is 6:3.

54 *PEER*, p. 53: to bless[you] ... [night] and day ... [you who made] heaven[and] all that is in [it, the earth and what is on earth,] seas and rivers and [all that is] in [them].

55 Had Strasbourg Papyrus, or the tradition it represented, influenced Egyptian Basil?

56 You are the only true Lord; you made the heaven and the heaven of heavens, and all their order, the earth, and all things that are in it, the seas, and all things in them; And you give life to everything, and the hosts of heaven worship you.

57 Bouley, *From Freedom to Formula*, pp. 106, 108.

58 Raymond E. Brown, *The Community of the Beloved Disciple* (London 1979), pp. 43–8. Cf. p. 91: 'What the Johannine Christians considered to be a tradition that had come down from Jesus seems to have been accepted by many other Christians as an embraceable variant of the tradition that they had from Jesus.'

59 'Discourses Against Judaising Christians', in Paul W. Hawkins, *The Fathers of the Church* (Washington 1979). Discourse 1.

60 *The Heavenly Hierarchy*, chap 7, sect. 4.

61 See chapter 5.

62 See below.

63 The Semitic form is plural, and may be rendered by the English singular or plural.

64 See W. E. Scudamore, *Notitia Eucharistica* (London 1876), p. 533; Bouyer, *Eucharist*, p. 352.

65 J. M. Harden, *The Anaphoras of the Ethiopic Liturgy* (London 1928), pp. 50ff.

66 E. Hammerschmidt, *Studies in the Ethiopic Anaphoras* (Berlin 1961), pp. 106–9.

67 *OC* 48 (1969), pp. 121–4.
68 M. Daoud, *The Liturgy of the Ethiopian Church* (Addis Ababa 1954), p. 59.
69 W. E. Crum, *Coptic Ostraca* (London 1902), p. 6, No. 4.
70 Werner, 'The Doxology in Synagogue and Church', in *Contributions*, p. 337.
71 Magne, 'Carmina Christo I', p. 19, suggested that the Egyptian sanctus was originally addressed to Christ, and the benedictus, also addressed to Christ, was originally recited after the words in St Mark: 'with theirs, receive also our sanctification, saying ... ', and that it has subsequently fallen out. This is quite preposterous.
72 Macomber, 'The Oldest Known Text', p. 363, note 9.

7 Developments in East and West to the Reformation

1 Alphonse Raes, *Anaphorae Syriacae*, I, Fasc. 1 (Rome 1939), pp. xxxix–xlii.
2 A. Vööbus, 'Discovery of the Anaphora by Johannan of Qartamin', *EL* 90 (1976), pp. 197–200.
3 E. Renaudot, *Liturgiarum Orientalium Collectio*, II (reprint, Farnborough 1970); see also note 1.
4 Michael Hayek, *Liturgiarum Maronite. Histoire et textes eucharistiques* (Paris 1964).
5 H. Fuchs, *Die Anaphora des monophysitischen Patriarchen Johannan I* (Münster, Westfalen, 1926), pp. xxxii, xliii.
6 *Ibid.*, p. xliv.
7 *Ibid.*, p. lii.
8 *Ibid.*, p. lxi.
9 *Ibid.*, p. lxvii.
10 *Ibid.*, p. lxxi.
11 *Ibid.*, pp. xliiiff.
12 Stevenson, *Eucharist and Offering*.
13 John Fenwick, 'Significance of Similarities in the Anaphoral Intercession Sequence in the Coptic Anaphora of St Basil and other Ancient Liturgies', in *SP*, forthcoming (communication read to the Oxford Patristic Conference, 1983).
14 The idea that man is the 'stuff' of the universe become conscious is commonplace in modern scientific textbooks. See chapter 11.
15 *On Divine Names*, chap. 4, sect. 7.
16 *Oration* 28:31, 38:9.
17 *On the Celestial Hierarchy*, 15:2.
18 M. Ormian, *The Church of Armenia* (London 1955), p. 3.
19 *Ibid.*, p. 8.
20 *Ibid.*, p. 8.
21 V. K. Sarkissian, *A Brief Introduction to Armenian Christian Literature* (London 1960), p. 14, note 7.
22 *Ibid.*; A. Atiya, *A History of Eastern Christianity* (London 1968), p. 317; G. Winkler, 'The Political Influence of the Holy See on Armenia and its Liturgy (XI – XIV centuries)', in Vellian (ed.), *The Romanization Tendency* (Kottayam 1975), pp. 110–25.
23 S. Salaville, *Introduction to the Study of Eastern Liturgies*, (London 1958), p. 16; King, *The Rites of Eastern Christendom*, II, (Rome 1948), p. 588.
24 A. Renoux, 'L'Anaphore Arménienne De Saint Gregoire L'Illuminateur', *Eucharisties d'Orient et d'Occident*, II (Paris 1970), pp. 83–108, 84.

25 Texts: Y. Catergian and P. J. Dashian, *Die Liturgies bei den Armeniern. Fünfzehn Texte und Untersuchungen* (Wien 1897).
26 Renoux, 'L'Anaphore'.
27 I am indebted to Professor Sir Harold Bailey of Cambridge who has kindly provided a literal translation of Gregory the Illuminator, Isaac, Gregory of Nazianzen and Cyril of Alexandria from Catergian-Dashian. For Athanasius I have used the ET in Brightman.
28 J. M. Harden, *The Anaphoras of the Ethiopic Liturgy* (London 1928), p. 1; Rufinus, *Hist.Eccl.* I, p. ix.
29 Hammerschmidt, *Studies in the Ethiopic Anaphoras*. Three of these – Our Lady by Gregory and its alternative, and shorter Cyril – have not been published.
30 Hammerschmidt, *Studies*, p. 44.
31 *Ibid.*, p. 45.
32 *Ibid.*, pp. 46–7.
33 *Ibid.*, pp. 47ff.
34 *Ibid.*, p. 82.
35 *Ibid.*, p. 49.
36 *Ibid.*
37 *Ibid.*, p. 80.
38 *Ibid.*, pp. 165–6.
39 G. Haile, 'Religious Controversies and the Growth of Ethiopic Literature in the Fourteenth and Fifteenth Centuries', *OC* 4th series 65 (1981), pp. 102–36.
40 *Ibid.*, p. 116.
41 *Ibid.*, p. 129.
42 Bouley, *From Freedom to Formula*, p. 228.
43 Harden, *The Anaphoras*, p. 63; Hammerschmidt, *Studies*, p. 74; Mercer, *Journal of the Society of Oriental Research* 1 (1917), p. 27; M. Daoud and H. E. Blatta Marsie Hazen, *The Liturgy of the Ethiopian Church*, (Addis Ababa, 1959), p. 102.
44 Harden, *The Anaphoras*, p. 114.
45 Hammerschmidt, *Studies*, p. 94.
46 Daoud–Hazen, *The Liturgy*, p. 296.
47 Harden, *The Anaphoras*, p. 16.
48 S. Euringer, *OC* 3.1. (1926–7), pp. 98–142; Daoud–Hazen, *The Liturgy*, p. 237.
49 Harden, *The Anaphoras*, p. 16; Hammerschmidt, *Studies*, pp. 56, 86; Daoud–Hazen, *The Liturgy*, p. 155.
50 See chapter 4.
51 Daoud–Hazen, *The Liturgy*, p. 237 (adapted).
52 Harden, *The Anaphoras*, p. 88.
53 Hammerschmidt, *Studies*, p. 56.
54 Harden, *The Anaphoras*, p. 110.
55 *Ibid.*, p. 97 (adapted).
56 *Ibid.*, p. 34; Daoud–Hazen, *The Liturgy*, p. 72, omit cherubim and seraphim, and simply qualify 'honourable creatures[beasts]' with 'each with six wings'.
57 Hammerschmidt, *Studies*, p. 90.
58 *Ibid.*
59 *PE* pp. 509–10.
60 L. C. Mohlberg, 'Das Fragment de Bruyne', *Missale Gallicanum vetus*, (Rome 1958), p. 97.
61 Bouley, *From Freedom to Formula*, pp. 177ff.

62 B. MacCarthy, *On the Stowe Missal*, *TRIA* 27 (1886), p. 207.
63 In W. K. Lowther Clarke (ed.), *Liturgy and Worship* (London 1932), p. 338.
64 For example, the Sarum and York missals.
65 Kenneth Levy, 'The Byzantine Sanctus and its Modal Tradition in East and West', in *Annales Musicologiques* 6 (1958–63), pp. 7–67.
66 Paul Evans, 'Some Reflections on the Origin of the Trope', in *Journal of the American Musicological Society* 14 (1961), pp. 119–30; Richard L. Crocker, 'The Troping Hypothesis', in *Musical Quarterly* 52 (1966), pp. 183–203.
67 E. Costa, *Tropes et séquences dans le cadre de la vie liturgique au moyen-âge*, Bibliotheca Ephemerides Liturgicae Subsidia 17 (Rome 1979), pp. 7–10.
68 Evans, 'Some Reflections', p. 121.
69 For these terms used by Jacques Chailley, see Guilio Cattin, *Music of the Middle Ages*, I (London 1984), pp. 110ff.
70 Costa, *Tropes et séquences*, pp. 6ff; W. H. Frere, *The Winchester Troper* (London 1894), p. viii.
71 *Analecta Hymnica Medii aeri*, ed. C. Blume and H. M. Bannister, vol. 47 (Leipzig 1905). Cited as AH.
72 Dr Gundilla Inversen of Stockholm and Dr Charles Atkinson of Ohio University are working in this area at the present.
73 AH, p. 320.
74 AH, p. 321.
75 Costa, *Tropes et séquences*, p. 53.
76 *Ibid*.
77 Cattin, *Music of the Middle Ages*, p. 113.
78 In Denmark and, apparently, Sweden. See chapter 8.

8 The Reformation rites

1 Rosamund McKitterick, *The Frankish Church and the Carolingian Reforms, 789–895* (London 1977), p. 142.
2 For the texts, see the American edition of *Luther's Works* (Philadelphia and St Louis 1955–) (*LW*), 36.
3 Text in E. Sehling, *Die Evangelischen Kirchenordnungen des XVI. Jahrhunderts*, 5 vols. (Leipzig 1902–13), I, pp. 697ff.
4 'Heyliger, heyliger, heyliger herre Gott Sabaoth; voll seind hymmel und erd deiner herlichkeit. Osanna in den hochsten, gebenedet sen, der da kompt in dem namen des herren. Gluck und heyl in den hochsten.' Text in J. Smend *Die Evangelischen Deutschen Messen bis zu Luthers Deutscher Messe* (Göttingen 1898; Nieuwkoop 1967), p. 75.
5 German text in Sehling, *Die Evangelischen*, I, pp. 497ff.
6 Heilger, heilger, heilger herre gott Sabaoth. Himmel und erde seint erfullet mit deinem preise. Ozianna in dem hochsten. Desegnet sei, der do kumpt in namen des hereen. Ozianna in den hochsten.' Smend, *Die Evangelischen*, p. 104. The German is given in order to compare with Kantz's rendering, note 4.
7 Texts *LW*, 53. See Spinks, *Luther's Liturgical Criteria and His Reform of the Canon of the Mass*, Grove Liturgical Study 30 (Bramcote 1982).
8 *LW*, 40, p. 141.
9 See below on Calvin and Farel.
10 *LW*, 53.

11 Y. Brilioth, *Eucharistic Faith and Practice, Evangelical and Catholic* (London 1930), p. 117.

12 *LW*, 16, p. 70.

13 I. Pahl (ed.), *Coena Domini I. Die Abendmahlsliturgie der Reformationskirchen im 16./17. Jahrhundert, Spicilegium Friburgense 29* (Freiburg 1983), p. 55.

14 A. E. Richter, *Die Evangelischen Kirchenordnungen*, 2 vols. (Weimar 1846), I, p. 106.

15 Sehling, *Die Evangelischen*, VII/I (Tübingen 1955ff), p. 224.

16 *Ibid.*, p. 75.

17 Sehling, *Die Evangelischen*, I, p. 271.

18 *Ibid.*

19 See below.

20 Text in Cuming, *A History of Anglican Liturgy* (London 1969), pp. 353–4.

21 *Ibid.*

22 E. E. Yelverton, *The Mass in Sweden 1531–1914*, HBS 57 (London 1920).

23 *Coena Domini I*, p. 69.

24 Richter, *Die Evangelischen*, I, p. 30; II, p. 67.

25 *Ibid.*, I, p. 207.

26 *Ibid.*, II, p. 28.

27 Sehling, *Die Evangelischen*, VII/I, pp. 379–81.

28 Richter, *Die Evangelischen*, I, p. 261.

29 *Ibid.*, p. 224.

30 Yelverton, *The Mass in Sweden*, p. 38.

31 *Ibid.*

32 *Ibid.*, p. 71; Brilioth, *Eucharistic Faith*, pp. 254ff.; Frank C. Senn, 'Liturgia Svecanae Ecclesiae: An Attempt at Eucharistic Restoration during the Swedish Reformation', *SL* 14(1980–1), pp. 20–36.

33 Sigtrygg Serenius, *Liturgia Svecanae ecclesiae catholicae et orthodoxae conformis: En liturgiehistorisk undersökning med särskild hänsyn till struktur och förlagor* (Åbo, 1966).

34 Oscar Quensel, *Bidrag till Svenska liturgiens historia*, II (Uppsala 1893), p. 122; Yelverton, *The Mass in Sweden*, pp. 73–4.

35 *Ibid.*, p. 71.

36 Brilioth, *Eucharistic Faith*, p. 260.

37 Richter, *Die Evangelischen*, I, p. 224.

38 *Coena Domini I*, p. 258.

39 Richter, *Die Evangelischen*, I, pp. 307ff.

40 *Ibid.*, p. 164.

41 *Coena Domini I*, p. 256.

42 *Danske Messeboger Fra Reformationstiden* (København 1959) for the Danish texts referred to in this section.

43 Sigurd Kroon, *Tibi Laus. Studier kring den Svenska Psalmen Nr. 199* (Lund 1953); Henrik Glahn, *Melodistadier Til Den Lutherske Salmesangs Historie Fra 1524 til Ca 1600* (København 1954) I, Plate 4. I am grateful to Henrik Glahn, former Karlsberg Fellow at Churchill College, Cambridge 1984, for guidance on the Danish material.

44 *Coena Domini I*, p. 66.

45 *Danske Messeboger*, p. 82.

46 Glahn, *Melodistadier*, p. 114.

47 *Danske Messeboger*, p. 82.

48 *Coena Domini I*, p. 174.

49 H. O. Old, *The Patristic Roots of Reformed Worship* (Zurich 1975).

50 F. Hubert, *Die Strassburger liturgischen Ordnungen im Zeitalter der Reformation* (Göttingen 1900); W. D. Maxwell, *An Outline of Christian Worship* (London 1936); René Bornert, *La Réforme Protestante du Culte à Strasbourg au XVIᵉ siècle. 1523–1598* (Leiden 1981).

51 Maxwell, *An Outline*, p. 90.

52 *Ibid.*, p. 94, note 1.

53 Text, Hubert *Die Strassburger*, pp. 64–5. I am indebted to my colleague, Dr Andrea Cervi, for the translation of this text, and that of 1525.

54 Hubert, *Die Strassburger*, p. 85.

55 Bornert, *La Réforme*, p. 543.

56 Smend, *Die Evangelischen*, pp. 51ff. The text of the sanctus given by Oecolampadius was: 'Heylig, heylig, heylig yst Got der almechtig. Hymel und erden ist vol deyner glory. Ach Got, hylf uns yn deyner hoch. Geben edeyet sey der, der da kumpt yn dem namen des herren Gyb gluck und heyl.'

57 *ET* in Bard Thompson, *Liturgies of the Western Church* (New York and Cleveland 1971), pp. 211–15.

58 *Coena Domini I*, pp. 185–8; ET, *PEER* pp. 130ff.

59 Smend, *Die Evangelischen*, pp. 196ff; ET in Thompson, *Liturgies*, pp. 151ff.

60 Leo Weisz, 'Heinrich Bullingers Agenda', in *Zwingliana* 10(1954–8), pp. 1–23.

61 See Old, *The Patristic Roots, passim.*

62 Spinks, *From the Lord and 'The Best Reformed Churches'. A Study of the Eucharistic Liturgy in the English Puritan and Separatist Traditions 1550–1633* (Rome 1985), pp. 46ff.

63 ET in Thompson, *Liturgies*, pp. 205–7, 219–23; Spinks, *From the Lord*, pp. 83–4.

64 Spinks, *From the Lord*, p. 63.

65 For these eucharistic liturgies, see Spinks, *From the Lord*.

66 See above, pp. 151–2.

67 I am indebted to Canon Dr Donald Gray for pointing out this and the ambiguity in the 1662 text. The 1549 rubric caused Bucer to remark that since clerks are often impatient and sing it before the priest has finished praying, a stricter rubric was necessary. E. C. Whitaker, *Martin Bucer and the Book of Common Prayer*, Alcuin Club Collection 55 (Great Wakering 1974), pp. 48–50.

68 W. H. Frere, *Some Principles of Liturgical Reform* (London 1911), p. 187–8; Cf. Maxwell, *An Outline of Christian Worship*, p. 149.

69 C. O. Buchanan, *What Did Cranmer Think He was Doing?*, Grove Liturgical Study 7 (Bramcote 1976), p. 27.

9 Protestant and Anglican liturgies 1662–1960

1 Edward T. Horn, *Outlines of Liturgics* (Philadelphia 1890), pp. 47–8.

2 L. D. Reed, *The Lutheran Liturgy* (Philadelphia 1960, 2nd edn), pp. 152–3.

3 W. Löhe, *Agende für christliche Gemeinden des lutherischen Bekenntsnisses* (Nordlingen 1844), pp. 26–30, 29.

4 Text in Yelverton, *The Mass in Sweden*.

5 *Ibid.*

6 Reed, *The Lutheran Liturgy*, p. 758.

7 H. Holloway, *The Norwegian Rite* (London 1934).

8 *Ibid.*

9 I am indebted to Professor H. Glahn and Revd Dr K. Stevenson for information and texts of the Danish rite.

10 Reed, *The Lutheran Liturgy, passim.* For the various churches and amalgamations, see Arthur C. Piepkorn, *Profiles in Belief. The Religious Bodies of the United States and Canada,* II (New York 1978).

11 I am grateful to Revd R. Feuerhahn of the Lutheran Seminary, St Louis, for kindly supplying me with the text. See also Reed, *The Lutheran Liturgy,* p. 168.

12 Horn, 'The Lutheran Sources of the Common Service', *Lutheran Quarterly* 21 (1891), pp. 239–68. For other Lutheran groups, see Reed, *The Lutheran Liturgy, passim.*

13 *Ibid.,* pp. 126, 211, 756.

14 Text in Bruno Bürki, *Cène du Seigneur – Eucharistie de l'Eglise,* 2 vols. (Fribourg 1985), vol. A.

15 *Ibid.,* vol. B, pp. 57ff.

16 *Ibid.,* vol. A, p. 18.

17 *Ibid.,* vol. B, p. 81.

18 *Ibid.,* vol. B, p. 82.

19 *Ibid.,* vol. B, p. 75.

20 See my review of Bürki in *JTS* NS 37 (1986), pp. 693–7; see also Spinks, *From the Lord.*

21 So H. Daniel (ed.), *Codex Liturgicus* (Leipzig 1853), III.

22 H. Hageman, *Pulpit and Table* (Richmond 1962), p. 61.

23 *Ibid.,* pp. 70ff.

24 Text in Bürki, *Cène du Seigneur.*

25 For a full discussion, see Bürki, vol. B, pp. 108ff.

26 Text in Bürki.

27 Bürki, vol. B, *passim.*

28 *Ibid.,* vol. A, p. 114.

29 *Ibid.,* vol. B, pp. 139ff.

30 See Bürki, vol. A.

31 For a full survey, see Stevenson, 'The Catholic Apostolic Eucharist', Ph.D. Thesis, University of Southampton, 1975; Stevenson, 'The Catholic Apostolic Church – its History and its Eucharist', *SL* 13 (1979), pp. 21–43. I am grateful to Kenneth Stevenson for his assistance with the background to this rite.

32 Stevenson, 'The Catholic Apostolic Church', p. 27.

33 *Ibid.*

34 *Ibid.,* p. 30.

35 *Ibid.,* pp. 35–9.

36 J. Cardale, *Readings upon the Liturgy and other Divine Offices of the Church,* 2 vols. (London 1874–5).

37 J. M. Maxwell, *Worship and Reformed Theology. The Liturgical Lessons of Mercersburg* (Pittsburgh 1976).

38 Scott F. Brenner, 'Philip Schaff the Liturgist', *Christendom* 11 (1946), pp. 443–56, 450.

39 See Maxwell, *Worship,* for details.

40 George W. Sprott, *The Worship and Offices of the Church of Scotland* (Edinburgh and London 1882), p. 118.

41 I am indebted to Professor J. M. Barkley who not only supplied me with the texts of these rites, but also offered helpful advice on them.

42 Private letter, 9 July 1985.
43 For details of these rites, see J. M. Barkley, *The Worship of the Reformed Church* (London 1966).
44 For full details, see Spinks, *Freedom or Order?* (Allison Park 1984).
45 Spinks, 'The Liturgical Revival amongst Nineteenth-Century English Congregationalists', *SL* 15 (1982–3), pp. 178–87.
46 Spinks, 'A Prescursor to Dr W. E. Orchard's Divine Service?', *Journal of United Reformed Church History Society* 2:3 (1979), pp. 73–5.
47 Spinks, *Freedom or Order?*, pp. 123ff.
48 For this title, see *ibid.*, pp. 165ff.
49 Text in W. Jardine Grisbrooke, *Anglican Liturgies of the Seventeenth and Eighteenth Centuries* (London 1958).
50 *Ibid.*
51 Itself probably a Puritan eucharistic prayer. Cuming, 'Two Fragments of a Lost Liturgy?', in *Studies in Church History*, 3 (Leiden 1966), pp. 247–53.
52 *Ibid.*, p. 51.
53 *Ibid.*, p. 240.
54 *Ibid.*, p. 263.
55 *Ibid.*, pp. 266–7.
56 *Ibid.*, pp. 273ff.
57 Marion J. Hatchett, *The Making of the First American Book of Common Prayer* (New York 1982).
58 *Ibid.*, pp. 26–7.
59 Texts in B. Wigan, *The Liturgy in English* (Oxford 1962).
60 W. H. Frere, *Some Principles of Liturgical Reform* (London 1911), p. 188.
61 *Ibid.*, p. 191.
62 Quoted in Cuming, *The Godly Order* (London 1983), p. 175.
63 See Cuming, *A History of Anglican Liturgy* (London 1968) for the influence of Frere on South Africa.
64 Texts in Wigan, *The Liturgy in English*; C. O. Buchanan, *Modern Anglican Liturgies 1958–1968* (Oxford 1968).
65 J. Winslow and E. C. Ratcliff, *The Eucharist in India: a Plea for a Distinctive Liturgy for the Indian Church* (London 1920).
66 Text in Thompson, *Liturgies of the Western Church*.
67 For details, see Cuming, *A History of Anglican Liturgy*, pp. 179–82.
68 Wesley F. Swift, 'The Sunday Service of the Methodists', *PWHS* 29 (1953–4), pp. 12–24; 'The Sunday Service of the Methodists. A Study of Nineteenth-Century Liturgy', *PWHS* 31 (1957–8), pp. 112–18.
69 See Elliot Peaston, *The Prayer Book Tradition in the Free Churches* (London 1964).
70 John C. Bowmer, 'Some Non-Wesleyan Service Books', *PWHS* 32 (1960–1), pp. 145–52.
71 Nolan B. Harmon, *The Rites and Ritual of Episcopal Methodism* (Nashville 1926).

10 The sanctus in some contemporary eucharistic prayers

1 Though of course new proper prefaces, for example St Joseph the Worker, Immaculate Conception, had been added subsequently.
2 For a discussion, see Bouyer, *Eucharist*, pp. 443ff.; L. Sheppard (ed.), *The New Liturgy* (London, 1970), pp. 161ff; John Barry Ryan, *The Eucharistic Prayer. A*

Study in Contemporary Liturgy (New York 1974); E. Mazza, *The Eucharistic Prayers of the Roman Rite* (ET Pueblo, New York 1986).

3 *Ibid.*

4 Bouyer in *The New Liturgy*, pp. 203ff.; Mazza, *The Eucharistic Prayers*, pp. 123ff.

5 *The New Liturgy*, pp. 213ff.; Mazza, *The Eucharistic Prayers*, pp. 154ff.

6 *Ibid.*, pp. 191ff., 225ff.

7 The prayers for the children's eucharistic prayers were only given a general outline in Latin, which had to be fleshed out.

8 For example, the prayer of the Swiss Synod, and the Anaphora for India.

9 Aidan Kavanagh, 'Thoughts on the New Eucharistic Prayers', *Worship* 43 (1969), pp. 2–12, 4.

10 Mazza, *The Eucharistic Prayers*, p. 163.

11 This question will be considered more fully in the final chapter.

12 *Ordo Missae* (Hilversum 1970).

13 *Ibid.*, p. 91.

14 See Mazza, *The Eucharistic Prayers*, p. 213.

15 Text in *News of Liturgy* 120 (December 1984).

16 International Commission on English in the Liturgy.

17 International Consultation on English Texts.

18 ICET, *Prayers we have in Common* (London 1975, 2nd edn), p. 15. W. J. Grisbrooke, 'Series II: The new Communion Service of the Church of England Examined', *SL* 7 (1970), pp. 2–36, makes this point. See chapter 5.

19 C. O. Buchanan (ed.), *Modern Anglican Liturgies 1958–1968* (Oxford, 1968) (*MAL*); *Further Anglican Liturgies 1968–1975* (Bramcote 1975) (*FAL*); *Latest Anglican Liturgies 1976–1984* (London 1985). (*LAL*) The abbreviations used in these volumes for the various Anglican rites have been utilised in this chapter.

20 So in England and Uganda; *MAL*, p. 47; Buchanan, *Anglican Eucharistic Liturgy 1975–1985*, Grove Liturgical Study 41 (Bramcote 1985), p. 10.

21 For these documents, see *MAL*, pp. 31–2; *FAL*, pp. 26–31.

22 See *MAL*, pp. 14–15.

23 *FAL*, p. 30.

24 *MAL*, p. 65.

25 Buchanan, *Recent Liturgical Revision in the Church of England*, Grove Booklet on Ministry and Worship 14 (Bramcote 1973) and Supplements 14A, 1973–4; 14B, 1974–6; 14C, 1976–8; *Latest Liturgical Revision in the Church of England 1978–1984*, Grove Liturgical Study 39 (Bramcote 1984).

26 *The Church of England Liturgical Commission. Alternative Services. Second Series* (London 1965), p. 147.

27 See the articles in *Theology* 69 (1966) and 70 (1967). See also the discussion in Stevenson, *Eucharist and Offering*, pp. 204ff.

28 G. G. Willis, *1966 and All That* (London 1969), p. 13.

29 *Ibid.* Grisbrooke, 'Series II'.

30 See Introduction.

31 Private letter to the writer, 10 September 1975.

32 See *MAL* and *FAL* for details.

33 Buchanan, *Latest Liturgical Revision in the Church of England 1978–1984*, pp. 8–12.

34 H. B. Porter, 'An American Assembly of Anaphoral Prayers', in Bryan D. Spinks (ed.), *The Sacrifice of Praise*, pp. 181–96.

35 *Ibid.*, p. 90.
36 *An Order of Public Worship* (Oxford 1970), p. 31.
37 See Introduction.
38 S. Gibbons, 'The Eucharistic Prayer' (Cyclostyled), p. 6.
39 *Ibid.*
40 Letter to the writer, 7 June 1974.
41 A private conversation with Dr Gregory in July 1976.
42 For Oosterhuis, see Ryan, *The Eucharistic Prayer*.
43 See Bürki, *Cène du Seigneur*, vol. A, pp. 155ff., and vol. B, pp. 164ff. Bürki points out that the chant book, *Louange et prière*, contains two versions of the sanctus set to music, one by Bach and the other by Bortniansky. *Ibid.*, vol. B, p. 168.
44 *Ibid.*, vol. A, pp. 172, 167.
45 I am grateful to Professor Bürki for drawing my attention to these rites.
46 Duncan Forrester, 'Recent Liturgical Work in Scotland', *The Expository Times* 91:2 (1979), pp. 39–44; Julius Melton, 'Presbyterian Worship in Twentieth-Century America' in Booty (ed.), *The Divine Drama*. I am indebted to Revd Dr H. Allen for kindly supplying me with the texts.
47 Text in *SL* 4 (1966).
48 O. Jordahn, 'The Ecumenical Significance of the New Eucharistic Prayers of the Roman Liturgy', *SL* 11 (1976), pp. 101–17; H. C. Schmidt-Lauber, 'The Eucharistic Prayers of the Roman Catholic Church Today', *ibid.*, pp. 159–76; J. Bergsma, 'The Eucharistic Prayer in Non-Roman Catholic Churches of the West Today', *ibid.*, pp. 177–85.
49 Philip H. Pfatteicher and Carlos R. Messerli, *Manual on the Liturgy: Lutheran Book of Worship* (Minneapolis 1979), p. 235.
50 For some details, see Spinks, *Luther's Liturgical Criteria and His Reform of the Canon of the Mass*, pp. 38–40; *Report and Recommendations of the Special Hymnal Review Committee*, 1978.
51 1975 according to *Baptism and Eucharist*, p. 140; 1976 according to the English translation of *Hogmaisa Med Naltvard* of the London Church!
52 I am indebted to Revd Dr Helge Faehn for details of recent revision. See also Arve Brunvoll, 'Tradition and Renewal: Recent Liturgical Work in the Church of Norway', I, *LR* 9 (1979), pp. 67–71; II, *LR* 10 (1980), pp. 23–32.
53 My thanks to Professor Glahn for the Danish text, and to Revd Leo Norja for the Finnish text.

11 The sanctus in perspective

1 For example, the prayers of Robert Hoey and Thiery Naetens, discussed by Ryan, *The Eucharistic Prayer*. Alan Gaunt's prayers in *New Prayers for Worship*, 1972 – the work of a United Reformed Church minister.
2 Ryan, *The Eucharistic Prayer*, p. 188.
3 J. J. Von Allmen, *Worship: Its Theology and Practice* (London 1965), p. 205.
4 *Ibid.*
5 Billy Graham, *Angels: God's Secret Agents* (London 1976), p. 25.
6 *Ibid.* The vicar of a parish to whom I was an assistant curate once claimed to see angels in the lavatory!
7 R. Bultmann, 'New Testament and Mythology', in *Kerygma and Myth* ed. H. W. Bartsch and R. H. Fuller (London 1964, 2nd edn.), I, pp. 1–16.

8 Karl Barth, *CD* III/3, p. 413, quoting Strauss, and p. 414 quoting Lipsius.
9 E. Langton, *The Ministries of the Angelic Powers according to the Old Testament and Later Jewish Literature* (London 1936); *The Angel Teaching of the New Testament* (London 1935). W. G. Heidt, *Angelology of the Old Testament* (Minnesota 1949). There are of course articles dealing with particular passages of the Bible and Intertestamental literature.
10 Barth, *CD* III/3, p. 371.
11 J. Macquarrie, *Principles of Christian Theology* (London 1966), pp. 215–18. Barth, *CD* III/3; Karl Rahner, *Theological Investigations* 19 (London 1983), pp. 235–74.
12 For example, Bultmann, *Theology of the New Testament*, I (London 1952); G. Caird, *Powers and Principalities* (Oxford 1956); A. W. Carr, *Angels and Principalities: The Background, Meaning and Development of the Pauline Phrase 'hai archai kai hai exousiai'* (Cambridge 1981).
13 It is well known that this was true for several of the authors of *The Myth of God Incarnate*.
14 J. A. Habgood, 'The Uneasy Truce between Science and Religion', in A. R. Vidler, (ed.), *Soundings* (Cambridge 1963), pp. 21–41.
15 T. F. Torrance, *Divine and Contingent Order* (London 1981), p. 2.
16 A. R. Peacocke, *Creation and the World of Science* (London 1979), p. 103.
17 Paul Davies, *God and the New Physics* (London 1983), pp. 218ff.
18 James Lovelock, *Gaia: A New Look at Life on Earth* (London 1982).
19 N. Henbest and H. Couper, *The Restless Universe* (London 1982), p. 204.
20 *Ibid.*, p. 205.
21 *Ibid.* Cf. H. Montefiore, *The Probability of God* (London 1985), pp. 166ff.
22 Torrance, *Divine and Contingent Order*, p. 73.
23 *Ibid.*, p. 83.
24 Jürgen Moltmann, *God in Creation* (London 1985), p. 71. F. Crick, an atheist (and a former Fellow of the College of which I am Chaplain), criticises organised religion for a lack of awe and wonder at the sheer size of the Universe. *Life Itself* (New York 1981), pp. 21ff.
25 This, according to David Brown (see below), is represented by Lampe's *God as Spirit* and Moule's *The Holy Spirit*.
26 David Brown, *The Divine Trinity* (London 1984); W. Kasper, *The God of Jesus Christ* (London 1984); Moltmann, *The Trinity and the Kingdom of God* (London 1981).
27 Brown, *The Divine Trinity*, p. 305.
28 Moltmann, *The Trinity and the Kingdom of God*, p. 153.
29 P. Toon, *Justification and Sanctification* (London 1983), p. 40.
30 Torrance, 'The Paschal Mystery of Christ and the Eucharist', in *Theology in Reconciliation* (London 1975).
31 Toon, *Justification*, pp. 141–2.
32 Moltmann, *God and Creation*, p. 169.
33 *Patterns for Worship*, GS 898 (London 1989); see also the commentary by the present writer and Dr K. W. Stevenson, GSMisc.333 *Patterns for Worship. Essays on Eucharistic Prayers* (London 1989).
34 See Spinks, *Freedom or Order?*, p. 209.
35 Rudolph Otto, *Die Christliche Welt*, 27 July 1911, p. 709, cited in Robert F. Davidson, *Rudolph Otto's Interpretation of Religion* (Princeton 1947), p. 78.

—————— ✿ ——————

Bibliography

Ackroyd, P. 'The Meaning of Hebrew DÔR Considered', *JSS* 13 (1968), pp. 5–8.

Albright, W. F. 'What were the Cherubim?', *The Biblical Archaeologist* 1 (1938), pp. 1–3.

Review of 'L'épithète divine Jahve Sᶜba'ot: Etude philologique, historique et éxégétique', *JBL* 67 (1948), pp. 337–81.

Allgeier, A. 'Das afrikanische Element im altspanischen Psalter', *Spanische Forschungen* 2 (1930), pp. 196–228.

Anderson, B. W. *The Living World of the Old Testament* (DLT, London 1978, 3rd edn).

Andrieu, M., and Collomp, P. 'Fragments sur papyrus de l'anaphore de Saint Marc', *Revue des sciences religieuses* 8 (1928), pp. 489–515.

Atiya, A. *A History of Eastern Christianity* (Methuen, London 1968).

Audet, J.-P. 'Literary Forms and Contents of a Normal *Eucharista* in the First Century', *TU* 18 (1959), pp. 643–62.

Auf der Maur, H.-J. *Die Osterhomilien des Asterios Sophistes als Quelle für die Geschichte der Osterfeier* (Paulinus-Verlag, Trier 1967).

Barkley, J. M. *The Worship of the Reformed Church* (Lutterworth Press, London 1966).

Barth, Karl. *Church Dogmatics* III/3 (T. and T. Clark, Edinburgh 1960).

Bates, W. H. 'The Composition of the Anaphora of Apostolic Constitutions VIII', *SP* 13 (1975), pp. 345–55.

'Thanksgiving and Intercession in the Liturgy of St Mark', in B. D. Spinks (ed.), *The Sacrifice of Praise*, pp. 107–19.

Baumstark, A. 'Die Chrysostomosliturgie und die syrische Liturgie des Nestorios', in *Chrysostomika* (Pustet, Rome 1908).

'Zwei nicht erkannte Bruchstücke früchristlich-griechischer Liturgie Ägyptens', *JLW* 1 (1921), pp. 132–4.

Beaurecueil, S de. 'La prière eucharistique dans la liturgie égyptienne de Saint Grégoire', *Les Cahiers Coptes* 7–8 (1954), pp. 6–10.

Beck, E. *Des Heiligen Ephraem des Syrers Hymnen de Nativité (Epiphania)* (CSCO, Louvain 1959).

Bergsma, J. 'The Eucharistic Prayer in Non-Roman Catholic Churches of the West Today', *SL* 11 (1976), pp. 177–85.

Bersier, E. *Projet de Révision de La Liturgie des Eglises Reformées de France* (Fischbacher, Paris 1888).

Bertholet, A., and Galling, K. *Hesekiel HAT* 13 (Mohr, Tübingen 1936).

Betz, H. D. *The Greek Magical Papyri in Translation*, I (University of Chicago Press, Chicago 1985).

Bickell, G. (ed.), *Première homélie sur la Pâque de Seigneur*, *ZDMG* 27 (1878), pp. 569–75.

Birdsall, J. N., and Thompson, R. W. (eds.). *Biblical and Patristic Studies in Memory of Robert Pierce Casey* (Herder, Freiburg 1963).

Bishop, E. *Liturgica Historica* (Oxford University Press, Oxford 1918).

Bishop, W. C. *The Mozarabic and Ambrosian Rites* (Mowbray, London 1924).

Black, M. *The Scrolls and Christian Origins* (Nelson, London 1961).

Bloch, P. 'Die Yordei Merkavah, die Mystiker der Gaonzeit und ihr Einfluss auf die Liturgie', *MGWJ* 37 (1893).

Blond, G. 'Clement of Rome' in *The Eucharist of the Early Christians* ed. W. Rordorf (ET Pueblo, New York 1978), pp. 24–47.

Blume, C., and Bannister, H. M. *Analecta Hymnica Medii aeri* 47 (Reisland, Leipzig 1905).

Bobrinskoy, B. 'Liturgie et Ecclésiologie Trinitaire de Saint Basile', in *Eucharisties d'Orient et d'Occident* II (Cerf, Paris 1970), pp. 197–240.

Booty, John E. (ed.) *The Divine Drama in History and Liturgy*, Pittsburgh Theological Monographs, New Series 10 (Allison Park, Pennsylvania 1984).

Bornert, R. *La Réforme Protestante du Culte à Strasbourg au XVIᵉ Siècle. 1523–1598* (Brill, Leiden 1981).

Botte, B. *Le Canon de la messe romaine* (Abbaye du Mont Cesar, Louvain 1935).
　　'L'Anaphore Chaldéene des Apôtres', *OCP* 15 (1949), pp. 259–76.
　　'L'Eucologe de Sérapion est-il authentique?', *OC* 48 (1964), pp. 50–7.
　　'Problèmes de l'Anaphore syrienne des Apôtres Addaï et Mari', *Or.Syr* 10 (1965), pp. 86–106.

Botte, B. and Mohrmann, C. *L'Ordinaire de la Messe* (Cerf, Paris and Louvain 1953).

Bouley, A. *From Freedom to Formula* (Catholic University of America Press, Washington 1981).

Bousset, W. *Eine jüdische Gebetssammlung im siebten Buch der Apostolischen Konstitutionen. Nachrichten Gesellschaft* (Göttingen, Berlin 1916).

Bouyer, L. *Eucharist* (ET. Notre Dame University Press, Indiana 1968).

Bowmer, J. C. 'Some Non-Wesleyan Service Books', *PWHS* 32 (1960–1), pp. 145–52.
　　'The Bible Christian Service Book', *PWHS* 33 (1961–2), pp. 1–3.

Box, G. H. *The Testament of Abraham* (SPCK, London 1927).

Bradshaw, P. F. 'The Search for the Origins of Christian Liturgy: some Methodological Reflections', *Gratias Agamus*, SL 17 (Jubilee Volume 1987), pp. 26–34.

Brann, M., and Rosenthal F. (eds.). *David Kaufman Memorial Volume* (Sches. Verlags-Anstalt v.s. Schottlaender, Breslau 1910).

Brenner, Scott F. 'Philip Schaff the Liturgist', *Christendom* 11 (1946), pp. 443–56.

Bright, J. *A History of Israel* (SCM, London 1960, 1st edn.).

Brilioth, Y. *Eucharistic Faith and Practice, Evangelical and Catholic* (SPCK, London 1930).

Brock, S. P. 'Studies in the Early History of the Syrian Orthodox Baptismal Liturgy', *JTS* ns 23 (1972), pp. 16–64.

Brown, David. *The Divine Trinity* (Duckworth, London 1985).

Brown, L. W. *Relevant Liturgy* (SPCK, London 1965).

Brown, R. E. *St John 1–12* (Anchor Bible, Chapman, London 1971).
   The Community of the Beloved Disciple (Chapman, London 1979).
   'Pre-Christian Semitic Concept of Mystery', *CBQ* 20 (1958), pp. 417–43.

Brun, P. Le. *Explication littérale, historique et dogmatique des prières et des cérémonies de la messe*, 4 vols. (Paris 1716–26).

Brunner, P. *Worship in the Name of Jesus* (ET. Concordia, St Louis Missouri 1968).

Brunvoll, Arve. 'Tradition and Renewal: Recent Liturgical Work in the Church of Norway', *LR* 9 (1979), pp. 67–72; 10 (1980), pp. 23–32.

Buchanan, C. O. *Modern Anglican Liturgies 1958–1968* (Oxford University Press, Oxford 1968).
   Recent Liturgical Revision in the Church of England (Grove Booklet on Ministry and Worship 14, Bramcote 1973); *Supplements* 14A, 14B, 14C.
   Further Anglican Liturgies 1968–1975 (Grove Books, Bramcote, 1975).
   Latest Liturgical Revision in the Church of England 1978–1984 (Grove Liturgical Study 39, Bramcote 1984).
   Anglican Eucharistic Liturgy 1975–1985 (Grove Liturgical Study 41, Bramcote 1985).
   Latest Anglican Liturgies 1976–1984 (Alcuin Club SPCK, London 1985).

Bultmann, R. *Theology of the New Testament*, I (SCM, London 1952).
   'New Testament and Mythology', in H. W. Bartsch and R. H. Fuller (eds.), *Kerygma and Myth* I, (SPCK, London 1964, 2nd edn.), pp. 1–16.

Bürki, B. *Cène du Seigneur-Eucharistie de l'Eglise*, 2 vols., Cahiers Oecumeniques (Editions Universitaires Fribourg Suisse, Fribourg 1985).

Burrows, M. *More Light on the Dead Sea Scrolls* (Viking, New York 1958).

Cabaniss, A. 'A Note on the Liturgy of the Apocalypse', in *Interpretation* 7 (1953), pp. 78–86.

Cagin, P. *Te Deum ou Illatio* (Scriptorium Solsmense, Abbaye de Solesmes, Oxford and Rome 1906).

Caird, G. *Powers and Principalities* (Clarendon Press, Oxford 1956).
   The Revelation of St John the Divine (A. and C. Black, London 1966).

Capelle, B. 'Problèmes textuels de la préface romaine. II. Caeli caelorumque virtutes', *RSR* 40 (1951–2), pp. 145–50.

'Les liturgies "basiliennes" et S. Basile', in J. Doresse and E. Lanne, *Un témoin archaïque de la liturgie copte de S. Basile* (Publications universitaires Louvain, Louvain 1960).

Cardale, J. *Readings in the Liturgy and Divine Offices of the Church*, 2 vols. (Thomas Bosworth, London 1874–5).

Carr, A. W. *Angels and Principalities: The Background, Meaning and Development of the Pauline Phrase 'hai archai kai hai exousiai'* (Cambridge University Press, Cambridge 1981).

Catergian, Y., and Dashian, P. J. *Die Liturgien bei den Armeniern. Fünfzehn Texte und Untersuchungen* (Gerold and Co., Vienna 1897).

Cattin, G. *Music of the Middle Ages I* (Cambridge University Press, London 1984).

Charles, R. H. *The Revelation of St John I* (T. and T. Clark, Edinburgh 1920).

Charlesworth, J. H. *The Pseudepigrapha and Modern Research. With a Supplement* (Scholars Press, Chico 1981).

'The SNTS Pseudepigrapha Seminars at Tübingen and Paris on the Books of Enoch', *NTS* 25 (1979), pp. 315–23.

'A Prolegomenon to a New Study of the Jewish Background of the Hymns and Prayers in the New Testament', *JJS* 33 (1982), pp. 265–85.

'Jewish Hymns, Odes, and Prayers', in R. A. Kraft and G. W. E. Nickelsburg (eds.), *Early Judaism and its Modern Interpreters* (Scholars Press, Atlanta, Georgia 1986), pp. 411–36.

Chavoutier, L. 'Un Libellus Pseudo-Ambrosien sur le Saint-Esprit', *SE* 11 (1960), pp. 136–91.

Clements, R. E. *God and Temple* (Oxford University Press, Oxford 1965).

Isaiah 1–39 (Marshall, Morgan and Scott, London 1980).

Coebergh, C. 'Sacramentaire léonien et liturgie mozarabe', in *Miscellanea Liturgica in honorem Cuniberti Mohlberg* (Edizioni Liturgiche, Rome 1949), pp. 295–304.

Comblin, J. 'La liturgie de la Nouvelle Jérusalem', *ETL* 29 (1953), pp. 5–40.

Connolly, R. H. *The Liturgical Homilies of Narsai*, Texts and Studies 8, (Cambridge University Press, Cambridge 1909).

'The Original Language of the Syriac Acts of John', *JTS* 8 (1906–7), pp. 249–61.

Connolly, R. H., and Codrington, H. W. *Two Commentaries on the Jacobite Liturgy* (Williams and Northgate, London 1913).

Cornet, L. 'Sanctus et Merkaba', *QL* 59 (1978), pp. 23–37.

Costa, E. *Tropes et Séquences dans le Cadre de la Vie Liturgique au moyen-âge* (CLV, Rome 1979).

Couratin, A. H. 'The Sanctus and the Pattern of the Early Anaphora: A Note on the Roman Sanctus', *JEH* 2 (1951), pp. 19–23.

'The Methodist Sunday Service', *CQ* 2 (1969), pp. 31–8.

'The Sanctus' (unpublished essay, typescript).

Couratin, A. H. and Tripp, D. H. (eds.), *Liturgical Studies* (SPCK, London 1976).

Crick, F. *Life Itself* (Simon and Schuster, New York 1981).

Crocker, R. L. 'The Troping Hypothesis', *Musical Quarterly* 52 (1966), pp. 183–203.

Cross, F. M. *Canaanite Myths and Hebrew Epic* (Harvard University Press, Cambridge Mass. 1973).

'The Council of Yahweh in Second Isaiah', *JNES* 12 (1953), pp. 274–7.

'Yahweh and the God of the Patriarchs', *HTR* 55 (1962), pp. 225–59.

Cross, Frank Leslie. *St Cyril of Jerusalem's Lectures on the Christian Sacraments* (SPCK, London 1966).

Cuming, G. J. *A History of Anglican Liturgy* (Macmillan, London 1969, 1st edn.).

Hippolytus: A Text for Students (Grove Liturgical Study 8, Bramcote 1976).

The Godly Order (Alcuin Club/SPCK, London 1983).

The Liturgy of St Mark (OCA 234, Rome 1990).

Cuming, G. J. (ed.). *Essays on Hippolytus* (Grove Liturgical Study 15, Bramcote 1978).

Cuming, G. J. 'Two Fragments of a Lost Liturgy?,' in *Studies in Church History* 3 (Brill, Leiden 1966), pp. 247–53.

'Egyptian Elements in the Jerusalem Liturgy', *JTS* ns 25 (1974), pp. 117–24.

Review Article in *Eastern Churches Review* 7 (1975), pp. 95–7. 'Thmuis Revisited: another look at the prayers of Bishop Sarapion', *TS* 41 (1980), pp. 568–75.

'The Early Eucharistic Liturgies in Recent Research' in B. D. Spinks (ed.), *The Sacrifice of Praise*, pp. 65–9.

'The Anaphora of St Mark: A Study in Development', *Mu* 95 (1982), pp. 115–29.

'Four Very Early Anaphoras', *Worship* 58 (1984), pp. 168–72.

'Pseudonymity and Authenticity, with special reference to the Liturgy of St John Chrysostom', *SP* 15 (1984), pp. 532–8.

'The Shape of the Anaphora', paper read at the Oxford Patristic Conference, 1987.

Cullman, O. *Christ and Time* (ET. SCM, London revised edition 1962).

Cutrone, E. C. 'Cyril's Mystagogical Catecheses and the Evolution of the Jerusalem Anaphora', *OCP* 44 (1978), pp. 52–64.

Daniel, H. (ed.) Codex Liturgicus (T. O. Weigel, Leipzig 1853).

Daniélou, J. *The Theology of Jewish Christianity* (DLT, London 1964).

Gospel Message and Hellenistic Culture (DLT, London 1973).

The Origins of Latin Christianity (DLT, London 1977).

Danske Messeboger Fra Reformationstiden (J. H. Schultz Forlag, Copenhagen, 1959).

Daoud, M., and Hazen, H. E. B. M. *The Liturgy of the Ethiopian Church* (The Egyptian Church Press, Addis Ababa 1959).

Davidson, R. F. *Rudolph Otto's Interpretation of Religion* (Princeton University Press, Princeton 1947).

Davies, P. *God and the New Physics* (Dent, London 1983).

Dean-Otting, M. *Heavenly Journeys. A Study of the Motif in Hellenistic Jewish Literature* (Verlag Peter Lang, Frankfurt am Main, Bern, New York 1984).

Dekkers, E. 'Van profetie tot canon', *TL* 25 (1946), pp. 8–25.

Dhorme, E. 'Le nom des chérubins', in *Recueil Edouard Dhorme* (Imprimerie nationale, Paris 1951), pp. 671–83.

Dibelius, M. *Die Geisterwelt im Glauben des Paulus* (Vandenhoeck and Ruprecht, Göttingen 1909).

'Die Mahl-Gebete der Didache', *ZNTW* 37 (1938), pp. 32–41.

Dix, G. *The Shape of the Liturgy* (Dacre, London 1945).

'Primitive Consecration Prayers', *Theology* 37 (1938), pp. 261–83.

Doresse, J. and Lanne, E. *Un Témoin archaïque de la liturgie copte de S. Basile* (Publications Universitaires, Louvain 1960).

Driver, G. R. 'Isaiah 6:1. His Train filled the Temple', in H. Goedicke (ed.), *Near Eastern Studies in Honor of W. F. Albright* (John Hopkins Press, Baltimore and London 1971).

Duchesne, L. *Christian Worship* (Christian Knowledge Society, London 1904).

Duchesne, L. (ed.). *Liber Pontificalis*, I (Bibliothèque des Ecoles françaises d'Athènes et de Rome, Paris 1955–7).

Dugmore, C. W. *The Influence of the Synagogue upon the Divine Office* (Oxford University Press, Oxford 1944; Faith Press, London 1964).

Dunn, J. D. G. *Unity and Diversity in the New Testament* (SCM, London 1981, 2nd edn.).

Eaton, J. H. *Kingship and Psalms* (SCM, London 1976).

Festal Drama in Deutero-Isaiah (SPCL, London 1979).

Vision in Worship (SPCK, London 1981).

Eichrodt, W. *Ezekiel* (SCM, London 1970).

Elbogen, I. *Der jüdische Gottesdienst in seiner geschichtlichen Entwicklung* (J. Kauffmann, Frankfurt 1931).

Emerton, J. A. 'The Origin of the Son of Man Imagery' *JTS* ns 11 (1958), pp. 225–42.

'New Light on Israelite Religion: The Implications of the Inscriptions from Kuntillet "Ajrud",' *ZAW* 94 (1982), pp. 2–20.

Engberding, H. *Das eucharistische Hochgebet der Basileiosliturgie* (Aschendorff, Münster 1931).

'Die syrische Anaphora der zwölf Apostel und ihre Paralleltexte', *OC* 12 (1937), pp. 213–47.

England *Church of England Liturgical Commission. Alternative Services. Second Series* (SPCK, London 1965).

Church of England Liturgical Commission, Patterns for Worship, GS 898 (Church House Publishing, London 1989).

Euringer, S. 'Die äthiopische Anaphora des hl. Epiphanius, Bischofs der Insel Cypern', *OC* 3:1 (1926–7), pp. 98–142.

Evans, E. *Tertullian's Tract on Prayer* (SPCK, London 1953).

Evans, Paul. 'Some Reflections on the Origin of the Trope', in *Journal of the American Musicological Society* 14 (1961), pp. 119–30.

Fallon, F. T. *The Enthronement of Sabaoth* (Brill, Leiden 1978).

Fenwick, J. R. K. *Fourth-Century Anaphoral Construction Techniques* (Grove Liturgical Study 45, Bramcote 1986).

'The Missing Oblation': the Contents of the Early Antiochene Anaphora, Alcuin/Grow Liturgical Study 11, (Grove Books, Bramcote 1989).

'An Investigation into the Common Origin of the Anaphora of the Liturgies of St Basil and St James', Ph.D. Thesis, London University 1985.

'Significance of Similarities in the Anaphoral Intercession Sequence in the Coptic Anaphora of St Basil and Other Ancient Liturgies', *SP* forthcoming.

Ferotin, M. *Le Liber Ordinum* (Libraire de Firmin-Didot, Paris 1904).

Le Liber Mozarabicus Sacramentorum (Libraire de Firmin-Didot, Paris 1912).

Fiensy, D. A. *Prayers Alleged to be Jewish. An Examination of the Constitutiones Apostolorum* (Brown Judaic Studies 65, Scholars Press, Chico 1985).

Finkelstein, L. 'The Development of the Amidah', *JQR* ns 16(1925–6), pp. 1–43, 127–70.

'The Birkat Ha-Mazon', *JQR* ns 19(1928–9), pp. 211–62.

'La Kedouscha et les Bénédictions du Schema', *REJ* 93(1932), pp. 1–26.

Fitzmyer, J. A. 'Implications of the New Enoch Literature from Qumran', *TS* 38(1977), pp. 332–45.

Fleischer, E. 'The Diffusion of the Qedushot of the Amidah and the Yozer in the Palestinian Ritual', *Tarbiz* 38(1968–9), pp. 255–84.

Flusser, D. 'Sanktus und Gloria', in O. Beta *et al.* (eds.), *Abraham unser Vater*, Festschrift Otto Michael (Brill, Leiden 1963), pp. 129–52.

Forrester, D. 'Recent Liturgical Work in Scotland', *The Expository Times* 91:2 (1979), pp. 39–44.

Frend, W. H. C. *Martyrdom and Persecution in the Early Church* (Oxford University Press, Oxford 1955).

Frendo, J. A. *The 'Post Secreta' of the 'Missale Gothicum' and the Eucharistic Theology of the Gallican Anaphora* (St Venera, Malta 1977).

Frere, W. H. *The Winchester Troper* (HBS 8, London 1894).

Some Principles of Liturgical Reform (John Murray, London 1911).

Fuchs, H. *Die Anaphora des monophysitischen Patriarchen Jôhannan I* (Liturgiegeschichtliche Quellen, Münster, Westfalen 1926).

Gamber, K. *Missa Romensis* (Pustet, Regensburg 1970).

Gärtner, B. *The Temple and the Community in Qumran and the New Testament* (Cambridge University Press, Cambridge 1965).

Gavin, F. *The Jewish Antecedents of the Christian Sacraments* (SPCK, London 1928).

Gerhards, A. *Die griechische Gregoriosanaphora* (Liturgiewissenschaftiche Quellen und Forschungen 65, Aschendorff, Münster 1984).

'Le Phénomène du Sanctus Addressé au Christ', in *Le Christ dans la Liturgie* (Conférences St Serge 1980, CLV, Rome 1981), pp. 65–83.

Gesenius, W. *Lexicon Manuale Hebraicum et Chaldaicum* (Vogel, Lipsiae 1885).

Gesenius, W. and Kautzch, E. *Hebrew Grammar* (ET. Clarendon Press, Oxford, 1898).

Glahn, H. *Melodistadier Til Den Lutherske Salmesangs Historie Fra 1524 til ca 1600* 2 vols. (Rosenkilde og Bagger, Copenhagen 1954).

Goodenough, E. R. *By Light, Light* (Yale University Press, New Haven and London 1935).

Jewish Symbols in the Greco-Roman Period, II (Pantheon Books, New York 1953).

Graham, Billy. *Angels: God's Secret Agents* (Hodder and Stoughton, London 1976).

Grant, R. M. 'The Early Antiochene Anaphora', *ATR* 30(1946), pp. 91–4.

Grant, R. M. and Graham, H. H. 'First and Second Clement', in Grant (ed.) The *Apostolic Fathers* (Harper and Row, New York 1965).

Gray, G. B. *Isaiah 1–25* (T. and T. Clark, Edinburgh 1912).

Gray, J. *1 and 2 Kings* (SCM, London 1964, 1st edn.).

Green, W. S. (ed.). *Approaches to Ancient Judaism: Theory and Practice* (Scholars Press, Missoula 1978).

Griffe, E. 'Aux origines de la liturgie gallicane' in *Bulletin de Littérature Ecclésiastique*, 1(1955), pp. 17–43.

Grisbrooke, W. J. *Anglican Liturgies of the Seventeenth and Eighteenth Centuries* (Alcuin Club/SPCK, London 1958).

'Series II: The new Communion Service of the Church of England Examined', *SL* 7(1970), pp. 2–36.

Grove *New Grove Dictionary of Music and Musicians*, vol. xix (Macmillan, London 1980).

Gruenwald, I. *Apocalyptic and Merkavah Mysticism* (Brill, Leiden 1980).

Gy, P.-M. 'La Sanctus Romain et les Anaphores Orientales', in *Mélanges Liturgiques offerts au R. P. Dom Bernard Botte* (Abbaye du Mont César, Louvain 1972), pp. 167–74.

Habgood, J. A. 'The Uneasy Truce between Science and Religion', in A. Vidler (ed.), *Soundings* (Cambridge University Press, Cambridge 1963), pp. 21–41.

Hagedorn, D. *Der Hiobkommentar des Arianers Julian* (De Gruyter, Berlin 1973).

Hageman, H. *Pulpit and Table* (John Knox Press, Richmond 1962).

Hagner, D. A. *The Use of the Old and New Testaments in Clement of Rome* (Brill, Leiden 1973).

Hahn, F. *The Worship of the Early Church* (Fortress Press, Philadelphia 1973).

Haile, G. 'Religious Controversies and the Growth of Ethiopic Literature in the Fourteenth and Fifteenth Centuries', *OC* 4th series 65(1981), pp. 102–36.

Hammerschmidt, E. *Die Koptische Gregoriosanaphora* (Berliner byzantinische Arbeiten 8, Berlin 1957).

Studies in the Ethiopic Anaphoras (Akademie-Verlag, Berlin 1961).

Hannover *Die Hannoversche Agende*. Kleine Texte für Vorlesungen und Ubengen herausgegeben von Hans Lietzmann, 125 (A. Marcus and E. Weber Verlag, Bonn 1913).

Hanson, R. P. C. 'The Liberty of the Bishop to Improvise Prayer in the Eucharist', *VC* 15(1961), pp. 173–6.

Hanssens, J. M. *La Liturgie D'Hippolyte* (OCA 155, Rome 1965).

Haran, M. *Temples and Temple-Service in Ancient Israel* (Oxford University Press, London 1978).

'The Ark and the Cherubim: Their Symbolic Significance in Biblical Ritual', *Israel Exploration Journal* 9 (1959), pp. 30–8, 89–94.

Harden, J. M. *The Anaphoras of the Ethiopic Liturgy* (SPCK, London 1928).

Harmon, N. B. *The Rites and Ritual of Episcopal Methodism* (Publishing House of the Methodist Episcopal Church, South, Nashville 1926).

Hatchett, M. J. *The Making of the First American Book of Common Prayer* (Seabury Press, New York 1982).

Hayek, M. *Liturgie Maronite. Histoire et textes eucharistiques* (Maison Mame, Paris, 1964).

Heaton, E. W. *Daniel* (SCM, London 1956).

Hedegard, D. *Seder R. Amran Gaon*, Part 1 (Ph. Lindstedts universitets-bokhandel, Lund 1951).

Heidt, W. G. *Angelology of the Old Testament* (The Catholic University of America. Studies in Sacred Theology, Minnesota 1949).

Heinemann, J. *Prayer in the Talmud* (De Gruyter, Berlin and New York 1977).

Henbest, N., and Couper, H. *The Restless Universe* (George Philip, London 1982).

Hengel, M. *Judaism and Hellenism: Studies in Their Encounter in Palestine During the Early Hellenistic Period*, 2 vols. (Fortress Press, Philadelphia 1974).

Herntrich, V. *Ezekielprobleme*, BZAW 61 (Topelmann, Giessen 1933).

Herrmann, J. *Ezechielstudien* (J. C. Hinrichs, Leipzig 1908).

Hoffman, L. A. *The Canonization of the Synagogue Service* (University of Notre Dame, Indiana 1979).

Holloway, H. *The Norwegian Rite* (Stockwell, London 1934).

Hölscher, G. *Hesekiel, der Dichter und das Buch*, BZAW 39 (Topelmann, Giessen 1924).

Hooke, S. H. *Myth, Ritual and Kingship* (Clarendon Press, New York and Oxford 1958).

Horn, E. T. *Outlines of Liturgics* (Lutheran Publication Society, Philadelphia 1890).

'The Lutheran Sources of the Common Service', *Lutheran Quarterly*, 21(1891), pp. 239–68.

Houssiau, A. 'The Alexandrine Anaphora of St Basil', in Sheppard (ed.) *The New Liturgy*, pp. 228–43.

Hubert, F. *Die Strassburger liturgischen Ordnungen im Zeitalter der Reformation* (Vandenhoeck and Ruprecht, Göttingen 1900).

ICET *Prayers We have in Common* (SPCK, London 1975 2nd edn.).

Idelsohn, A. Z. *Jewish Liturgy and its Development* (Schocken, New York, 1960).

Jacob, E. *Theology of the Old Testament* (Hodder and Stoughton, London 1958).

James, M. R. *The Lost Apocrypha of the Old Testament* (SPCK, London 1920).

Janeras, S. 'L'Original grec del fragment copte de Louvain Num.27 en l'Anafora di Barcelona', in *Miscellania Liturgica Catalana*, 3(1984), pp. 13–25.

Johnson, A. R. *Sacral Kingship in Ancient Israel* (University of Wales, Cardiff 1967).

Joines, K. R. 'Winged Serpents in Isaiah's Inaugural Vision', *JBL* 86 (1976), pp. 410–15.

Jones, C. *et al.*, *The Study of Liturgy* (SPCK, London 1978).

Jonge, M. de *The Testament of the Twelve Patriarchs: A Study of their Text, Composition and Origin* (Van Gorcum, Assen 1953).

Studies on the Testaments of the Twelve Patriarchs: Text and Interpretation (Brill, Leiden 1975).

'Once More: Christian Influence in the Testaments of the Twelve Patriarchs' *Nov.T.* 5(1962), pp. 311–19.

Jordahn, O. 'The Ecumenical Significance of the New Eucharistic Prayers of the Roman Liturgy', *SL* 11 (1976), pp. 101–17.

Jungmann, J. A. *The Mass of the Roman Rite*, 2 vols. (Benzinger, New York 1955).

The Place of Christ in Liturgical Prayer (Geoffrey Chapman, London 1965, 2nd edn.).

Kahle, P. E. *Bala'izah Coptic Texts from Deir el Bala'izah in Upper Egypt* (Oxford University Press, London 1954).

Kahler, E. *Studien zum Te Deum* (Vandenhoeck and Ruprecht, Göttingen 1956).

Kaiser, O. *Isaiah 1–12* (SCM, London 1972, 1st edn.; 1983 2nd edn.).

Kapelrud, A. S. 'The Gates of Hell and the Guardian Angels of Paradise', *Journal of the American Oriental Society*, 70(1950), pp. 151–6.

Kasper, W. *The God of Jesus Christ* (SCM, London 1984).

Kavanagh, A. 'Thoughts on the New Eucharistic Prayers', *Worship* 43 (1969), pp. 2–12.

Keel, O. *The Symbolism of the Biblical World*, (SPCK, London 1978).

Keifer, R. A. 'The Unity of the Roman Canon: An Examination of its unique structure', *SL* 11(1976), pp. 39–58.

Khouri-Sarkis, G. 'L'Origine syrienne de l'anaphore byzantine de saint Jean Chrysostome', *Or.Syr* 7 (1962), pp. 3–68.

Kilmartin, E. 'Sacrificium Laudis: Content and Function of Early Eucharistic Prayers', *TS* 35 (1974), pp. 268–87.

King, A. A. *The Rites of Eastern Christendom*, 2 vols. (Catholic Book Agency, Rome 1948).

Liturgies of the Primatial Sees (Longmans, London 1957).

Kingsbury, E. C. 'The Prophets and the Council of Yahweh', *JBL* 83(1964), pp. 279–86.

Klauser, T. *A Short History of the Western Liturgy* (Oxford University Press, Oxford 1979, 2nd edn.).

Knibb, M. A. 'The Date of the Parables of Enoch: A Critical Review', *NTS* 25(1978–9), pp. 345–59.

Kohler, K. *The Origins of the Synagogue and the Church* (Macmillan, New York 1929).

'The Origins and Composition of the Eighteen Benedictions with a Translation of the Corresponding Essene Prayers in the Apostolic Constitutions', *HUCA* 1 (1924), pp. 387–425.

Kraft, R. A. *The Testament of Job* (Scholars Press, Missoula, Montana 1974).

Kraus, H.-J. *Worship in Israel* (ET. Blackwell, Oxford, 1966).

Kretschmar, G. *Studien zur frühchristlichen Trinitätstheologie* (J. C. B. Mohr, Tübingen 1965).

'Die frühe Geschichte der Jerusalemer Liturgie', in *Jahrbuch für Liturgik und Hymnologie*, (1956), pp. 22–46.

Kronholm, T. *Seder R. Amran Gaon*, Part II (C. W. K. Gleerup, Lund 1974).

Kroon, S. *Tibi Laus. Studier Kring den Svenska Psalmen Nr.199* (Lunds universistits Arsskrift, Lund 1953).

Kropp, A. *Demotische und Koptische Texte*, 3 vols. (Ausgewählte Koptische Zaubertexte, Brussels 1930–1).

Kuhn, K. G. 'The Lord's Supper and the Communal Meal at Qumran', in K. Stendahl (ed.), *The Scrolls and the New Testament* (SCM, London 1958).

Lacan, M.-F. 'Caeli caelorumque virtutes', *RSR* 51(1963), pp. 240–6.

Lang, A. P. *Leo der Grosse und die Texte des Altgelasianums* (Pontifical Gregorian University, Steyl 1957).

'Leo der Grosse und die Dreifaltigkeitspräfation', *SE* 9(1957), pp. 116–62.

Langton, E. *The Angel Teaching of the New Testament* (J. Clarke, London 1935).

The Ministries of the Angelic Powers according to the Old Testament and Later Jewish Literature (J. Clarke, London 1936).

Leak, N. 'Recent Developments in Public Worship and Aids to Devotion – Presbyterian Church of England', *LR* 3(1973), pp. 26–31.

Leaney, A. R. C. *The Rite of Qumran and its Meaning* (SCM, London 1966).

Ledogar, J. *Acknowledgement: Praise Verbs in the Early Greek Anaphoras* (Herder, Rome 1968).

Leiser, B. M. 'The Trisagion of Isaiah's Vision', *NTS* 6(1959–60), pp. 261–3.

Lengeling, E. 'Le problème des nouvelles prières eucharistiques dans la liturgie romaine', *QL* 53(1972), p. 51.

Levey, S. *The Targum of Ezekiel* (T. and T. Clarke, Edinburgh 1987).

'The Targum of Ezekiel', *HUCA* 46(1975), pp. 139–58.

Levy, K. 'The Byzantine Sanctus and its Modal Tradition in East and West', *Ann.M.* 6(1958–63), pp. 7–67.

Liebreich, L. J. 'An Analysis of U-Ba' Le-Ziyyon', *HUCA* 21(1948), pp. 176–209.

Lietzman, H. *Mass and Lord's Supper: A Study in the History of Liturgy* (Brill, Leiden 1979).

Lightfoot, J. B. *The Apostolic Fathers* (Macmillan, London 1907).

Ligier, L. 'From the Last Supper to the Eucharist', in Sheppard (ed.) *The New Liturgy*, pp. 113–50.

'Anaphores orientales et prières juives', *Proche-Orient Chrétien* 13(1963), pp. 3–20.

'The Origins of the Eucharist Prayer: From the Last Supper to the Eucharist', *SL* 9(1973) pp. 176–85.

Lincoln, A. T. *Paradise Now and Not Yet* (Cambridge University Press, Cambridge 1981).

Lohe, W. *Agende für Christliche Gemeinden des luthischen Bekenntnisses* (Beck, Nordlingen 1844).

Lovelock, J. *Gaia: A New look at Life on Earth* (Oxford University Press, London 1982).

Lowther Clarke, W. K. (ed.). *Liturgy and Worship* (SPCK, London 1932).

Luther's Works (Fortress Press, Philadelphia: Concordia, St Louis 1955–).

MacCarthy, B. *On the Stowe Missal*, (*TRIA* 27 1886).

McNamara, M. *The New Testament and the Palestinian Targum to the Pentateuch* (Pontifical Biblical Institute, Rome 1966).

Macomber, W. F. *Six Explanations of the Liturgical Feasts by Cyrus of Edessa*, vols. 155–6 (CSCO, Louvain 1974).

'The Oldest Known Text of the Anaphora of the Apostles Addai and Mari', *OCP* 32 (1966), pp. 335–71.

'A Theory on the Origins of the Syrian, Maronite and Chaldean Rites', *OCP* 39 (1973), pp. 235–42.

'An Anaphoral Prayer Composed by Theodore of Mopsuestia', *Parole de l'Orient* 6–7 (1975–6) (Mélanges offerts au R. P. François Graffin, sj), pp. 341–7.

'The Ancient Form of the Anaphora of the Apostles' in *East of Byzantium, Syria and Armenia in the Formative Period* (Dumbarton Oaks, Washington 1982).

Macquarrie, John. *Principles of Christian Theology* (SCM, London 1966).

Magne, J. 'Carmina Christo I. Le "Sanctus" de la Messe Latine', *EL* 100 (1986), pp. 3–27.

'Carmina Christo II. Le "Te Deum",' *EL* 100 (1986), pp. 113–37.
'L'anaphore nestorienne dite d'Addée et Mari et l'anaphore maronite dite de Pierre III', *OCP* 53 (1987), pp. 107–59.
Mann, J. 'Geniza Fragments of the Palestinian Order of Service', *HUCA* 2 (1925), pp. 269–338.
Mansoor, M. *The Thanksgiving Hymns* (Brill, Leiden 1961).
Marmorstein, A. 'L'Age de la Kedouscha de l'Amidah', *REJ* 97 (1934), pp. 176–209.
Marshall, I. H. *The Gospel of Luke* (Paternoster Press, Exeter 1978).
Martin, R. P. *Worship in the Early Church* (T. and T. Clark, Edinburgh 1965).
Maxwell, J. M. *Worship and Reformed Theology. The Liturgical Lesson of Mercersburg* (Pickwick Press, Pittsburgh 1976).
Maxwell, W. D. *An Outline of Christian Worship* (Oxford University Press, London 1936).
Mazza, E. *The Eucharistic Prayers of the Roman Rite* (ET Pueblo, New York 1986).
'Una Anafora Incompleta? Il Papiro Strasbourg Gr.254', *EL* 99 (1985), pp. 425–36.
Mearns, C. L. 'The Parables of Enoch – Origin and Date', *Expository Times* 89 (1978), pp. 118–19.
'Dating the Similitudes of Enoch', *NTS* 25 (1978–9), pp. 360–9.
Melton, J. 'Presbyterian Worship in Twentieth-Century America', in J. E. Booty (ed.), *The Divine Drama in History and Liturgy* (Pickwick Publications, Allinson Park 1984), pp. 179–99.
Mettinger, T. N. D. *The Dethronement of Sabaoth. Studies in the Shem and Kabod Theologies*. Coniectanea Biblica Old Testament Series 18 (C. W. K. Gleerup, Lund 1982).
Metzger, B. *A Textual Commentary on the Greek New Testament* (United Bible Society, New York and London 1971).
Metzger, M. *Königsthron und Gottesthron*, 2 vols. (Verlag Butzon and Bercker, Kevelaer 1985).
Metzger, Marcel 'The Didascalia and the Constitutiones Apostolorum', in *The Eucharist of the Early Christians*, ed. W. Rordorf (Pueblo, New York, 1978), pp. 194–219.
Milik, J. T. *The Books of Enoch: Aramaic Fragments of Qumran Cave 4* (Oxford University Press, Oxford 1976).
'Problèmes de la littérature hénochique à la lumière des fragments araméens de Qumrân', *HTR* 64 (1971), pp. 333–78.
Miller, P. D. *The Divine Warrior in Early Israel* (Harvard Semitic Monographs 5, Harvard University Press, Cambridge, Mass. 1973).
Milne, A. A. *Winnie-The-Pooh* (Methuen, London 1926).
Mitchell, G. A. 'Firmilian and Eucharistic Consecration', *JTS* ns 5 (1954), pp. 215–20.
Mohlberg, L. C. *Missale Gallicanum Vetus* (Rome, Herder 1958).

Mohrmann, C. *Liturgical Latin* (Catholic University of America Press, Washington 1957).

'Les origines de la latinité chrétienne à Rome', *VC* 3 (1949), pp. 47–106, 163–83.

Moltmann, J. *The Trinity and the Kingdom of God* (SCM, London 1981). *God in Creation* (SCM, London 1985).

Montefiore, H. *The Probability of God* (SCM, London 1985).

Morgenstern, J. 'The Gates of Righteousness', *HUCA* 6 (1926), pp. 1–37.

Mowinckel, S. *The Psalms in Israel's Worship* (Blackwell, Oxford 1982).

Mowrey, L. 'Revelation 4–5 and Early Christian Liturgical Usage', *JBL* 71 (1952), pp. 75–84.

Mullen, E. T. *The Assembly of the Gods* (Harvard Semitic Monographs 24, Scholars Press, Chico 1980).

Murray, R. *Symobls of Church and Kingdom* (Cambridge University Press, London 1972).

'Hellenistic-Jewish Rhetoric in Aphrahat', *Symposium Syriacus 1980* (OCA 221, Rome 1983), pp. 79–85.

Musurillo, H. *The Acts of the Christian Martyrs* (Oxford University Press, Oxford 1972).

Nassau *Liturgie bei dem öffentlichen Gottesdienste der evangelisch-christlichen Kirche im dem Herzogthum Nassau* (Wiesbaden 1843).

Neale, J. M. and Forbes G. H. *Ancient Liturgies of the Gallican Church* (Pitsligo Press, Burntisland 1855).

Neuberg, F. J. 'An Unrecognised Meaning of Hebrew DÔR', *JNES* (1950), pp. 215–17.

Neusner, J. *A Life of Rabban Yohanan Ben Zakkai Ca.1–80CE* (Brill, Leiden 1962).

A History of the Jews in Babylonia. I The Parthian Period (Brill, Leiden 1969, 2nd edn.).

Aphrahat and Judaism. The Christian–Jewish Argument in Fourth Century Iran (Brill, Leiden 1971).

News of Liturgy (Bramcote, Nottinghamshire) 120 (Dec. 1984), 154 (Oct. 1987).

Noth, M. 'God, King and Nation in the Old Testament', in *The Laws in the Pentateuch and other Studies* (Oliver and Boyd, Edinburgh 1966).

Odeberg, H. *3 Enoch*, revised by J. Greenfield (Ktav, New York 1973).

Oesterley, W. O. E. *The Jewish Background of the Christian Liturgy* (Oxford University Press, Oxford 1925).

Old, H. O. *The Patristic Roots of Reformed Worship* (Theologischer Verlag, Zurich 1975).

Ordo Missae Dutch Church (N. V. Gooi and Sticht, Hilversum 1970).

Ormanian, M. *The Church of Armenia* (Mowbray, London 1955).

Pahl, I. (ed.). *Coena Domini. I. Die Abendmahlsliturgie der Reformationskirchen im 16./17. Jahrhundert*. Spicilegium Friburgense 29 (Universitätsverlag, Freiburg Schweiz 1983).

Paredi, A. *I Prefazi ambrosiani* (Società editrice vita e pensiero, Milan 1937).

Paverd, F. Van de. *Zur Geschichte der Messliturgie in Antiocheia und Konstantinopel gegen Ende des vierten Jahrhunderts* (OCA 187, Rome 1970).

Peacocke, A. R. *Creation and the World of Science* (Oxford University Press, London 1979).

Peake *Peake's Commentary on the Bible* (Nelson, London 1962).

Peaston, A. E. *The Prayer Book Tradition in the Free Churches* (J. Clarke, London 1964).

Peterson, E. *The Angels and the Liturgy* (DLT, London 1964).

Petuchowski, J. (ed.). *Contributions to the Scientific Study of Jewish Liturgy* (Ktav, New York 1970).

Pfatteicher, P. H., and Messerli, C. R. *Manual on the Liturgy: Lutheran Book of Worship* (Augsberg, Minneapolis 1979).

Pfeiffer, R. H. 'Cherubim', *JBL* 41 (1922), pp. 249–50.

Piana, G. La. 'The Roman Church at the End of the Second Century', *HTR* 18 (1925), pp. 201–77.

Piepkorn, A. C. *Profiles in Belief. The Religious Bodies of the United States and Canada*, II (Harper and Row, New York 1978).

Pinell, J. 'De liturgiis occidentalibus' (manuscript, 2 vols. Rome 1967).

Piper, O. 'The Apocalypse of John and the Liturgy of the Ancient Church', *Church History* 20 (1950), pp. 10–22.

Pitt, W. E. 'The Origin of the Anaphora of St Basil', *JEH* 12 (1961), pp. 1–13.

Porteous, N. *Daniel* (SCM, London 1965).

Porter, H. B. 'An American Assembly of Anaphoral Prayers', in B. D. Spinks (ed.), *The Sacrifice of Praise*, pp. 181–96.

Price, C. P. 'Jewish Morning Prayers and Early Christian Anaphoras', *ATR* 43 (1961), pp. 153–68.

Prigent, P. *Apocalypse et liturgie* (Delachaux and Niestle, Neuchâtel 1964).

Quensel, O. *Bidrag till Svenska liturgiens historia*, II (Lundequistska, Uppsala 1893).

Rad, G. Von. *Old Testament Theology*, I and II (ET Oliver and Boyd, Edinburgh 1962).

Raes, A. 'L'Authenticité de la Liturgie byzantine de S. Jean Chrysostome', *OCP* 24 (1958), pp. 5–16.

Raes, A. (ed.). *Anaphorae Syriacae* (Pontifical Institute of Oriental Studies, Rome 1939–   ).

Rahner, K. *Theological Investigations* 19 (DLT, London 1983).

Ratcliff, E. C. 'The Original Form of the Anaphora of Addai and Mari: A Suggestion', *JTS* 30 (1928–9), pp. 23–32.

'The Institution Narrative of the Roman Canon Missae: its beginnings and Early Background', *SP* 2 (1957), pp. 64–82.

'A Note on the Anaphoras described in the Liturgical Homilies of Narsai', in Birdsall and Thompson (eds.), *Biblical and Patristic Studies in Memory of Robert Pierce Casey*, 235–49.

Ratcliff, E. C. and A. H. Couratin. 'The Early Roman Canon Missae', *JEH* 20 (1969), pp. 211–24.

Reed, L. D. *The Lutheran Liturgy* (Fortress Press, Philadelphia 1960, 2nd edn.).

Renaudot, E. *Liturgiarum Orientalium Collectio*, 2 vols. (Gregg International reprint, Farnborough 1970).

Renoux, A. 'L'Anaphore Arménienne de Saint Grégoire l'Illuminateur', *Eucharisties d'Orient et d'Occident*, II (Cerf, Paris 1970), pp. 83–108.

Richard, M. *Asteri Sophistae Commentariorum in Psalmos quae supersunt accedunt aliquot homiliae anonymae* (Symbolae Osloenses, Oslo 1956).

Richter, A. E. *Die Evangelischen Kirchenordnungen*, 2 vols. (Verlag des Landes-industriecomptoirs, Weimar 1846).

Robinson, H. Wheeler, *Inspiration and Revelation in the Old Testament* (Oxford University Press, Oxford 1946).

'The Council of Yahweh', *JTS* 45 (1944), pp. 151–7.

Robinson, J. M. *et al. The Nag Hammadi Library in English* (Brill, Leiden 1977).

Rordorf, W. 'Les Prières Eucharistiques de la Didache', in *Eucharisties d'Orient et d'Occident*, I (Cerf, Paris 1970), pp. 65–82.

Rowland, C. C. *The Open Heaven* (SPCK, London 1982).

'The Visions of God in Apocalyptic Literature', *JSJ* 10 (1979), pp. 137–54.

Rudolph, W. *Micha-Nahum-Habakuk-Zephanja Kommentar zum Alten Testament* (Mohn, Gütersloh 1975).

Ryan, J. B. *The Eucharistic Prayer. A Study in Contemporary Liturgy* (Paulist Press, New York 1974).

Salaville, S. *Introduction to the Study of Eastern Liturgies* (Sands and Co., London 1938).

Sánchez Caro, J. M. *Eucharistia E Historia de la Salvacion* (Biblioteca de Autores Christianos, Madrid 1983).

'La anafora de Addai y Mari y la anafora meronita Sarrar: intento de reconstruccion de la fuente primitiva comun', *OCP* 43 (1977), pp. 41–69.

Sanders, J. A. *The Dead Sea Psalms Scroll* (Cornell University Press, New York 1967).

Sandmel, S. *The First Christian Century in Judaism and Christianity: Certainties and Uncertainties* (Oxford University Press, London 1969).

Sarason, R. S. 'On the Use of Method in the Modern Study of Jewish Liturgy' in W. S. Green (ed.), *Approaches to Ancient Judaism: Theory and Practice* (Scholars Press, Missoula 1978), pp. 97–172.

Sarkissian, V. K. *A Brief Introduction to Armenian Christian Literature* (Faith Press, London 1960).

Savignac, J. de. 'Les "Seraphim"', *VT* 22 (1972), pp. 320–5.

Schafer, P. *Synopse zur Hekhalot Literatur* (Mohr, Tübingen 1982).

Schecher, A. I. *Studies in Jewish Liturgy* (The Dropsie College for Hebrew and Cognate Learning, Philadelphia 1930).

Schmidt-Lauber, H. C. 'The Eucharistic Prayers in the Roman Catholic Church Today', *SL* 11(1976), pp. 159–76.

Scholem, G. *Jewish Gnosticism, Merkabah Mysticism, and Talmudic Tradition* (Jewish Theological Seminary of America, New York 1965, 2nd edn.).

Sehling, E. *Die Evangelischen Kirchenordnungen des XVI. Jahrhunderts*, 5 vols. (Reisland, Leipzig 1902–13).

Senn, F. C. 'Liturgia Svecanae Ecclesiae: An Attempt at Eucharistic Restoration during the Swedish Reformation', *SL* 14 (1980–1), pp. 20–36.

Serenius, S. *Liturgia Svecanae ecclesiae catholicae et orthodoxae conformis: En liturgiehistorisk undersokning med sarskild hansyn till struktur och forlagor* (Acta Academiae Aboensis, Abo Akademi, Abo 1966).

Shepherd, M. H. 'The Formation and Influence of the Antiochene Liturgy', in *Dumbarton Oaks Papers* 15(1961), pp. 25–44.

'Eusebius and the Liturgy of Saint James' in *Yearbook of Liturgical Studies* 4(1963), pp. 109–23.

Sheppard, L. (ed.). *The New Liturgy* (DLT, London 1970).

Smend, J. *Die Evangelischen Deutschen Messen bis zu Luthers Deutscher Messe* (Reprint De Graff, Nieuwkoop 1967).

Smith, M. A. 'The Anaphora of Apostolic Tradition Re-considered', *SP* 10 (1970), pp. 426–30.

Smolarski, D. C. *Eucharistia. A Study of the Eucharistic Prayer* (Paulist Press, New York 1982).

Spinks, B. D. *Addai and Mari – The Anaphora of the Apostles: A Text for Students* (Grove Liturgical Study 24, Bramcote 1981).

Luther's Liturgical Criteria and His Reform of the Canon of the Mass (Grove Liturgical Study 30, Bramcote 1982).

Freedom or Order? The Eucharistic Liturgy in the English Congregationalist Tradition 1645–1980 (Pickwick Publications, Allinson Park, 1984).

From the Lord and 'The Best Reformed Churches'. A Study of the Eucharistic liturgy in the English Puritan and Separatist Traditions 1550–1633 (CLV, Rome 1985).

Spinks, B. D. (ed.) *The Sacrifice of Praise* (A. H. Couratin *Festschrift*) (CLV, Rome 1981).

Spinks, B. D. 'The Consecratory Epiklesis in the Anaphora of St James', *SL* 11(1976), pp. 19–38.

'The Original Form of the Anaphora of the Apostles: A Suggestion in the Light of Maronite Sharar', *EL* 91(1977), pp. 146–61.

'A Precursor to Dr W. E. Orchard's Divine Service?', *Journal of United Reformed Church History Society* 2:3 (1979), pp. 73–5.

'A Note on the Anaphora outlined in Narsai's Homily XXXII', *JTS* ns 31(1980), pp. 82–93.

'The Jewish Liturgical Sources for the Sanctus', *HJ* 21(1980), pp. 168–79.

'The Cleansed Leper's Thankoffering Before the Lord: Edward Craddock Ratcliff and the Pattern of the Early Anaphora', in *The Sacrifice of Praise*, pp. 161–78.

'The Liturgical Revival amongst Nineteenth-Century English Congregationalists', *SL* 15(1982–3), pp. 178–87.

'A Complete Anaphora? A Note on Strasbourg Gr.254', *HJ* 25(1984), pp. 51–9.

'Eucharistic Offering in the East Syrian Anaphoras', *OCP* 50(1984), pp. 347–71.

'Beware the Liturgical Horses! An English Interjection on Anaphoral Evolution', *Worship* 59(1985), pp. 211–19.

Review of Bruno Bürki, *Cène du Seigneur*, *JTS* ns 37(1986), pp. 693–7.

'The East Syrian Anaphora of Theodore: Reflections upon its Sources and Theology', *EL* 103(1989), pp. 441–55.

'The Jerusalem Liturgy of the Catecheses Mystagogicae: Syrian or Egyptian?', forthcoming in *SP*.

Spinks, B. D. and Stevenson, K. W. *Patterns for Worship. Essays on Eucharistic Prayers* GSMisc.333 (Church House, 1989).

Sprott, G. W. *The Worship and Offices of the Church of Scotland* (Blackwood, Edinburgh and London 1882).

Stalker, D. M. G. *Ezekiel* (SCM, London 1968).

Stevenson, K. W. *Eucharist and Offering* (Pueblo, New York 1986).

'The Catholic Apostolic Eucharist'. Ph.D. Thesis, Southampton University, 1975.

'The Catholic Apostolic Church – its History and its Eucharist', *SL* 13(1979), pp. 21–43.

Stone, M. E. *The Testament of Abraham. The Greek Recensions.* (Scholars Press, Missoula, Montana 1972).

Strugnell, J. 'The Angelic Liturgy at Qumran – 4Q Šîrôt Ôlat Haššabbât', in *Congress Volume Oxford 1959* (VT Supplement 7, Brill, Leiden 1960).

Sutcliffe, E. F. 'Sacred Meals at Qumran', *HJ* 1(1960), pp. 48–65.

Suter, D. W. *Tradition and Composition in the Parables of Enoch* (SBL Dissertation Series 47, Scholars Press, Missoula, 1979).

Swaans, W. J. 'A propos des "Catéchèses Mystagogiques" attribuées à S. Cyrille de Jérusalem', *Mu* 55(1942), pp. 1–43.

Swift, W. F. 'The Sunday Service of the Methodists', *PWHS* 29 (1953–4), pp. 12–24.

'The Sunday Service of the Methodists. A Study of Nineteenth-Century Liturgy', *PWHS* 31(1957–8), pp. 112–18.

Taft, R. F. 'The Authenticity of the Chrysostom Anaphora Revisited. Determining the Authorship of Liturgical Texts by Computer', *OCP* 56 (1990) 5–51.

Talley, T. J. 'The Eucharistic Prayer of the Ancient Church According to Recent Research: Result and Reflections', *SL* 11(1970), pp. 138–58.

'From *Berakah* to *Eucharistia*: A Reopening Question', *Worship* 50(1976), pp. 115–37.

'The Eucharistic Prayer: Directions for Development', *Worship* 51(1977), pp. 316–25.

'The Eucharistic Prayer: Tradition and Development', in Kenneth W. Stevenson (ed.), *Liturgy Reshaped* (In honour of G. J. Cuming) (SPCK, London 1982), pp. 48–64.

'The Literary Structure of the Eucharistic Prayer', *Worship* 58(1984), pp. 404–20.

Talmon, S. 'The Emergence of Institutionalized Prayer in Israel in the Light of the Qumran Literature' in M. Delcor (ed.), *Qumran: Sa piété, sa théologie et son milieu* (Duculot, Paris 1978), pp. 265–84.

Tarby, A. *La Prière Eucharistique de L'Eglise de Jérusalem* (Beauchesne, Paris 1972).

Theissen, G. *Sociology of Early Palestinian Christianity* (Fortress Press, Philadelphia 1978).

The Social Setting of Pauline Christianity (T. and T. Clark, Edinburgh 1982).

Thompson, B. *Liturgies of the Western Church* (The World Publishing Company, New York and Cleveland 1971).

Thurian, M., and Wainwright, G. *Baptism and Eucharist. Ecumenical Convergence in Concelebration* (WCC, Geneva; Eerdmans, Grand Rapids 1984).

Toon, P. *Justification and Sanctification* (Marshall, Morgan and Scott, London 1983).

Torrance, T. F. *Divine and Contingent Order* (Oxford University Press, London 1981).

Theology in Reconciliation (Geoffrey Chapman, London 1975).

Tov, E. *The Septuagint Translation of Jeremiah and Baruch* (Scholars Press, Missoula 1976).

Unnik, W. C. Van '1 Clement 34 and the Sanctus', *VC* 5(1951), pp. 204–48.

Urbach, E. E. 'The Traditions about the Merkabah Mysticism in the Tannaitic Period', in *Studies in Mysticism and Religion Presented to Gershom G. Scholem on his Seventieth Birthday* (Magnes Press, Jerusalem 1967).

The Sages – Their Concepts and Beliefs (Magnes Press, Jerusalem 1975).

Vellian, J. 'The Anaphoral Structure of Addai and Mari Compared to the Berakoth Preceding the Shema in the Synagogue Morning Service', *Mu* 85(1972), pp. 201–23.

Von Allmen, J. J. *Worship: Its Theology and Practice* (ET. Lutterworth, London 1965).

Vööbus, A. 'Discovery of the Anaphora by Johannan of Qartamin', *EL* 90(1976), pp. 197–200.

Wagner, G. *Der Ursprung der Chrysostomusliturgie* (LQF 59 Aschendorff, Münster 1973).

Walker, N. 'The Origin of the "Thrice Holy"', *NTS* 5(1958–9), pp. 132–3.

Wegman, H. 'Pleidoor voor een Tekst de Anaphora van de Apostelen Addai en Mari', *Bijdragen* 40(1979), pp. 15–43.

'Généalogie hypothétique de la prière eucharistique', *QL* 61(1980), pp. 263–78.

'Une anaphore incomplète?', in R. Van Den Broek and M. J. Vermaseren (eds.), *Studies in Gnostic and Hellenistic Religions* (Brill, Leiden 1981), pp. 432–50.

Christian Worship in East and West (Pueblo, New York 1986).

Weinfeld, M. 'Traces of Kedushat Yozer and Pesukey De-Zimra in the Qumran Literature and in Ben-Sira', *Tarbiz* 45(1975–6), pp. 13–26.

Weisz, L. 'Heinrich Bullingers Agenda', *Zwingliana* 10(1954–8), pp. 1–23.

Werner, E. 'The Doxology in Synagogue and Church', *HUCA* 19(1945–6), reprinted in J. Petuchowski (ed.), *Contributions to the Scientific Study of Jewish Liturgy*, pp. 318–70.

Wevers, J. W. *Ezekiel* (Oliphants, London 1969).

Whitaker, E. C. *Martin Bucer and the Book of Common Prayer* (Alcuin Club, Mayhew-McCrimmon, Great Wakering 1974).

Wigan, B. *The Liturgy in English* (Oxford University Press, Oxford 1962).

Willis, G. G. *Essays in Early Roman Liturgy* (Alcuin Club, SPCK, London 1964).

1966 and All That (Faith Press, London 1969).

Wilson, J. A. 'The Assembly of a Phoenician City', *JNES* 4(1945), p. 245.

Winkler, G. *Das Armenische Initiationsritual* (OCA 217, Rome 1982).

'The Political Influences of the Holy See on Armenia and its Liturgy (XI–XIV Centuries)' in J. Vellian (ed.), *The Romanization Tendency* (The Syrian Churches Series 8, Kottayam 1975), pp. 110–25.

Winslow, J., and Ratcliff, E. C., *The Eucharist in India: a Plea for a Distinctive Liturgy for the Indian Church* (Longmans, London 1920).

Wright, G. E. *The Old Testament Against its Environment* (SCM, London 1950).

Wright, W. *The Apocryphal Acts of the Apostles* 2 vols. (Williams and Norgate, London 1871).

Yarnold, E. 'The Authorship of the Mystagogic Catecheses attributed to Cyril of Jerusalem', *HJ* 19(1978), pp. 143–61.

Yelverton, E. E. *The Mass in Sweden 1531–1914* (HBS 57, London 1920).

Zimmerli, W. *Ezekiel 1* (Chapters 1–24) (Fortress Press, Philadelphia 1979).

Zunz, L. *Die Gottesdienstlichen Vorträge der Juden* (J. Kauffmann, Frankfurt 1892).

Index of modern authors

255

Index of eucharistic prayers and liturgical rites

258